University of Liverpool

Withdrawn from stock

PERGAMON OXFORD GEOGRAPHY SERIES
Editor: W. B. FISHER

Other Titles in the Series

CLARK, J.I.
Population Geography, 2nd edition

CLARK, J.I.
Population Geography and the Developing Countries

CLOUT, H.D.
Rural Geography

CLOUT, H.D.
The Geography of Post-War France

COOKE, R.U. & JOHNSON, J.H.
Trends in Geography: An Introductory Survey

COPPOCK, J.T. & SEWELL, W.R.D.
Spatial Dimensions of Public Policy

DEWDNEY, J.C.
A Geography of the Soviet Union, 2nd edition

GILCHRIST SHIRLAW, D.W.
An Agricultural Geography of Great Britain, 2nd revised impression

JOHNSON, J.H.
Urban Geography, 2nd edition

McINTOSH, I.G. & MARSHALL, C.B.
The Face of Scotland, 3rd edition

O'CONNOR, A.M.
The Geography of Tropical African Development

SUNDERLAND, E.
Elements of Human and Social Geography
Some Anthropological Perspectives

Frontispiece. The EEC Headquarters group of buildings in Brussels. *Centre:* Berlaymont. *Centre right foreground:* three smaller Commission buildings. *Bottom right:* original EEC building. *Centre left:* Council building. Other Commission services operate in Luxemburg City and other parts of Brussels. (By courtesy of the Information Office, EEC, Brussels)

The Common Market and How It Works

BY

ANTHONY J. C. KERR

PERGAMON PRESS

OXFORD · NEW YORK · TORONTO · SYDNEY
PARIS · FRANKFURT

U.K.	Pergamon Press Ltd., Headington Hill Hall, Oxford OX3 0BW, England
U.S.A.	Pergamon Press Inc., Maxwell House, Fairview Park, Elmsford, New York 10523, U.S.A.
CANADA	Pergamon of Canada Ltd., 75. The East Mall, Toronto, Ontario, Canada
AUSTRALIA	Pergamon Press (Aust.) Pty. Ltd., 19a Boundary Street, Rushcutters Bay, N.S.W. 2011, Australia
FRANCE	Pergamon Press SARL, 24 rue des Ecoles, 75240 Paris, Cedex 05, France
WEST GERMANY	Pergamon Press GmbH, 6242 Kronberg-Taunus, Pferdstrasse 1, Frankfurt-am-Main, West Germany

First edition 1977

Library of Congress Cataloging in Publication Data

Kerr, Anthony J C
The Common Market and how it works.

(Pergamon Oxford geographies)
Bibliography: p.
1. European Economic Community. I. Title.
HC241.2.K45 1977   341.24'2   76-43324
ISBN 0-08-021142-9 (Hardcover)
ISBN 0-08-021141-0 (Flexicover)

Printed in Great Britain by A. Wheaton & Co., Exeter

Contents

List of Figures

List of Plates

Acknowledgements

My thanks are due first of all to Mme Renée van Hoof, Director of the Interpreting and Conference Service of the European Commission, since it would not have been possible for me to write this book without the knowledge and experience acquired over a period of years as an interpreter at the Common Market,* and, secondly, to the Rt. Hon. Commissioner George Thomson, several members of his personal staff, and others involved in the Commission's work—in particular the Hon. Christopher Layton (Director, Industry and Technology), Dr. Richard Mayne (Head of the Commission's London Office), and Mr. Hugh McLean (Social Affairs). It is, however, impossible to list them all, since nearly every chapter of this book involved obtaining information and in most cases documentation from people working for one or other of the EEC institutions. I should also like to acknowledge the help given by the Statistical Offices of the Community itself and of its nine member-states.

My thanks are also due to Professor J. D. B. Mitchell, Director of the Centre for European Governmental Studies at Edinburgh University, for his very helpful advice and for giving me access to his Centre's library.

*It should be noted that I am not a member of the Common Market Staff but a freelance interpreter. Any views I may have expressed in this book are purely my own, and do not commit the EEC Commission or any of its officials, in particular those mentioned above. No confidential information, obtained in the course of my work, has been included in this book.

Introduction

Britain's decision to stay in the European Community, for better or for worse, has established that body on a reasonably secure basis. It is too early to say more, but it does not look as though the Community, or the Common Market as it is more popularly known, is now likely to break up. It may be more or less successful, it may develop faster or slower, it may or may not evolve as its founders hoped and intended. But in the foreseeable future it will always be there and we shall be part of it. Membership will increasingly affect our daily lives; decisions on the price of food, the amount of coal and steel to be produced, and how energy is to be provided, used, and conserved being taken by the Common Market authorities rather than by national governments and parliaments.

Another way in which membership affects our lives is through the removal of trade barriers—a protection to some and a nuisance to others—and of nearly all legal and practical obstacles to the free movement of persons whether in search of work or for other purposes. With a few significant exceptions, any citizen of a member-state may travel, settle, and work anywhere in the Community. The only restrictions on this freedom are that certain named individuals (mainly political extremists) are excluded from some countries for the sake of public order, that British "non-patrials" (e.g. Kenya Asians) are not regarded by continental Europeans as citizens of the Community, and that people who come to any EEC country to seek work but fail to find it may be sent home after three months.

As regards freedom to work, there are more limitations: civil servants (including teachers in some countries) and army officers, for instance, must in general be citizens of the state which employs them, while doctors and lawyers, among others, may be required to have qualified in the country in which they practise.* But a steelworker, a farmer, an engineer, or a typist, among others, can make their living anywhere.

*There are changes in this field, though progress has been rather slow due to differences in the period of study and training, the structure of the professions (barristers or advocates and solicitors are separately organized in Scotland, England and Wales, and Ireland, while the legal profession is unified in other EEC states) and in the status of some professional people. Thus university professors in the United Kingdom are on the staff of autonomous institutions in receipt of state funds, and need not be British, but in France they are employed by the Government and must normally be French. See also Appendix A (Recent and Projected Developments).

They will, of course, encounter various problems if they choose to move from their own country to any of the others. The language and the food may be different. A higher cost of living, especially while they find their feet, may cancel out their higher incomes. Children may have to be left behind with relatives or fitted into an entirely different educational system: the age of transfer from primary to secondary schools, for instance, may be as early as 10 or as late as 14, and schools are single-sex in some countries and mixed in others. Social security arrangements are not identical: in Britain you get free medical treatment while in West Germany you pay first and get a refund later. Most people therefore find it convenient to stay where they belong: but the essential point is that they are free to move if they are prepared to adapt.

The removal of trade barriers has exposed many small firms producing for a local market to severe competition. Some have survived and have taken advantage of new openings, especially where their local area has a frontier running through it which previously cut them off from otherwise accessible suppliers and customers. Others have gone down, often because their plant was obsolete and their methods were inefficient.

In fact not all trade barriers have been removed as yet. Beside customs duties and quota restrictions, abolished under the Treaty of Rome, one may find varying safety standards, voltages, and plug sizes, and national tastes and preferences, which make it difficult to sell products in any country other than the one for which they were originally manufactured. Some of these barriers, known to the Common Market authorities as "non-tariff obstacles", are gradually being phased out; others, especially those depending on tastes and preferences, will probably continue in the foreseeable future. Nevertheless, it must now be accepted as a fact of life that no job is safe in an industry which is completely thirled to a local market and depends on the continued exclusion of rival products. This may, of course, change if transport costs rise much higher, but in that event the whole tempo of economic activity will slow down very considerably, with many other effects on our way of life.

Whether we like it or not, and whether or not we are fully aware of it, our lives will not be the same in the Common Market as they would have been if we had remained on our own. Indeed, its continued existence and our membership of it will also make a considerable difference to many others, not least to the developing nations of Africa, the Caribbean, and the Pacific, now linked with it by the Lomé Convention.

It is quite clear that the Common Market and the way it works is something we ought to know and care about. What is less clear is how to explain the matter to those who are not thoroughly familiar with it. Basically I had to choose between the traditional approach and the more modern way. The first involved giving the historical background, basic details of the nine member-states, and an outline of the main Community institutions and of the decision-making process, this being followed up by some account of what the Community does about farming, regional and social problems, world trade, relations with developing countries, etc. The second would have involved trying to take the reader's place and asking: How does the Common Market affect me as an Irish farmer? As a Motherwell steelworker? A London secretary? An African coffee-grower?, and then seeking to answer these questions. I have decided to stick to the way I know because (a) I do not happen to be any of these people, (b) it is much easier to put the facts in this way as a coherent and consistent whole, and (c) I am more used to it in any event. The other way, possibly more attractive to some, would have involved a great deal of tedious repetition. Either way it is impossible to cover the whole ground in one volume of readable length, but those who really want to learn will probably learn more from the traditional presentation.

Whichever way one looks at it, the Common Market is a very complex subject, and it is quite unlike any other organization the world has known up till now. It is more than a customs union but it is not a federation. It has authorities, rules, and procedures but no army or police. It has a Court of Justice but sends nobody to jail. It works mainly by using other people's employees. It consists of independent nations but they are no longer free to do whatever they like except ultimately at the cost of withdrawing from the Community, foregoing the advantages of membership, and most probably disrupting their own economy. It cannot be defined, only described, and the best way to describe it in its present form is as a group of states working closely together and arriving at some of their decisions jointly through common institutions, of which the most important are the Commission, which prepares them, and the Council, which actually takes them, both after a great deal of consultation with experts from all the member-states. In some fields the Community has its own policy (agriculture and foreign trade being the most important); in others it co-ordinates and provides support for the national policies of its member-states (regional development and protection of the environment are obvious cases in point).

This, in any event, is the situation as of now. Many Europeans would like the Community to grow into a United States of Europe with a Federal Government responsible to a Federal Parliament. A whole range of subjects would then be taken out of the hands of the existing member-states and of their national authorities. Others prefer the Common Market much as it is, possibly subject to Scotland and Wales becoming member-states in their own right, and regard a Federal Europe as unacceptable or at least unrealistic in our time. They want the present system to continue with some improvements here and there to make it more efficient and more democratic, and to get rid of embarrassing side-effects such as wine lakes and butter mountains.

There are solid arguments on both sides; enough to say at this stage that "pro-marketeers" are not necessarily federalists, and it is by no means a foregone conclusion that western Europe will ultimately become a kind of super-state. We are concerned here with the Common Market as it is, and for the time being at least it consists of countries.

Finally, a word about the layout of this book. It seemed natural to begin from the beginning and to show how the present set-up grew out of an age-old feeling that western Europe somehow belongs together and that there is a "European thing", the successor to the *res Romana,* which, like the Community itself, cannot be defined but can to some extent be described and is certainly worth defending.

The next step, since the Community is what it is, whatever it may become in the future, was to look at the individual states, describe them briefly, and explain how they fit into the whole scheme.

At this point is seemed appropriate to use statistical material: this is the most recent available at the time of writing, but it should be considered as indicating an order of magnitude rather than as conveying exact information. We should further bear in mind that the figures supplied by national statistical offices, and used by the EEC authorities, are not fully comparable. Thus terms such as "working population" and "economically active population" do not always cover the same people in every country. Very small-scale sub-sistence farmers, living partly from pensions and other welfare benefits, and on remittances from their children, may be regarded as working in one country and retired or unemployed in another. Again, the same individual may be salaried in one capacity (e.g. as a teacher or local authority official) and self-employed in another (running a small shop, restaurant, or café).

Again, the traditional division between agriculture, industry, and services is not altogether relevant. It ignores the fact that food-processing industries, the manufacture of agricultural equipment, and a substantial part of the services sector in rural areas and small towns are so closely linked with farm-ing that they must be regarded as part of "the agricultural interest". The political importance of the agricultural sector is therefore far greater than might appear from the number of people who are directly involved as farmers, members of their families working alongside them, and wage-earning farm workers.

The third obvious step was to describe the Common Market institutions and *their* place in the scheme without going into excessive detail and using a minimum of technical language. This third chapter is essential to a proper understanding of the subject, and may also be of interest to those who are thinking of a possible career as "Eurocrats". I must stress, however, that openings are very limited at present. There are fewer officials running the Common Market as such, with its 258 million people, than there are running Scotland with 5 million or Ireland with 3 million. Most of the Community's administrative work is in fact carried out by customs officials, agricultural inspectors, and others who are employed by national, regional, or local authorities. Much of the policy-making is done in the same way, at the intermediate stage, when proposals are discussed, criticized, and improved by government officials and scientific experts who come to Brussels or Luxemburg City for this purpose and then return home to get on with their regular job; typically they may spend a couple of days a month at EEC headquarters and the rest of their working time in their own countries.

The fourth, and in my view as author the most important, chapter of this book deals with the way decisions are prepared and taken, and shows how the various institutions are involved at different stages of this process.

The remaining chapters are concerned with some of the main sectors in which the Common Market authorities are active, though one should bear in mind that they seldom if ever act on their own. It was impossible to cover the whole ground, and I have therefore kept to what the Community itself regards as the most important aspects—those for which one or other of the commissioners is specifically responsible. Each of these chapters, in general, deals with the sphere of influence of one commissioner, though there is some inevitable overlap, for instance between competition policy and the internal market, or between external relations and overseas development. I have departed from this pattern in two instances only. Economic and financial affairs and taxation are at present the responsibility of two commissioners, but it seemed more logical to combine them in one chapter. Similarly, coal, iron, and steel, and the workers in those industries, now fall within the sphere of influence of several commissioners, and more particularly those in charge of energy, industry and technology, and social policy. The Commission deals with them under a different treaty, however, and has more power to help them as a result. It therefore seemed appropriate to consider ECSC matters as a whole in one chapter.*

The concluding chapter is an attempt, but no more than an attempt, to consider how far the Community has achieved and is achieving the objectives set by its founders, and how it appears to be evolving. It is an assessment rather than a judgement, and it may be futile at this stage to argue whether the Common Market is "a good thing" or "a bad thing". What matters is that it is there, and that on the whole it works.

---

*Since this book was written, there has been some rearrangement of Commission portfolios. The structure of Chapters 5–17 is based on the responsibilities of individual Commissioners in 1973–76.

CHAPTER 1

The Historical Background

The Common Market in its present form is less than twenty years old, but the underlying idea goes back fifteen centuries to the last days of the Roman Empire. This underlying idea is, quite simply, that western Europe belongs together and should stick together.

It goes without saying that men like Alaric, Aetius, Clovis, and Theodoric did not think exactly in those terms: for a start Aetius was the only one among them who was educated enough to realize there was such a part of the world as "Europe". But they recognized the existence of a Western civilization—the *Res Romana* or "Roman Thing" as they called it, in which Latins, Latinized Celts, Greeks, and incoming Germanic nations all had a share. They also recognized that it was worth defending against outsiders who only knew how to plunder and destroy but not how to keep it going. In that knowledge they fought side by side at Châlons, scattering the Huns and their allies in the greatest cavalry action of all time.

The "Roman Thing" was then kept alive, somewhat inefficiently but with greater success than was at one time supposed* by the East Goths and the Lombards in Italy, by the West Goths in Spain, and by the Franks in France, the Low Countries, and west Germany. In every case a Germanic ruler and his warriors maintained some sort of order, often better than the Romans had done in the last generations of imperial rule, while priests and monks provided the Civil Service, such as it was, and ran what was left of the educational system.

The main weakness of the whole set-up was that the royal families, especially among the Franks, were constantly afflicted by internecine quarrels, but the "Roman Thing" only had to meet one major threat from

---

*Until quite recently, historians felt obliged to glorify the Renaissance and the modern period by overstressing the ignorance and brutality of the Dark Ages (450–1000) and of the Middle Ages (1000–1450). In fact the barbarian invasions were not all equally destructive: town life and trade continued, especially in southern France and Italy, well after the fall of the Western Empire, and indeed tended to revive in the sixth century and again in the eighth. The process of decline was very slow, reaching its nadir about 850–950. From 950 onwards there was a generally rising tendency as the Viking, Saracen, and Magyar raids all ceased and as the French and German kings restored order in their respective territories.

1

outside, the Arab invasion of 711–732. Most of Spain was lost in a year, but the Gothic resistance at Covadonga (near Santander) saved the northern fringe and began the long process of reconquest as early as 718; then, at Poitiers (732) Charles Martel dispersed the Moorish cavalry in a battle which ranks with Marathon and Châlons as one of the major victories of our civilization.

Twenty years later, Martel's son Pepin took over the Frankish kingdom from the degenerate heirs of Clovis. His son Charlemagne reconstructed a "Roman Empire" out of this kingdom and his own conquest. Though smaller than the old Roman Empire, and indeed smaller than the old western half following on the division made by Diocletian in 304, it included territories of great strategic value which Rome had never ruled. Its eastern boundary virtually coincided with the present Iron Curtain, falling a few miles short of it in Austria and going a few miles beyond it in East Germany. With very minor exceptions, the most important being the heel and toe of Italy, it took in the six original founder-states of the Common Market, together with Switzerland, most of Austria, and north-eastern Spain. Britain was never part of this empire, but Charlemagne maintained friendly contact with Offa, the most powerful of the English rulers at the time, and

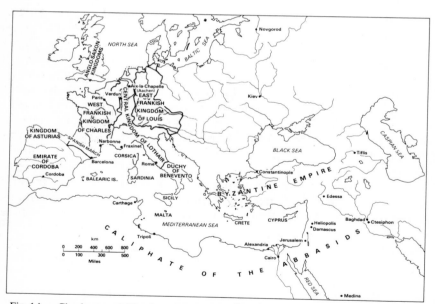

Fig. 1A.   Charlemagne's Empire AD 814. Boundary fixed on the division of Charlemagne's empire by the Treaty of Verdun, AD 843. (*Atlas of Man and Religion,* Hawes & Knight, Pergamon Press.)

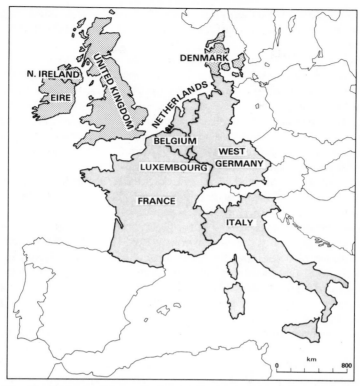

Fig. 1B.   The European Community showing the six original members and the three later members. (La Communauté Européenne, Information Office, European Communities, Paris).

"imported" Alcuin of York, Head Master of St. Peter's School, as his chief educational adviser (Figs. 1A and 1B).

Charlemagne left only one son when he died in 814, but the Empire was divided among his grandsons by the Treaty of Verdun in 843, the same year in which Scotland became a nation-state through the union of the Picts and the Scots. The western part, from which France developed, went to Charles the Bald: it also included the Spanish March (Catalonia and northern Aragon) and a small part of present-day Belgium. The Middle Kingdom consisted of the rest of Belgium, Holland, Luxemburg, Germany west of the Rhine, North Italy, the French-speaking part of Switzerland, and the eastern provinces of present-day France: in other words it included bits (and in two cases the whole) of all the original Common Market states. It went to Lothar, Charlemagne's eldest grandson, along with the imperial title, and is now the most "European-minded" part of the Common Market. Lewis the German got the remainder of West Germany, from the Rhine to the Curtain, together with most of Switzerland, most of Austria, and an outlet to the Mediterranean at Trieste.

Subsequently the eastern and middle kingdoms were reunited as the "Holy Roman Empire", while France went her own way. This revived empire was definitely Germanic rather than multi-national like Charlemagne's and later spread out to cover present-day East Germany. At times, for instance under Frederick Barbarossa (d. 1190), it was a genuine and very powerful state; at other times the Emperor only had a shadowy primacy over a host of princes, counts, bishops, and free cities, but nobody, from Charlemagne to Napoleon, succeeded in ruling both Germany and France as a whole.

Though politically divided, medieval and early modern Europe always remained something of an informal community. Educated men understood one another, through Latin until the Reformation and through French thereafter. Most people lived and died within a few miles of the town or village where they were born, but for those who travelled at all, frontiers were not in general a major obstacle, and for those who chose or were forced to leave home, there were few problems apart from that of staying alive until they found work and a place to live. There were no immigration laws in the modern sense: if the local ruler liked you, he would let you stay; if not, you had to move on. But if a man had a trade, or some education, or looked a likely soldier, the chances were he would be allowed to stay. Similarly, there were no work permits in the modern sense, though it was often necessary to join a guild in order to work at a particular trade in a particular town. Nationality was not a major consideration on the Continent at any rate; what mattered was allegiance to a king, bishop, or prince, given in return for the ruler's protection, and this did not involve the same complicated procedures as naturalization does today.

These rulers, however, spent a great deal of time fighting one another, and the material damage this caused was often very severe. Because the whole economy was less well developed, and in particular because storage facilities and the transport system were grossly inadequate by our standards, recovery from this damage took a great deal longer than after the two world wars for instance. Moreover, the death rate from natural causes was far higher than it has been since about 1800, and additional losses from war and from war-induced famine and epidemics therefore took a great deal longer to make up.

Because of this, some of Europe's most far-sighted rulers (e.g. James IV of Scotland and Henry IV of France) as well as thinkers such as Dante and the Abbé St. Pierre, propounded various schemes for a European Confederation to establish peace between western kingdoms and common defence against outsiders such as the Turks and the Barbary pirates. These schemes all came to nothing, but they had one positive element in common; they were based on the principle of independent states agreeing to work closely together through some sort of collective leadership rather than any one ruler asserting his power over all the rest who would never have allowed it—as has been proved repeatedly whenever anybody has tried.

The name "Common Market" itself was coined by the French statesman Aristide Briand, who submitted a detailed scheme for a European union, first to the League of Nations Assembly in 1929,* and then to all the European governments in the following year. He was a few years too late: the rise of Fascism in Italy and of National Socialism in Germany, together with the stresses of the Great Depression, made it impossible for the governments to get together and make a practical start on his scheme. In any event, the lesson of 1914–18 had not been fully learnt: another and even more terrible war was necessary to convince them that Europe could only survive by becoming united, or at any rate more united than it was.

The decisive impulse was in fact given by Europe's need for outside aid after 1945. This aid, offered by America, was subject to certain conditions, the main one being that the states which were to receive it should set up a joint organization to manage the resources thus made available and to work out a common economic policy. The Marshall Plan thus led to the establishment of the Organization for European Economic Co-operation (OEEC) which later became the Organization for Economic Co-operation and Development (OECD) and now serves to bring Europeans, Americans, and Canadians together.

At the same time, following on the Communist take-over in Czechoslovakia and Hungary, western defence became a matter of some urgency. It could not be effective without German participation, but France could not take the risk of another war with a rearmed Germany. Some way had to be found of making such a war not merely impossible but unthinkable. One obvious way was to integrate the coal, iron, and steel industries of the two countries, because you cannot make war without steel (and vast quantities of it) and you cannot make steel without coal and iron. This was what the French Foreign Minister, Robert Schuman, proposed in his declaration of 9 May 1950, after consultation with the West German Government. Italy, Belgium, Holland, and Luxemburg—this last an important steel producer despite its very small size as a country—also came in on this scheme, which took definite shape as the European Coal and Steel Community, later merged with the European

---

*The League was set up in 1919 by the Treaty of Versailles. It was wound up in 1945, being replaced by the United Nations. The purposes of the two organizations were broadly similar but the League had no means of taking military action and its decisions therefore had moral force only. The International Labour Organization, originally an offshoot of the League, continued to operate as a "Specialized Agency" of the United Nations. The other Specialized Agencies (UNESCO, FAO, etc.,) are generally more recent and were set up together with the United Nations or some time after.

Economic Community (the Common Market) and the European Atomic Energy Community (Euratom), which originally consisted of the same six countries.

The essential features of the ECSC were as follows:

1. All three industries, in all six countries, were placed under the overall supervision of a supra-national High Authority which served as the prototype for the EEC Commission and was later merged with it.

2. To ensure that vital national interests were not ignored or overridden by this body, a Council of Ministers, representing the six member-states, was set up with the exclusive right to take certain major decisions.

3. A parliamentary assembly was also set up to provide some measure of democratic control (but not a great deal), together with a consultative assembly bringing together producers (nationalized and other industries workers and users), and a European Court of Justice to ensure that the rules were kept. All these institutions were copied or simply used as they stood by the EEC when it was established a few years later.

4. Among the High Authority's powers were those of setting production quotas for the six countries,* deciding on rail freight charges for the products which it controlled, and preventing various forms of unfair competition. It also financed retraining schemes for workers made redundant by rationalization and by pit closures, and helped to rehouse them if necessary.

5. The ECSC was not dependent on financial contributions from the member-states but had its own resources from the start in the form of a levy on the turnover of the nationalized and other firms whose activities it controlled, and a special levy on sales of scrap within the Community. This, however, was used to subsidize imports of scrap from other countries.

It is worth noting that the ECSC had greater powers under the Treaty of Paris than the Common Market authorities under the Treaty of Rome, essentially because these powers were intended to prevent another war (the last being scarcely over at the time, and much of the damage still visible), and were only exercised over a narrow though very important sector of economic activity rather than over the whole of agriculture, industry, and trade. Because the High Authority was a specialist body, the six governments were more willing to delegate powers to it than to the EEC Commission a few years later.

Again, to prevent another war, these same governments were quite prepared to look at the idea of a European Army, integrated right down to company level, with a French captain giving orders through German sergeants to Italian and Dutch soldiers. From a language standpoint alone, this scheme was an obvious non-starter and was, in fact, rejected by the

*This has never in fact been done, even as a crisis measure.

French National Assembly in 1954. With it, the idea of a European Government responsible to a Federal Parliament also had to be shelved, at least for the time being, and those who wanted a political union had to seek a more realistic way—to widen the existing Coal and Steel Community into an Economic Community and build on from there.

After lengthy negotiations, the prime ministers and foreign ministers of the six ECSC countries signed the Treaty of Rome (1957), setting up the European Economic Community with the institutions described in Chapter 3. These were copied from the ECSC, but the two communities remained quite distinct for some years, the older body having more extensive powers but in a narrower field. Another treaty, signed at the same time, established the European Atomic Energy Community (Euratom).

The EEC, popularly known as the Common Market, was basically an economic union, ultimately requiring a political union to make it work: its founders intended and stated that there should be such a political union in due course, but without specifying exactly what form it would take. The Treaty's immediate objectives, however, were to get rid of all obstacles to the free movement of people and of resources between the member-states, and to promote economic growth throughout the Community.

This meant, in the first instance:

1. No customs duties, "equivalent taxes", or quota restrictions on goods crossing from one member-state to another.*

2. Uniform customs duties for goods entering any member-state from the outside. Otherwise American cars, for instance, might enter Germany at a lower rate of duty than they would pay on arrival at a French port, cross the Rhine freely, and then flood the French market.

3. The right of any citizen of any one member-state to work in any of the other five and to enjoy the same pay, working conditions, and social security benefits as the citizens of the country to which he moved.

4. The right of any firm established in any one member-state to operate in any of the others, subject to the same laws and the same taxation as firms originally registered in that country.

5. Rules preventing any government from unfairly helping its citizens and the businesses which they controlled in competition with the citizens of other member-states, e.g. by charging higher freights on its railways for imports than for exports, or by giving higher subsidies to its farmers than were received by farmers in the other states.

---

*An example of an "equivalent tax" was the "statistical tax" levied on goods entering Italy from France. This was supposed to pay for the cost of keeping statistics of Franco–Italian trade. In fact it was a useful source of revenue for the Italian Government and discriminated against French products. It was therefore ruled out of order by the European Court.

6. No restrictions on the free transfer of funds from one member-state to another. This, however, could only work if all the member-states had one currency, which in turn would presuppose a single West European Government to decide on the value of that currency. Failing this it would be necessary to impose restrictions from time to time to prevent too much money going out of one country (or coming in, which can also be inconvenient): the French, Italian, and British governments have all had to impose restrictions on outgoing funds at one time or another, and West Germany has occasionally had to stop money coming in.

There is as yet no common currency, but some transactions are carried out in the "Units of Account" which were originally worth the same as the US dollar, but kept their value when the dollar was devalued. The UA is a very odd "currency" in that you never actually see it (at present anyway) but only use it to work out sums. You cannot go into a bank and ask for ten, a hundred, or a thousand units of account: wherever you are it has to be "translated" into a national currency. It is in practice worth about 3 German marks or 50 Belgian francs. Its value in sterling is difficult to express because there are three rates of exchange for different types of transaction and because sterling does not have a fixed or nearly fixed value in relation to other currencies.

Some of the Common Market rules came into force at once, e.g. freedom to work anywhere in the EEC (with certain exceptions, of which public service is the most important); for others a transitional period was provided, during which customs duties were gradually abolished between the member-states and external duties (e.g. on goods imported from America to Germany or Spain to France) were brought into line with the Common Customs Tariff. One exception to the CCT rules is still in force: goods coming from East Germany to West Germany pay no duty, but they pay CCT duties if they continue from there to France or are imported from East Germany straight into Denmark, for instance. This could lead to serious "distortions of traffic", as there need be nothing to show that goods entering France from West Germany were in fact made there and not on the other side of the Curtain, where wages are considerably lower. In practice this problem is not as serious as it looks, but the West Germans derive some unfair advantage from being able to import cheap East German components which they then incorporate into their own products, and there has been some dissatisfaction about this.

Britain did not join the EEC at the time, any more than she had joined the ECSC. There were many reasons, traditional distrust of foreigners and reluctance to hand over *any* powers to a supra-national authority being the most important. Instead, she combined with most of the other states of western Europe to create EFTA (the European Free Trade Association), a less ambitious and less "political" body, whose members abolished customs duties and quota restrictions on trade in manufactured (but not agricultural) products between themselves, but did not, for instance, do away with work permits or immigration formalities.

In its early years, the Common Market worked more smoothly than it has done since. Recent memories of the war helped; so did the fear of Communism and the fact that a mainly Catholic party, the Christian Democrats, formed part or most or the whole of the government in all six countries—as Christian Democrats in Italy, Luxemburg, and most of West Germany; Social Christians in Bavaria and Belgium; the Popular Republican Movement in France; and the Catholic People's Party in the Netherlands.

The first serious difficulties arose with Britain's application to join in 1962–63. Five of the six countries wanted her in, but President de Gaulle feared that France would lose her leading position in the Community and that the United Kingdom would serve as a bridgehead for American influence, making Europe less distinctly "European". He therefore vetoed the application just as negotiations seemed about to succeed. This caused much bitterness among the other five states, and for a while France refused to co-operate and sent no representatives to meetings of the Council of Ministers. A second British application in 1967 was never accepted nor formally rejected.

Another problem at this stage was General de Gaulle's fear that the Community would evolve into a federal super-state. The French "policy of the empty chair" had as much to do with this as with difficulties over Britain's entry. It ended with the Luxemburg Compromise (1965), whereby the present rule of unanimity was established, even though the Treaty provides for weighted majority voting in most cases.

In 1970 Britain applied a third time, along with Ireland, Denmark, and Norway. This time France raised fewer difficulties, partly because de Gaulle was no longer there and largely because West Germany was by now a great deal more powerful and seemed likely to assume the leadership of the whole Community if the United Kingdom did not join. An interesting feature of the negotiations was that the existing six member-states spent far more time arriving at a common position than talking to the British or anyone else. Whenever the applicant states were present, the French Ambassador or Foreign Minister alone spoke in the name of the Six.* The British (or the Irish, Danes, or Norwegians as the case might be) remained for half an hour,

---

*France held the Council Presidency during the most important part of the negotiations (January–June 1971). Germany chaired some of the earlier meetings, Italy several of the latter; but at that stage the political decisions to admit the applicant states had been taken, and it was essentially a matter of tying up the loose ends.

perhaps less; the two spokesmen exchanged prepared statements and the applicants then withdrew while the Six got together again for another two or three hours. During this part of the proceedings every country had its say, generally more than once.

The negotiations with Britain were considerably more difficult than with the other three, largely because any concessions the Irish, the Danes, or the Norwegians might seek, if granted, would only have a marginal effect on the economy of the Common Market as a whole, and the Six were therefore more willing to make such concessions, especially as they knew these smaller countries would only join subject to referendum, and the governments would therefore have to sell the terms to their people. Secondly, the three minor applicants had no colonies or ex-colonies apart from Greenland (Danish)* and the Norwegian sector of Antarctica. The former had about 30,000 inhabitants, the latter none.

Britain, on the other hand, wanted special terms for imports both from the old White Dominions and from the new Commonwealth countries: Caribbean sugar, in particular, caused serious problems at one stage. Finally, the other applications stood or fell with that of the United Kingdom: if Britain did not join, the others would stay out; if she joined, Ireland at least could not afford to remain on her own. In the event all four applications were accepted by the existing member-states, but the Norwegian people, by a narrow majority, refused to go along with their Government, which then resigned.

The former French and Belgian colonies were already linked with the old Community of Six by the two *Yaoundé Conventions*; Nigeria and the East African states entered into similar arrangements with the EEC even before Britain joined. These agreements were all due to run out in 1975 and were therefore re-negotiated, this time to include nearly all the Commonwealth countries and territories in Africa, the Caribbean, and the Pacific.

The merger of the three communities (ECSC, EEC, and Euratom) has already been mentioned. It took place in 1969 and involved the following arrangements:

1. The same *Council* became the supreme decision-making body of all three communities. However, as we shall see in Chapter 3, the Council itself does not always consist of the same individuals. This depends on the business in hand.

2. The *EEC Commission* took over the job of the Euratom Commission and of the ECSC High Authority. Its members were all due for reappointment at the time, and the new Commission was somewhat larger than the old.

---

*Originally a colony, now a province of Denmark, but with various special arrangements in force, and the possibility of "Home Rule" along much the same lines as the Faroes, in a few years' time.

3. The *"European Parliament"* and the *Court of Justice* were already the same for all three communities. They soldiered on with their permanent home in Luxemburg City with the Parliament's plenary sessions mainly in Strasbourg. Brussels, however, became the headquarters of the combined communities and specifically of the Council and of the Commission. Luxemburg was compensated for losing the ECSC headquarters by getting all the Council meetings in April, June, July, and September and by retaining some Commission departments.

4. The *ECSC Consultative Committee,* however, remained distinct from the *Economic and Social Committee* of the EEC because it was a highly specialist body. It still meets in Luxemburg.

Some further reorganization was necessary when the new member-states joined, partly because the Community took on fresh interests (e.g. regional and social policy) and largely to enable those states to get their fair share of senior posts on the Commission and Council staff. This involved persuading many officials to retire early or to return home to appointments in their national Civil Service, the universities, and industry.

Britain's accession had not been welcomed as warmly in the United Kingdom itself as on the Continent, partly because Mr. Heath had undertaken only to negotiate and not to go further without seeking "the full-hearted consent" of the people. It was widely felt this should mean either a special general election or a referendum, preferably the latter, since an election would inevitably have been bedevilled by many side-issues.* Local polls in two small towns showed majorities of 80% against the Common Market and for a national referendum, and Labour won the 1974 general elections† largely on Mr. Wilson's pledge to put Britain's continuing membership to the vote after seeking better terms. This pledge was redeemed by some months of "re-negotiation" ending with a meeting of the French President and of the nine prime ministers in Dublin, followed by the United Kingdom referendum on 5 June 1975. Whether the terms obtained by Mr. Wilson were objectively much better than those accepted by Mr. Heath is open to argument: what mattered was that the people felt entitled to vote on this issue and were given the opportunity.

---

*A special election was in fact a non-starter because all the parties were divided on this issue. It would have been necessary to create two special parties for this occasion and prohibit all others, and independent candidates, from standing. The special parties, being disunited on all other issues, would then have had to dissolve themselves, yet another election being held with the normal parties. Parliament would never have accepted such a scheme.

† The first 1974 election (28 February) was a draw in Labour's favour. The Tories had more votes, but Labour had more seats, and no party gained a clear majority in Parliament. The second election (17 October) was a narrow victory for Labour, but with less than 40% of the popular vote.

The referendum turn-out was not quite as high as in a general election but a great deal higher than had been expected: the majority (nearly 70% in England and Wales, nearly 60% in Scotland, 67% for the United Kingdom as a whole) was convincing enough. What is less clear is how far this was a vote for the Common Market as it stood and how far it indicated support for a future political union. This book does not attempt to answer the question: the debate is still open.

CHAPTER 2

The Member-states of the Community

European Community

Area 1,528,900 sq. km (approx.)

Population 258,377,000 approx.

Density 169 per sq. km

Age distribution of population (%)
   Under 15   23.8
   15–64   63.2
   65 +   13.0

Economically active population 104,881,000 approx.
   Economically active persons as percentage of total population   40.7
   Percentage of women in economically active population   35.2
   Percentage of economically active persons in female population 27.9
      (in 15–64 age group 42% approx.)

Distribution of economically active population (%)
   By status
      Employers, self-employed, and family workers   17.1
      Wage and salary earners   82.9
   By sectors
      Agriculture   8.9
      Industry   42.6
      Services   48.5

GNP per head 3561 UA

Agricultural self-sufficiency 96% approx.

Imported energy dependence 60% approx.

The first thing to remember about the Common Market is that it is not a country but consists of countries, or to be more accurate, of states. It has no independent means of carrying out its policies and enforcing its decisions, and could only be given these means by the unanimous agreement of its nine member-states.

We cannot begin to understand the Community unless we know something about all the states of which it is made up: their essential geography, their agriculture and industries, their standard of living, their political institutions, and, above all, their people, because the whole set-up works on the basis of compromise between national interests as the ministers see them.

France

Area	547,000 sq. km
Population	52,566,000 (1975)*
Density	96 per sq. km

Age distribution of population (%)
Under 15	24.2
15–64	62.5
65 +	13.3

Economically active population (1975)   21,700,209
  (+ 98,065 seeking first job)

Economically active persons as percentage of total population	39.4
Percentage of women in economically active populations	38.0 approx.
Percentage of economically active persons in female population	23.9
(in 15–64 age group 43% approx.)	

Distribution of economically active population (%)
By status
Employers and self-employed including those working in family farms, shops, craft workshops, etc.	22.2
Wage and salary earners (1974)	77.8
Unemployed (November 1975)	4.8 approx.

By sectors
Agriculture	12.0 approx.
Industry	39.2
Services	49.2·†

GNP per head   4056 UA (sixth out of nine states)

Degree of agricultural self-sufficiency   126%
(average of wheat, potatoes, vegetables, sugar, butter, and meat)

Degree of dependence on imported energy   82.3%

---

*Resident population only. In addition there are some 44,000 soldiers and diplomats stationed abroad.

† These figures are taken from the EEC Social Report for 1975. They add up to 100.4%. The probable explanation of this excess is that some people work in two sectors, usually agriculture and services (e.g. small farmers operating a petrol station, shop, or café). It should be noted that in France, as elsewhere, fisheries and forestry are counted with agriculture, and the same Commission Department (DG VI) is responsible for them.

First in size and political importance—though West Germany, the United Kingdom, and Italy all have larger populations—is the French Republic. About a quarter of the French people live in and around Paris, but there are several other major centres of activity, some of them a considerable distance from the capital. Lille is only 150 miles from Paris, Lyons is 300 miles away, and Marseilles and Toulouse about 500 miles. The underpopulated and declining regions are not necessarily on the fringes, as in Britain, but mainly in the centre and west centre, starting about 200 miles from Paris. What is wrong with them is also quite different, in general, from what is wrong with comparable areas of the United Kingdom. Their climate is no worse than that of more prosperous regions, and there has been very little artificial depopulation of the type brought about in the Highlands by absentee landowners because most French farmers are freeholders. What has happened, more often than not, is that farms have become too small to be efficient and to provide an adequate living for farmers at a time when other people are much better off than they used to be and when their own expectations are therefore higher. Younger people have moved to the cities: the elderly cling on to their land because it is theirs and because they know no other way to live. But they have little to spend, so the market towns languish through lack of business. The excessively small size of farms is itself due (as in Italy) to the equal division of property among a man's heirs: the eldest son (or the one most interested in farming) may buy his brothers out if they are willing and if he can raise the mortgage, but this is not always the case.

In general, however, the French economy is better balanced than the German, the Italian, or the British, mainly because the distribution of people between cities and industrial areas, smaller towns, and the countryside is approximately right. Germany, and still more Britain, are over-urbanized: Italy remains excessively rural except in the north, and at the same time much of the country is mountainous and not very productive. France has the further advantage of close links, generally closer than Britain's with her former colonies.

The French political and administrative system has in the past been highly centralized, but the people at the centre were probably in closer touch with what was happening in the country at large than was the case in the United Kingdom, for instance, because many MPs and even some ministers remained active in local government as mayors or as councillors. There was a good deal of frustration at the fact that even quite minor decisions had to be taken in Paris, involving considerable delays, but they were taken by people who knew and understood small towns and villages. In any event there has been a tendency over the past few years to transfer much of the routine decision-making to regional and local authorities.

Politically, the distinctive features of the French Constitution are the powers of the President and the two-stage electoral system.

The French President has slightly less authority than his American counterpart, but not much less, and considerably more than any of the other heads of state (sovereigns or presidents) in the Community. He is the real head of the Government even though there is also a Prime Minister whom he can appoint and remove, and he can in the last resort appeal to the French people over the heads of the Assembly and Senate by holding a referendum on any issue he considers vital. The French Parliament, on the other hand, cannot get rid of him. His powers, his security of tenure, and the importance of his country together make him the first citizen of the Community, no matter who may hold the Council Presidency for the time being.

The Assembly is elected, like the President, by a method which normally involves a second round. That is to say, if any candidate get a clear majority in the first round he is declared elected, but in most cases this does not happen.

The next stage in a presidential election is that the two leading contenders fight it out, the remaining candidates being eliminated. In an Assembly election, the procedure is not quite so simple. Candidates with fewer than 10% of the vote are eliminated, but this may still leave four or five of them in any given constituency. Those who have more than 10%, but clearly do not stand a chance, often withdraw in favour of better-placed candidates with broadly similar views. In the end there may still be three candidates, and the one with the largest vote wins, as in the United Kingdom, even though he may be short of a clear majority.

Under this system the Communists get very few members elected except those who make it in the first round. If a Communist is eliminated or withdraws, nearly all his supporters will vote Socialist, but the converse does not hold true; when a Socialist goes out in the first round he may indeed advise his supporters to elect the Communist, but half of them, if not more, will vote for a Centre candidate.

As a result the Communists, with about 20% of the vote in the first round, only get a handful of seats, and this, incidentally, leads to reduced Communist representation in the "European Parliament", which at present consists of delegates from the national parliaments in rough proportion to the parties' strength in each of them.

The French Senate is elected in the same way but with smaller "constituencies", each consisting of all the mayors and councillors in a department, not the electorate as a whole. It has delaying powers similar to those of the House of Lords but stronger. De Gaulle tried to abolish this body as it was an obstacle to some of the reforms he wished to carry out, but this involved a constitutional amendment and therefore a referendum in which he was defeated, and it was on this issue that he resigned.

On the whole France has gained substantially from being in the Common Market, but there have been problems. One of them is that Italy can produce ordinary wines cheaper and in larger quantities though France remains supreme where quality wines are concerned. There is no legal way by which France, as a member-state of the Community, can prevent Italian wine from coming in, but farmers can overturn the lorries which bring it in or demolish the shops where it is sold, and the French Government then intervenes to restore public order by stopping the lorries—contrary to Community law.

Another problem is that the existence of the Common Market has tended to encourage economic growth in regions close to its centre. This includes Paris and much of northern and eastern France, but outlying areas, as in other countries, have suffered except where they had a well-entrenched speciality (Bordeaux wine, Toulouse aircraft) or a major port handling much of the Community's trade with the outside world (Marseilles). The Regional Policy, described in Chapter 8, is intended to redress the balance, it being recognized that excessive growth can be as damaging as economic decline.

Thirdly, a few small areas along the Belgian, German, and Swiss frontiers have difficulties due to these frontiers, or rather to what happens on the other side. Along the Belgian frontier the main difficulty has been that nobody wants to invest in economic development on the French side, as the Belgian Government is more helpful and, under the Treaty of Rome, capital flows freely from one side to the other. In Alsace-Lorraine the problem is that wages are far higher in Germany, so French industrialists cannot get labour. The same thing happens close to Basel and Geneva, with the added complication that Swiss taxes are far lower than in France. People who work in Switzerland, though living in France, bank their money on the Swiss side and do most of their shopping there; local shopkeepers on the French side are therefore ruined. Again the Regional Policy should help France to do something about this frontier decay.

French is the main administrative language of the Community, in which most policy documents are usually thought out and drafted. This is a tradition which became firmly entrenched in the first twenty years of the ECSC and of the EEC in its original form, before the new members joined, French being used by Belgium and Luxemburg as well as by France, and by nearly all the African states associated with them: it was also the second language of most educated Italians and of many Dutchmen and Germans. This linguistic bias has been a considerable advantage to France.

West Germany

West Germany has the largest population (though at present declining slightly) and is generally regarded as the second of the four major member-states. Her economy is the most powerful, though heavily dependent on imported energy and on imported labour, but her elongated shape is something of a drawback, greatly adding to transport costs. Another problem is that she is very vulnerable from a military point of view. Russian and East German forces could overrun Lübeck and Wolfsburg (the home of the giant

Area	248,600 sq. km
Population	62,054,000 (1974)
Density	250 per sq. km

Age distribution of population (%)
- Under 15   22.4
- 15–64   63.8
- 65 +   13.9*

Economically active population   26,271,000

Economically active persons as percentage of total population	42.3
Percentage of women in active population	37.0 approx.
Percentage of economically active persons in female population	30.6
(in 15–64 age group 45% approx.)	

Distribution of economically active population (%)
By status

Employers, self-employed, and family workers	15.8
Wage and salary earners (1974)	84.2
Unemployed (November 1975)	4.0 approx.

By sectors

Agriculture	7.3
Industry	47.6
Services	45.1

GNP per head   4915 UA (first out of nine states)

Agricultural self-sufficiency   86

Imported energy dependence   51.1

---

*Slight discrepancy due to rounding-up. Figures from EEC Social Report.

Volkswagen firm) in a matter of minutes, break into Hamburg in two hours and, in theory, reach almost anywhere except Munich, Saarbrucken, and Aachen within six or seven hours. In practice they would probably take longer, and nobody knows how many would desert instead of fighting. But the map does not look at all reassuring.

No one city has the same importance for West Germany as London for Britain or Paris for France. Bonn, the Federal capital, is relatively small and at some distance from any of the main centres of economic activity. These are Hamburg, the country's largest city and port, the Ruhr Valley, an industrial cluster similar to the English Midlands but even more heavily populated; the Rhine–Main–Neckar triangle with Frankfurt, Wiesbaden, Mannheim, Heidelberg, and several smaller cities, Stuttgart, and Munich. West Berlin, an "island" in East Germany, is about the same size as Hamburg, though losing steadily, but is not fully part of the Federal Republic. Its MPs do not vote, its young men are not liable for military service, and its inhabitants do not pay the same taxes as those of West Germany proper. The Allied Military Commanders, moreover, have special rights there and may, for instance, prevent the semi-Nazi NDP from holding rallies. But West

Berlin is part of the Common Market and included as a West German *Land,* not as a member-state in its own right.

West Germany is the only federal state in the Community at present. Including West Berlin it is divided into eleven self-governing provinces, or *Länder* (the city-states of Berlin, Hamburg, and Bremen, together with Schleswig-Holstein, Lower Saxony, North Rhine-Westphalia, Hessen, Rhineland-Palatinate, the Saar, Baden-Wurtemberg, and Bavaria. The city-states, Schleswig-Holstein, Lower Saxony, and Hessen are Protestant; North Rhine-Westphalia, Rhineland-Palatinate, the Saar, and Bavaria are Catholic (but much of northern Bavaria is Protestant): Baden-Wurtemburg is divided fairly evenly between the two religions, as is the country taken as a whole. Each of these *Länder* has its own Parliament (*Landtag*) and Government, these two bodies being known as the Council and Senate in the city-states, responsible for many matters including education, housing, health, and local government, but there are federal co-ordinating bodies (e.g. the Conference of Ministers of Education) which try to ensure that *Land* policies do not diverge excessively. The Federal Parliament consists of two houses, the *Bundestag,* elected by the people, and the *Bundesrat,* elected by the parliaments of the *Länder.*

The method of election to the *Bundestag* is a curious one. Half the members are elected by constituencies as in the United Kingdom and using the same system, though the constituencies themselves are much larger, averaging 180,000 voters each rather than 65,000. But everybody has a second vote, and it is these second votes which decide how many MPs each party is to have. Thus if the Christian Democrats (similar to the Tories and largely Catholic) have 45% of the B votes while the Social Democrats (Labour) also have 45% and the Free Democrats (Liberals) have 10%, the Free Democrats will get 10% of all the seats even though they have not won any constituencies. These MPs will be the candidates standing near the top of the party's general list in each *Land,* the order in which they appear (and therefore their chances of election) being determined by the party executive. The other parties will also have their seats made up to 45% of the total in each case, but since, with the same number of votes, the Christian Democrats gain more constituencies than the Social Democrats,* they will be awarded fewer extra seats to arrive at the same figure. This arrangement, however, only works in favour of parties which can take 5% of the national vote or gain three constituencies outright: this rule is intended to keep Communists and Nazis out of the *Bundestag* and prevent too many small parties from appearing on the scene.

*There are two reasons for this. In the first place the Christian Democrats are stronger in rural areas which have lost much of their population. Secondly (as in the United Kingdom) the left-wing party "waste" many votes on excessively large majorities in their traditional strongholds.

The *Land* parliaments are elected in the same way as the *Bundestag*: the majority party or coalition in each *Land,* however, elects all the *Bundesrat* members for that *Land.* It follows that by carrying the four Catholic *Länder* and Baden-Wurtemberg the Christian Democrats may get a majority in the *Bundesrat* even though the Social Democrats and Liberals together have more votes and a majority in the *Bundestag.** This is an important point because the *Bundestag* does not automatically get its way after a certain time like the United Kingdom's House of Commons. If there is a deadlock it has to be resolved by a joint sitting of both houses in which the opposition may have a majority. The Government must then either drop a proposed legislation on which it has been outvoted or arrange to have itself defeated on a vote of confidence in the *Bundestag,* which entitles it to call a general election. This procedure, however, has two snags. In the first place, the Government may lose the election and, secondly, it may win but still be short of a majority at a joint sitting, since the *Bundesrat* is not renewed at a general election. It must then wait until it captures a *Land* from the other side, whereupon the *Bundesrat* delegation from that *Land* will be replaced.

West Germany does not have the same problem of large, semi-derelict areas as France, let alone Italy. But she has others: small, languishing districts along the Iron Curtain, over-development and pollution in some of the industrial areas, and excessive dependence on imported labour.

To begin with the frontier districts, these have in many cases been cut off from sizeable towns which provided a market and a shopping centre for their farmers—places like Schwerin, Magdeburg, and Eisenach, now in East Germany. At the sale time the presence of Russian tanks a few miles away, with little to block their advance, discourages investment and is rather depressing for the local people in any event. Hence there is a tendency for young people to move away, leaving the elderly behind, and the economy has been run down except in Lübeck and Wolfsburg, which were already places of some importance before Germany was divided. The West German Government, and those of the *Länder* concerned, try to overcome this handicap by investing relatively large sums of public money in these areas and the Treaty of Rome specifically allows them to receive exceptional aids which would otherwise be prohibited under the competition rules.

Over-development is a problem in the Ruhr, along the Rhine, and in Munich especially. It is self-correcting to some extent: when life begins to deteriorate seriously, people move away, and this is already happening in Munich. But this means, of course, that much of the money spent in providing schools, houses, hospitals, roads, etc., is wasted, and that more has to be spent in creating the same infrastructure elsewhere.

*Voting does not absolutely follow religious lines: North Rhine-Westphalia in fact tends to put the Social Democrats in while Schleswig-Holstein supports the CDU. But the practical effect can be the same.

Finally, there is the problem of the "guest workers", most of whom now come from outside the Community. Originally they came to do the rough jobs which the Germans did not want, and moved into the poorer city districts which the Germans did not want either. By and large they have not fitted in very well because they were too "different". With rising unemployment the Federal Government have therefore tried to reduce their numbers by sending them home when they lost their jobs or when their work permits expired, and refusing to admit any more. At the same time they have closed the door on other "non-Community" workers already in France, Belgium, or Luxemburg, so that a common labour market cannot be said to exist in the EEC.

Several Community policies—the agricultural policy and the regional policy in particular—involve Germany in paying quite heavily for help given to other countries, mainly France (agricultural support), Italy and Scotland (regional aid), and Ireland (both types of aid). This has naturally given rise to some resentment. On the other hand, the existence of the Community itself provides German industry, generally the most efficient in the nine states, with a home market of over 250 million consumers and the Federal Republic itself with far greater weight in the world than it would otherwise have. For this reason it is probably the most "European-minded" of the four major states.

The United Kingdom

Area	244,000 sq. km
Population	56,056,000
Density	230 per sq. km

Age distribution of population (%)
Under 15	23.6
15–64	62.6
65 +	13.8

Economically active population 25,310,000
Economically active persons as percentage of total population	45.2
Percentage of women in active population	38.0 approx.
Percentage of economically active persons in female population	33.3
(in 15–64 age group 52% approx.)	

Distribution of economically active population (%)

By status
Employers, self-employed, and family workers	8.0
Wage and salary earners (1974)	92.0
Unemployed (November 1975)	4.7 approx.

By sectors
Agriculture	2.8
Industry	42.3
Services	54.9

GNP per head 2700 UA (seventh out of nine states)

Agricultural self-sufficiency 59%

Imported energy dependence 50.3% (at time of writing)

Scotland

The basic statistics for Scotland differ quite substantially from those for the United Kingdom as a whole, as may be seen from the details given.

Area   78,774 sq. km

Population   5,226,400

Density   67 per sq. km

Age distribution of population (%)
  Under 15   25.0
  15–64   62.0
  65 +   13.0

Economically active population   2,273,000
  Economically active persons as percentage of total population   43.5 approx.
  Percentage of women in economically active population   38.5 approx.
  Percentage of persons economically active in female population   38.32 approx.
    (in 15–64 age group 52% approx.)*

Occupational distribution of economically active population (%)
  By status
    Employers, self-employed, and family workers   5.7
    Wage and salary earners   94.3
    Unemployed (November 1975)   5.8

  By sectors
    Agriculture, forestry, fishing   2.5
    Industry   42.2
    Services   55.3

  No accurate figure exists for the Scottish GNP. The gross domestic product per capita in 1975 was estimated at 92.2 of the United Kingdom figure; the GNP per capita may have been a little higher, perhaps 95%. At the time of publication, due to oil developments, the balance has possibly shifted in Scotland's favour: 100 and 105% approximately would seem to be credible figures.

Agricultural self-sufficiency   86% approx. (with room for expansion)

Imported energy dependence. Not accurately known: probably close to zero at the time of writing and negative (as for Holland) at the time of publication.

---

*The age of pensionable retirement for women in Scotland is 60, as in the rest of the United Kingdom. Since this varies from state to state, however, the 15–64 age group has been retained here in order to maintain comparability with other EEC countries. In any event, many women of 60–64 are still working.

Politically Britain has been up till now one of the more solid and stable member-states of the Community: economically she is among the weakest. This may seem a paradox and calls for some explanation.

All the present member-states except Britain and Ireland were overrun by Germany or the Allies, and most of them by both, during the Second World War. Belgium, Holland, and some parts of Germany have been invaded repeatedly over a period of centuries. An invasion usually means loss of life and extensive damage. It also creates a great deal of hostility between those who remain loyal to their own side at all costs and those who for any reason choose to co-operate with the enemy. These wounds take many years to heal: even when the remaining "war criminals" have been amnestied, a legacy of bitterness remains. England has not gone through this kind of trauma since the civil wars of the seventeenth century; Scotland has not known it since the eighteenth.

At the same time the British political system, with two or three parties, has generally ensured greater stability and a more judicious balance between Parliament and Government than is found in most continental countries. In some of them there are so many parties that no government expect to stay in office more than a few months: in others, though France is the only one now in the Common Market, a natural reaction has led to undue strengthening of the Government's powers, so that Parliament is no longer an effective body.

For this reason Britain's accession has made the "European Parliament" a more credible body, though it will never be fully credible until it is directly elected. It has also led to some useful rethinking of the Community's approach to many problems because the British are less inclined to look at first principles all the time, and more willing to consider whether proposed measures will actually work.

On the other hand, the British economy has not been as great an asset to the Common Market as Britain has been to the political Community. There are several reasons for this, the most important being the existence of a number of problem regions and the survival of many "lame ducks".

We shall come back to the problem regions in Chapter 8. In general their problems in the United Kingdom are due to their dependence on declining industries or to severe depopulation rather than to inefficient farming.

The lame duck is not a purely British creature; but whereas in France one finds an excessive number of Civil Service posts, created or maintained to mop up unemployment in the otherwise largely unproductive cities or regions, the industrial lame duck, i.e. the firm which is persistently unable to pay its way because it carries too many passengers, is a United Kingdom speciality, in western Europe at least.* This did not matter so long as Britain

---

*Soviet and east European industries, however, are generally inefficient even by British standards and would certainly be classed as "lame ducks" if they had to compete on the open market and pay Western-type wages and fringe benefits. A far greater number of workers are generally required to produce the same quantity of goods than anywhere in western Europe, but their wages (calculated on any realistic rate of exchange) and their standard of living are appreciably lower. The distribution of labour is quite different, manufacturing industries being grossly overmanned while the services sector is seriously undermanned and quite inadequate by our standards. The reason is probably that it is felt morally "better" for people to be engaged in producing something than in making life more comfortable. The atmosphere of a factory encourages them to think and to feel in a Communist way: working in a shop or a restaurant they would be more tempted to revert to Western-type ideas.

had a large protected market overseas, or while she could afford a permanent trade deficit because of her "invisible" earnings from banking, shipping, insurance, and overseas investments, but it is a serious handicap now.

At the same time Britain's accession has not been as disastrous for the Common Market, even economically, as de Gaulle had feared. She has in fact contributed three important assets: a large number of substantial and efficient farmers, a considerable quantity of coal just when it was needed, and a small but useful group of high-technology industries.

The British political system is familiar enough to most of us but still needs to be described briefly for the sake of comparison with the others. It is far and away the oldest in the Community. Its three major institutions—the Crown, the Lords, and the Commons—go back to the ninth century in the case of the first two—the House of Lords is historically the continuation of the Witan and the Anglo-Norman "Great Council"—and to the end of the thirteenth century for the House of Commons. The two-party system dates back to about 1640 though the parties have changed more than once. It is based on a theological view of life as a perpetual conflict between "good" and "evil", the "good" side being one's own party. As most people no longer see life in these terms, its time seems to be running out, but it made politics and political choices simple and straightforward while it lasted: ordinary voters felt more involved even if they were not politically active, and the Government did not seem quite so remote and impersonal as in other countries.

The Cabinet form of government, with a Prime Minister who appoints his colleagues and dismisses them or gets them to resign if they fall out with him, and with the whole group going out of office if they lose a vote of confidence or a major piece of legislation, has been functioning since 1720 or thereabouts. It has been copied by most European countries, but Switzerland, closely linked with the Community by a free-trade agreement, has a different and unique arrangement. The Swiss Federal Executive is elected for four years by a joint sitting of the Swiss House of Representatives and Senate, in proportion to the strength of the major parties. It remains in office for that period, regardless of what happens to its legislation, and the premiership, which is at the same time the federal presidency, rotates annually according to rather complex rules.

Over the centuries there have been many changes in the British system but as a rule they have been gradual. The Sovereign is not now completely powerless and has, like the Queen of the Netherlands and the King of the Belgians, the considerable advantage of having been in office a great deal longer than any of her ministers: on the other hand, Britain, which did not exist as a state before 1707, has never been an absolute monarchy (nor was Scotland at any time in her history as an independent kingdom) and England only for a few years under Henry VIII.

The House of Lords is the only parliamentary body in the world that still consists mainly of hereditary members (though bishops, judges, and life peers make up about half of those who regularly attend). It is less powerful than most other Second Houses in countries that have one, but contains many people with expert qualifications of one kind or another, and is therefore a useful revising body. Its members have no constituencies to look after and can thus find more time for other activities: hence several of them have been included in British delegations to the European Parliament.

The House of Commons, with 635 members, is slightly larger than the corresponding Italian body and considerably larger than any other elected house anywhere in western Europe. (The House of Lords has over 1000 members, but half at most are active: the Supreme Soviet of the USSR is larger still but is more of a rubber stamp than anything else.) It has only been able to override the Lords since 1911, but has in practice been the more powerful of the two Houses since the seventeenth century, simply because the Government needed money every year and could only get the amount which it needed from the Commons. Before 1640 a careful king could rule for years using his own resources and taxes granted to him for the whole of his reign.

From the Community's standpoint it is essential to bear in mind that no Parliament can bind its successor and that there can be no such thing as an illegal Act of Parliament in the absence of a written constitution. This has several important consequences:

   (i) Britain could, in theory withdraw from the Community at any time if Parliament were to pass an Act to that effect. In practice this is unlikely to happen since her membership was confirmed, in the 1975 referendum, by a majority far larger than any party has ever obtained in a general election.

   (ii) Parliament could at any time pass an Act to say that a particular regulation (which, under the Treaty of Rome, immediately becomes law throughout the Community) is not to be enforced. It would then be impossible to enforce that regulation. In practice this is unlikely to arise so long as member-states remain individually free to veto any regulation which they regard as contrary to their vital interests. But it could become a matter of some importance if Council regulations were no longer subject to veto or if Commission regulations could no longer be challenged in the Council.

   (iii) Similar considerations apply to Community directives; but this is true of all the member-states. If Parliament refuses to "translate" a directive into legislation, there is no way it can be compelled to do so.

   (iv) Decisions of the European Court could not be enforced in Britain if judges refused to enforce them or were ordered by Parliament to ignore them.

What all this means is that, in the last resort, the Community authorities do not have—or at any rate cannot use—the same powers in the United Kingdom as in the other member-states, where the Constitution has been amended to transfer certain matters from national to Community jurisdiction. There is no such document as "The British Constitution" and Parliament always retains ultimate control. But since these authorities work on a basis of compromise and mutual concessions, rather than by asserting their rights under the Treaty, there is no immediate likelihood of conflict.

Britain's accession to the Community brought a large part of the Commonwealth into the network of the associated states. As a result there are now as many people living in these states as in the EEC as such (255 million in each case) whereas, until 1973, Europeans in the Common Market outnumbered Africans in the former French and Belgian colonies by more than two to one. This may in the long term prove to be an even more significant change than the enlargement of the Community itself.

Italy

Area 301,300 sq. km

Population 55,412,000

Density 184 per sq. km

Age distribution of population (%)
  Under 15 24.3
  15–64 64.3
  65 + 11.4

Economically active population 19,275,000
  Economically active persons as percentage of population 34.8
  Percentage of women in economically active population 28.5 approx.
  Percentage of economically active persons in female population 19.2
    (in 15–64 age group 30% approx.)

Distribution of economically active population (%)
  By status
    Employers, self-employed, and family workers 28.2
    Wage and salary earners (1974) 71.8
    Unemployed (September 1975) 5.9
  By sectors
    Agriculture 16.6
    Industry 44.1
    Services 39.3

GNP per head 2163 UA (eighth out of nine states)

Agricultural self-sufficiency 80.0%

Imported energy dependence 83.1%

Italy has the interesting distinction of being the guardian of the Treaty of Rome. This was signed in her capital, and the original copies in French, German, Italian, and Dutch are therefore lodged with her Government along with the Treaties of Accession signed fifteen years later by Britain, Denmark, and Ireland.

Economically, as well as politically, however, she is the weakest of the present member-states. Politically her main handicaps are the existence of too many parties and the considerable strength of the extreme left and the extreme right. Between them they have about 40% of the popular vote and a similar proportion of the parliamentary seats in both Houses.

The Italian Parliament consists of two Houses as in all the major member-states: the Chamber of Deputies with 630 members and the Senate with 315 elected members and a few life members. Both Houses are elected directly by proportional representation, though the two systems are not quite identical; they have equal powers and can block each other. The President may then call a general election to resolve the deadlock.

A curious feature of the system is that deputies and senators generally vote by secret ballot. Hence neither their party leaders nor the people at large know whether, on any particular occasion, they have voted in accordance with their party's policy. This may seem undemocratic, but is sometimes necessary for their personal safety since extremists are not only more numerous but more extreme than in any other EEC country taken as a whole.

Italy is divided into twenty regions, each with an elected Assembly and an executive responsible to it. Five of these regions have more self-government than the rest, either because they are large islands (Sardinia and Sicily) or because many of their people speak a language other than Italian, but they do not have the same entrenched rights as the German *Länder*: their assemblies may be dissolved by the central government (though an election must then be held within three months) and their legislation may be overruled by the Italian Parliament.

Economically, Italy suffers from her elongated shape. The south is too far away from the industrialized north, which also has the best agricultural land, and further still from the prosperous core of the Community. It faces countries which are even poorer, and its own agriculture is handicapped by poor soil, mountainous and rocky terrain, inadequate rainfall, and farms which are often so small that they cannot provide anybody with a decent living: indeed, they are in many cases not expected to do so, but are worked by women whose husbands send them money from Milan, Switzerland, or Germany, or by elderly couples mainly dependent on remittances from their children. In Calabria—the extreme case—the average income per head is about one-fifth of what it is in Hamburg, and the average standard of living, if not the actual money income, is below that of the better-off areas in West Africa.*

Central Italy, from Cassino Hill to Florence, is already much better off— roughly on a level with Scotland though still well below the Community average,† It produces most of Italy's wine and contains most of the places tourists want to see. The climate and soil are generally better, there is more industry, and the heartland of the Common Market is a few hundred miles nearer.

The north, above a line from Pisa to Rimini, has most of Italy's industries, the best land, and a far better network of roads and railways than the peninsula. Indeed, it has some advantages even compared with other industrial areas of the Community: thus its labour force is entirely Italian and does not cause the same social problems as North Africans in France or "guest workers" in West Germany. But it also includes mountain areas which have suffered from depopulation and especially from the loss of their younger people. Switzerland has been more successful in dealing with this problem; many young workers remain in their mountain villages and help their parents with hay-making and the harvest but have jobs in small industrial towns to which they commute daily. This saves valuable agricultural land in the Rhone Valley which would otherwise be needed for housing, and helps to keep the villages alive.

In past years Italy has been at odds with the EEC authorities more often than any other member-state and, indeed, more often than the rest put together. The reason is that there was less in the Common Market for her farmers than for the French, who produced more of the things the Germans, the Belgians, and the Dutch want to eat, and were much closer to them; while her industrialists, though some of them gained from membership, were not, taken as a whole, in any position to compete with the Germans unless they got some help from their Government. At the same time, for political reasons, the Italian Government was extremely reluctant to introduce value-added tax, since this tends to hit poorer people relatively harder than those who are fairly well off, and also involves a great deal of tedious work for small shop-keepers, many of whom are elderly while others are not very well educated. The Community, however, may call on this tax for part of its budget, and even though it received a direct contribution from Italy instead, there was no

---

*The reason is that *food* is usually cheaper in Africa, and more of it is produced locally, at least in areas with an adequate rainfall, while *services* are often performed on an exchange basis rather than directly paid for. The same money income therefore stretches further.

† Direct comparisons are difficult to establish, and consumer goods are more readily available in a small town in Scotland than in a comparable town in Italy. On the other hand, the Italians, who spend relatively more of their income on food, almost certainly eat better and, except in Naples, Italian housing is seldom as bad as in the worst parts of Glasgow.

way of telling whether this brought in as much money as a share of the country's VAT would have done.*

At present, however, Italy seems to fit in a little more easily because the advantages of EEC membership are beginning to show even in the south. In the first place the Community can help with regional problems which Italy could not handle adequately on her own. Forty per cent of the Regional Fund is earmarked for Italian projects, i.e., a sum of £100 million a year. This is not enough, but it is a start, and other resources are available from FEOGA and the Social Fund. Secondly, the enlarged Association with the ACP states places her, to some extent, in a more favourable position. This could be helpful to some Italian industries, particularly in the south, and should provide careers in "technical co-operation" for many Italian engineers and agricultural scientists. With Europe and Africa drawing closer together there could be advantages in being the southernmost of the EEC states.

The oil crisis could also, in the long term, strengthen Italy's position within the Common Market not only because she is a minor but useful producer of oil and of natural gas, but because she is a major producer of hydroelectricity and is better placed than any other member-state to collect and use solar energy once this can be done on a worthwhile scale. This particular technology was first developed in Sicily by Archimedes over 2000 years ago. It has only been revived in the past few years, and its applications are at present limited to domestic heating and cooking, but the Community is taking an interest in further research.

*Value Added Tax (VAT) is a tax on most goods and services, payable sometimes at a uniform rate, sometimes at a higher rate on luxury products. It is payable all along the line but can be reclaimed by everybody except the final consumer. Thus a wholesaler buys writing paper from a manufacturer and pays VAT on it, but gets it back. The stationer who buys it from the wholesaler also pays VAT but gets it back after filling in his tax returns. But the consumer who ultimately gets it for his own use cannot recover the tax. The equivalent of a 1% rate of VAT is earmarked for the Common Market authorities. Thus if VAT stands at 18% the Government takes 17% and the EEC may claim the other 1%. If the tax is levied at 25% it is divided in the proportion of 24 to 1. However, some goods pay VAT in one country and not in another; this is the case of food and children's clothes, for instance. This means that the EEC authorities get less than what they consider their fair share of tax from the countries which do not levy VAT on everything. This figure of 1% is a maximum, which the Community may call up if this is necessary in order to balance its budget. At present, however, no agreement having been reached on what goods and services should be taxed, the Community collects, in its place, a contribution based on the GNP.

Belgium

Area	30,500 sq. km
Population	9,788,248
Density	320 per sq. km

Age distribution of population (%)
    Under 15   22.8
    15–64   63.4
    65 +   13.8

Economically active population   3,895,000
    Economically active persons as percentage of total population   39.9
    Percentage of women in active population   35.0 approx.
    Percentage of economically active persons in female population 27.1
        (in 15–64 age group 45% approx.)

Distribution of economically active population (%)
    By status
        Employers, self-employed, and family workers   16.7
        Wage and salary earners (1974)   83.2
        Unemployed (November 1975)   6.2 approx.

    By sectors
        Agriculture   4.2
        Industry   43.3
        Services   52.5

GNP per head   3407 UA (fourth out of nine states)

Agricultural self-sufficiency (combined with Luxemburg)   119%

Imported energy dependence   91.1%

Belgium, the home of the main Common Market institutions, is in a sense far more European than Belgian. It has no language of its own—even Luxemburg can do better—and its borders with France, the Netherlands, and Germany are less significant than the language frontier running east and west from Mouscron through Brussels to the outskirts of Aachen.* Two very great Europeans—Charlemagne and the Emperor Charles V—were born within its present territory, but it has no national heroes of its own comparable with William Tell, Wallace and Bruce, St. Joan of Arc, or Garibaldi, for instance.

The Belgians were originally the largest and most warlike of the Gallic tribes, controlling not only present-day Belgium but much of northern France together with Kent, London, and Essex. They made two important contributions to British history: first by bringing the heavy plough which made it possible to cultivate fertile clay soils, and, secondly, by provoking the first

---

*In theory Brussels is a bilingual enclave surrounded by Flemish territory. In fact the nominally Flemish suburb of Rhode St. Genese, between the capital and the dual language frontier, is now predominantly French-speaking, as is Brussels itself.

Roman invasion, which was intended to prevent the Kentish clans from helping those on the mainland. Defeated by Caesar a few miles from Namur, in 57 BC, they only recovered their independence in 1830. In between times they had been subject to the Romans, the Franks, the French kings and the German emperors, the Spaniards, the Austrians, the French revolutionaries, Napoleon, the Dutch and a whole host of princes, dukes, bishops, and counts, and their country had been fought over and over again.

The battle of Waterloo, a few miles south of Brussels, ushered in the longest period of peace western Europe has known up till now. Belgium was transferred from Austrian to Dutch rule, Austria getting compensation in Italy. The Dutch king, however, gave too many of the top jobs to his own countrymen: this offended the upper class, who had done better under the Austrians, and the middle class, who had done much better under the French. In parts of the north, however, the common people supported the Dutch, who spoke their language, against the aristocracy, who spoke French among themselves and Flemish only to their servants, and Belgium emerged as an officially French-speaking state even though half the population spoke Flemish. This caused a great deal of bitterness which endures to this day, and the language issue bedevils Belgian politics in a way that only makes sense when one realizes that it is in fact the extension of a long drawn-out class struggle, at least so far as the Flemish people are concerned. It is also the continuation of a religious conflict, the Flemish being Catholics while many of the French-speakers are anti-clerical, but this aspect is less important now.

Most political parties exist in duplicate with a separate organization on either side of the internal frontier: a few are based on linguistic nationalism and only operate on their own side. This means that no government can ever count on a secure majority since it always consists of three or four parties which agree or at least find an acceptable compromise on social and economic policies but may fall out on educational issues or the transfer of a few villages from one province to another. The internal frontier is also the approximate dividing line between older and often declining industries (coal, steel, textiles) and modern light industries, which moved into the northern half of the country at a time when wages were generally lower there, and the influence of the Church could keep the Socialists and Communists down, which meant fewer strikes. As a result the south now has far more unemployed than the north; but Walloons do not move into Flanders in search of work—not in large numbers anyway—because the law would then require them to use the language of the land just as if they migrated to a foreign country.

The Constitution provides for a king, a senate, a chamber of deputies and two cultural councils. Deputies, of whom there are 212 at present, are elected by constituencies using proportional representation. In the same way, 106 senators are elected and a further 48 by the provincial councils with a mini-mum of three senators for each province. Another 24 senators are then co-opted by their 154 elected colleagues. The cultural councils consist of all the senators and deputies from the French-speaking and Flemish-speaking regions respectively; Brussels is not represented in either of them as it is officially bilingual though in practice about 75% French-speaking. They can make laws applicable within their own region: one example being a law which requires employers in the north to speak and write Dutch (Flemish) only in their dealings with their staff. This has caused some inconvenience and resentment: in American firms, for instance, the boss would normally speak English to other managerial staff, while many North African and Spanish workers have some French but no Dutch. In practice it has not been con-sistently applied.

Until 1962 Belgium possessed a large colonial empire with over eighty times her land area and about three times her population. This provided opportunities for administrators and businessmen and gave the country some sense of purpose. In some sense it held Flemings and Walloons together as Belgians. The winds of change swept it away rather suddenly with very little preparation for independence. As a result the loss of the colonies was a more traumatic experience for Belgium than for Britain and France, which in any event carried more weight in the world even without them, while independence itself caused far greater chaos in the Congo than in the former British and French colonies, and trading and other links were more severely disrupted.

Without the Congo, Belgium has found a new role as the centre of the Community. On a political level, Paul-Henri Spaak, Prime Minister after the Second World War, played a leading part in setting it up, and Jean Rey, one of the small minority of Belgian Protestants, was the first President of the Commission. More recently, Leo Tindemans, the present Prime Minister (1976), has toured all the EEC capitals to see what progress could be made towards the goal of a European Union. On an administrative level, many Belgians now choose to make their career in the EEC's Civil Service rather than in their own country's and 10,000 people of various nationalities are employed by the Community institutions, while many more are involved in providing services of one kind or another for them and for the institutions themselves.

The Netherlands

Most people think of The Netherlands simply as "Holland" and the two provinces of North and South Holland have, in fact, over four-fifths of the country's population and the lion's share of industry and trade, but there are

Area   40,800 sq. km

Population   13,545,000

Density   332 per sq. km

Age distribution of population (%)
   Under 15   26.0
   15–64   63.4
   65 +   10.4

Economically active population   4,724,000 approx.
   Economically active persons as percentage of total population   34.9
   Percentage of women in economically active population   26.2*
   Percentage of economically active persons in female population   18.1*
   (in 15–64 age group 29% approx.)*

Distribution of economically active population (%)
   By status
      Employers, self-employed, and family workers   15.7
      Wage and salary earners (1974)   83.2
      Unemployed (November 1975)   4.7
   By sectors
      Agriculture   6.6
      Industry   35.5
      Services   57.9

GNP per head   4094 UA (fifth out of nine states)

Agricultural self-sufficiency   170%

Imported energy dependence   minus 9.1% (= 109.1% self-sufficiency)

---

*These figures may be slightly out of date, but are the most recent available, and given in the EEC Social Survey. In the light of continuing trends, the true figures are probably 27%, 19%, and 30% respectively, or a shade above.

nine others: Zeeland, North Brabant, Limburg, Gelderland, Utrecht, Overijssel, Groningen, Drenthe, and Friesland. The country as a whole is the most thickly populated in Europe and, indeed, in the world apart from ministates such as Malta and Hong Kong, and the Dutch countryfolk were farmers producing for the urban market when nearly all the rest—French, Germans, Italian, and English—were peasants producing mainly for themselves and for their local lord.

At the start of the Reformation, The Netherlands formed part of Charles V's empire, but he ruled the various provinces through different officials and councils as duke of this and count of that, not as a country; he was at the same time German Emperor, King of Spain, and several other princes rolled into one. On his abdication they were transferred, along with Belgium, to his son Philip, who tried to rule them simply as part of his Spanish realm. This did not work, and within a few years they rose in revolt. William of Orange, a German prince taking his title from a small town in the south of France, which he also ruled, was invited by the insurgents to become their leader, and accepted after some hesitation, but was unable to retain control of the Belgian provinces. These put their Catholic religion first, and came to terms with Philip, who restored the system of government operated by his father.

The Dutch, on the other hand, became a confederation of self-governing provinces, each ruled by the merchant upper class of its towns and cities rather than by landed noblemen. William did not take the title of king but that of stateholder (governor) borne in turn by most of his descendants, but not all the time; for years on end there was no stateholder, only a committee of the States-General. The country only became a constitutional monarchy in 1815, essentially because the major European powers felt that everybody ought to have a king except the Swiss, who had never had one. Republics were considered by them to be somewhat untidy and dangerous, and the House of Orange therefore took the royal title.

During the wars of independence, fought against Spain from 1570 to 1648, the Dutch acquired a large part of the Portuguese colonial empire, Portugal being at the time joined with Spain. They lost it in 1947, but the experience was not as humiliating for them as for Belgium a few years later, nor did it inflict the same damage on the economy. It did, however, involve the absorption of several hundred thousand Indonesians and part-Indonesians into Dutch society. With few exceptions, they have been successfully integrated.

From a political standpoint Holland is unique in having parties, and much else besides, organized largely on a religious basis. While there is only one national language (plus Friesian in the north-east, but the Friesians all speak Dutch as well), there are three main religious communities or "pillars": Catholics, Protestants, and neutrals; these may have no religious background, or be non-practising Christians or Jews. The Protestants are further subdivided into two main denominations corresponding almost exactly to the Church of Scotland and the Free Kirk. Until recently members of the three communities had little to do with each other socially: segregation extended to such activities as tennis, chess, amateur photography, and stamp collecting, this in order to discourage mixed marriages, regarded as undesirable by all three communities. These sharp lines have become rather blurred, but politics remain largely sectarian. Thus a conservative-minded Dutchman will probably vote for the People's Party if he is a Catholic, for the "Liberals" if he is a neutral, for the Christian Historical Party if he is Reformed, and for the Anti-Revolutionary Party if he is a Free Kirker.

The Dutch electoral system, also used in Israel, encourages this fragmentation. There are no constituencies in elections for the Second Chamber (the Dutch equivalent of the House of Commons). Parties, rather than candidates, are directly elected on a national list. A party which gets 10% of the votes gets 10% of the seats, and the first fifteen candidates on its list are elected. The order in which they appear on the list is determined by the party itself: the voters cannot elect individual MPs. A party which gets 1% of the vote is still entitled to a couple of seats: there is no "5% hurdle" as in West Germany.

The First Chamber (Senate) is indirectly elected by the provincial councils. Again the list system is used, but since each province only elects a few senators, there are not so many parties.

It is generally impossible to form a stable government because the Catholics will line up with the Socialists on some issues (e.g. social welfare) and with the other religious parties on other issues (e.g. education). Depending on what the Government is trying to do at any given time, therefore, it is sure to be out-voted by one combination or another. This instability, however, does not have the same disastrous effects as it has done in other countries from time to time, because provincial and local authorities carry on regardless, because the Civil Service is efficient, and because the Queen is always around. With nearly thirty years on the throne she has considerably more experience than any of her ministers, as well as immense personal wealth: she is the biggest shareholder in Shell and has many other business interests. Top civil servants and provincial administrators can still report to her when there are no ministers, and some Dutchmen say the country runs better without a government than with one.

Dutch industry is heavily dependent on imported raw materials, as it has been for centuries. On the other hand, internal communications by road, rail, or inland waterways are less of a problem than anywhere else in Europe because most of the country is absolutely flat, or gently undulating. Transport costs are therefore not as high as elsewhere, and are further reduced by the fact that most of the manufacturing towns are very close to each other. This cluster of cities and towns, usually known as "Randstad Holland", makes for serious pollution problems, however.

The Common Market has given the Dutch economy a considerable boost because Holland serves as Germany's main outlet to the sea, handling even more of her foreign trade than Hamburg, and as the main distribution centre for Middle East oil coming to Europe. This arrives at Rotterdam, one of the few ports capable of handling giant tankers, and is then filtered out in various directions through pipelines and in smaller tankers. Dutch drivers, with their juggernaut lorries, have taken over a large share of Europe's road transport. Finally, it may be worth noting that Holland is a major producer of natural gas, while it is not impossible that oil will be found in her sector of the North Sea.

Denmark

Area	43,100 sq. km
Population	5,045,000
Density	118 per sq. km

Age distribution of population (%)
Under 15	22.7
15–64	64.1
65 +	13.1

Economically active population   2,444,000
Economically active persons as percentage of total population	48.4
Percentage of women in active population	42.0 approx.
Percentage of economically active persons in female population	39.9
(in 15–64 age group 63% approx.)	

Distribution of economically active population (%)
By status
Employers, self-employed, and family workers	18.2
Wage and salary earners (1974)	71.8
Unemployed (November 1965)	4.4

By sectors
Agriculture	9.6
Industry	32.3
Services	58.1

GNP per head   4846 UA (second out of nine states)

Agricultural self-sufficiency   180%

Imported energy dependence   99.5%

With the same Royal House on its throne for over a thousand years, Denmark is the oldest state in Europe. It has never formed part of any other (though it was briefly occupied by the Germans in 1940–5) but was, under Canute and again in the later Middle Ages, the centre of a larger northern empire. Most of its European territory is continental—the Jutland peninsula —but a majority of the people live on the three main islands and a host of smaller ones. In addition, it retains one ex-colony, Greenland, which has fifty times the area of the mother country but the population of a medium-sized town, while the Faroes have the same sort of relationship with it as the Channel Isles have with the United Kingdom. They are self-governing for most purposes, but foreign affairs and defence are a Danish responsibility. They have remained outside the Common Market, but have free trade with Denmark, and through Denmark with the Community as a whole. Since their only export is fish, this does not give rise to any serious problems— certainly none comparable with those caused by East Germany's free access via West Germany—the EEC being a heavy importer in any event mainly from Norway and Iceland.

Denmark has a single-house Parliament, the *Folketing*, with 179 members. Two of them represent Greenland, another two the Faroes: the remaining 175 are elected by the Danish people, using proportional representation. There are ten parties, which has led in recent years to the same instability as in Belgium and Holland. Earlier on the Social Democrats, with help from the Left Centre, were more or less permanently in office: they created an elaborate system of social welfare which brought them many votes: unfortunately it also cost a great deal of money and thus became rather unpopular with those who felt they were paying more for it than they were getting out of it, and those who felt this way became increasingly numerous as taxes went up. An anti-tax party, which proposed to disband the army and most of the Civil Service, did very well in the 1973 general election; since then it has lost some ground but remains a substantial force.

Most people think of Denmark as an agricultural country: it is in fact more industrial than agricultural, but the Danish farmers give the nation its distinctive character, and much of Danish industry consists of processing various agricultural products which are then exported as bacon, butter, cheese, or beer. Even in the cities—and Copenhagen is the only really large one—the link with the land remains strong, and farming interests carry a great deal of weight in Danish politics.

This was clearly seen when Denmark joined the Common Market. It went in because the farmers and the food-processing industries could not afford to find themselves on the wrong side of a tariff barrier separating them from both their main customers, Britain and West Germany. Had Britain not joined it would have been a matter of deciding which was more valuable—the British or the German trade. In that case the verdict would probably have gone against joining, because the "non-food" industries had much to fear from German competition, and Germany's accession was in fact followed by a steep rise in unemployment. How far this was due to EEC membership is arguable: Denmark, producing neither coal nor hydro-electricity, suffered badly from the oil crisis; the country which suffered least was France, which has both and gets oil from Algeria rather than from the Middle East.

Denmark belongs at the same time to the EEC and to the Nordic Council, whose other members are Norway, Sweden, Finland, and Iceland. All these countries, except Iceland, have free trade agreements with the Community. In addition, citizens of any of the Nordic countries may take up most jobs in all the others: the main exceptions are Civil Service posts and commissions in the armed services. Danes (but not other Scandinavians) may also take up jobs anywhere in the Community, so these two arrangements give them complete freedom of movement from Hammerfest, well above the Arctic Circle, to western Sicily, almost within sight of Africa, and the run of thirteen countries. The Nordic Council does not have authorities similar to the EEC

Commission, Council, and Court, but works on a more informal basis: the five prime ministers meet at certain times, the ministers of Agriculture, Industry, Education, etc., at other times, and similar meetings of senior civil servants and parliamentary delegations are also organized. No joint decisions are taken: it is more a matter of co-ordinating national decisions and seeing that policies do not conflict.

Ireland

Area   70,300 sq. km*

Population   3,086,000

Density   44 per sq. km

Age distribution of population (%)
- Under 15   31.2
- 15–64   57.7
- 65 +   11.1

Economically active population   1,111,000

Economically active persons as percentage of total population	36.0
Percentage of women in economically active population	26.0 approx.†
Percentage of economically active persons in female population	20.0 approx.
(in 15–64 age group 35% approx.)	

Distribution of economically active population (%)

By status
- Employers, self-employed, and family workers   28.9
- Wage and salary earners (1974)   71.1
- Unemployed (November 1975)   9.7

By sectors
- Agriculture   24.3
- Industry   31.1
- Services   44.6

GNP per head   1725 UA (ninth out of nine states)

Agricultural self-sufficiency   136%

Imported energy dependence 81.5%

*These figures refer to the Republic of Ireland only. The six counties of Northern Ireland are included in the United Kingdom. Figures for Northern Ireland on its own, population density, age distribution, employment structure, etc., are generally intermediate between those given for the United Kingdom and for the Republic.

†There are no recent figures for the economical activity of women. Those given here date back to 1971 but there has in fact been very little change in the general structure of employment since that time, and they are unlikely to be far out.

The states which created or later joined the Community nearly all sacrificed a measure of national sovereignty for the sake of something else which they regarded as more important. Ireland is unique in that she joined for the sake of greater independence, hoping to gain what the others gave up. The reason is that her economy was seriously unbalanced by the United Kingdom's massive share in her foreign trade, both as a customer (essentially for agricultural products and high-quality textiles) and as a supplier (of nearly everything else). The British were more or less in a position to decide how much they were prepared to pay for her beef, butter, and bacon: all other customers were much farther away and on the far side of a tariff wall. They could also dictate the price she would have to pay for their cars, washing machines, and television sets, again because other suppliers were much farther away and transport costs would have made up for any difference in the factory price of the goods.

This economic inferiority was humiliating in itself, but it also meant that Ireland was vulnerable to political pressures and that others—specifically the United Kingdom Treasury—decided what her money was worth.* From joining the Common Market, Ireland hoped above all to gain a more diversified economy and a more balanced relationship with the United Kingdom: both are minorities within the Community whereas, when they are face to face, Britain has twenty times Ireland's wealth and fifteen times per population. For this reason some of the largest majorities for the EEC, in the 1972 referendum, were recorded in areas with a strong Nationalist tradition, such as Donegal.

Like most of the EEC states, Ireland has a two-House Parliament, known as the Oireachtas. The Dail, or House of Representatives, consists of 145 members elected by 38 constituencies of varying size (2–5 members each). Proportional representation is used but does not result, as in some other countries, in a multiplicity of parties: in fact there are only three that matter, Fianna Fail, Fine Gael, and Labour, which is considerably smaller than the other two, but sometimes holds the balance of power between them. Only an Irishman can tell the difference between Fianna Fail and Fine Gael, and it is largely a matter of history and personalities rather than policy and interests. Fine Gael is the continuation of the moderate Nationalist Party which, under the leadership of Collins, Griffith, and the elder Cosgrave, accepted dominion status as the Irish Free State, and the partition of Ulster, six of whose nine counties remained within the United Kingdom. Its present leader is Cosgrave's son. Fianne Fail is the continuation of the more radical party, led by De Valera and the elder Childers, which refused to accept the Treaty of London and fought on for an independent republic including all thirty-two counties. De Valera lived on to be Taoiasach (Prime Minister), then President, dying in 1975 at the age of 92; Erskine Childers senior was shot on Cosgrave's orders but his son, as President, swore in the younger Cosgrave as Prime Minister. Since Ireland is now an independent republic, one of the

*This is still the case at present (1976), but there is increasing support for an independent currency, and little doubt that Ireland will in due course choose to have one. It is generally thought that the Irish £ would be worth a little more than the £ sterling: this would make exports to Britain more expensive but would be advantageous in other respects.

issues over which they quarrelled is no longer relevant; the other is something about which both parties have agreed there is little to be done for the moment. However, it may be said, to establish the difference, that Fianna Fail is a little more *consciously* Irish than Fine Gael, and in particular more concerned with the status of the Irish language.

Irish, which is very similar to Scottish Gaelic, and akin to Breton and Welsh, is one of the oldest languages in Europe. If St. Patrick were to come back and preach in Connemara or the Aran Islands, nobody would have much difficulty in understanding him except, of course, any foreign tourists who happened to be around at the time. Everybody agrees that it is an essential part of Ireland's Irishness, and must be preserved; but very few people *habitually* speak it: perhaps 50,000 out of 3 million (much the same proportion as speak Gaelic in Scotland and well below the corresponding figure for Wales). Many more have *some* knowledge of it, and street signs are generally bilingual. EEC documents, or some of them, are translated into it, but Irish representatives in the Common Market institutions speak and generally listen to English. Danish representatives usually do likewise, but their own language is provided for at the most important meetings, and some of them use French or German instead of English when Danish is not available.

Although there is a "language question", essentially concerned with the use of Irish in official correspondence, and how far it should be compulsory at school, to the possible detriment of other subjects, this is not a major issue to the same extent as in Belgium, and there is no visible language frontier. Similarly, though the Church has a great deal of influence (95% of the population are Catholics, and most of them still attend Mass regularly), politics do not divide on religious lines, as in Northern Ireland or Holland. Protestants may be found in all three major parties, and two of the first three presidents were among them.

Ireland's accession to the Common Market had immediate and beneficial consequences for her farmers, but was less helpful to manufacturing firms, producing mainly for the protected Irish market. Hence unemployment, which has always been relatively high, continued to rise. This, however, was partly due to the fact that young Irish workers, who had previously emigrated to England, or worked there on a seasonal basis, now had more confidence in their own country's future and preferred to stay at home until a job was available locally. Other reasons included higher unemployment in the United Kingdom, and the fact that many British employers, because of the Ulster troubles, were reluctant to take on Irishmen in any event. The situation might well have been worse had Ireland not joined the EEC: as a member-state she qualifies for help under the Regional and Social Funds, which should go a long way towards repairing any temporary damage to her industries.

From a political standpoint she carries far more weight as a member of the Community than she did on her own as a small country very much under Britain's shadow. This was particularly obvious in the first half of 1975, when her Foreign Minister held the Council Presidency and acted as the Community's spokesman on the international stage.

Luxemburg

Area	2600 sq. km
Population	357,000
Density	136 per sq. km

Age distribution of population (%)
Under 15	20.2
15–64	66.9
65 +	12.9

Economically active population   151,000
Economically active persons as percentage of total population	42.3
Percentage of women in economically active population	26.9
Percentage of economically active persons in female population	20.3
(in 15–64 age group 30% approx.)	

Distribution of economically active population (%)
By status
Employers, self-employed, and family workers	15.9
Wage and salary earners (1974)	84.1*
Unemployed (October 1975)	0.4

By sectors
Agriculture	6.6
Industry	49.0
Services	44.4

GNP per head   4761 UA (third out of nine states)

Agricultural self-sufficiency (combined with Belgium)   119%

Imported energy dependence   99.4%

*These appear to be the figures for the *whole* population, including foreigners. For the *citizen* population they are somewhat different: employers, self-employed, and family workers 21.2%; wage and salary earners 78.8%. This seems to be the only explanation for the very substantial differences to be found between two sets of equally official statistics.

Luxemburg is the smallest member-state of the Community: it is not, however, a relic of the Middle Ages like San Marino or Lichtenstein. Originally part of the Spanish and Austrian Netherlands, it was transferred to Dutch rule with Belgium in 1815 and joined in the Belgian revolt of 1830. It was only split off from Belgium a few years later, more or less along linguistic lines: the French-speaking areas remained part of Belgium as the Province of Luxemburg, while the Letzeburgish-speaking areas became an independent Grand Duchy. The reigning family is a Catholic branch of the Dutch royal house and the flag is similar to Holland's, though with a pale blue stripe.

There is only one House of Parliament, consisting of 59 elected members, but the Council of State, with 21 members nominated by the Grand Duke, has some of the functions of a senate in other countries. It considers all proposed legislation and major government regulations, acts as a court of law for some purposes (e.g. to consider complaints against senior civil servants), and gives advice on all matters submitted to it by the Government.

The Cabinet itself is very small, with nine members whose portfolios are sometimes combined in a peculiar way. Thus one might expect wine-growing to belong with agriculture, but it is such an important subject in its own right that it has been handed over to the Minister of Public Works, who would otherwise have little to do in a country with fewer people than Edinburgh or Bristol. Similarly, the Foreign Minister is also responsible for the Civil Service and for sport.

The country is so small that most of what it produces is exported, while most of what it consumes is imported, the proportion in both cases being well over 80%. Another peculiar aspect of its economy is that it makes a relatively large income simply by being there and by levying less tax than its three neighbours, for instance on petrol bought by motorists passing through, and on companies registered there. It would lose heavily if these matters were ever standardized under Community law; in the meantime it does very well by housing three of the Community's institutions—the Parliament, the Court of Justice, and the European Investment Bank.

General Considerations

All the present member-states have three things in common at least beside the fact of being in Europe. In the first place they all have a per capita income and, what is more important, a standard of living well above the world average.* This is true even of Italy as a country, though possibly not of its poorest regions. Secondly, by comparison with the rest of the world, they all have a very high proportion of their working population in manufacturing industries and the services sector, and a relatively low proportion in agriculture. This is less true of Italy and of Ireland than of the other seven, but even they have a minority of their population on the land.† Thirdly, every one of

*These are not necessarily the same thing. In the first place, exchange rates may be rather deceptive, especially when comparing Communist and Western states. Secondly, we must consider not only money incomes but the cost of living, and to do this we must first decide what items are part of the cost of living. National statistics are not fully comparable in this respect. Thirdly, in countries where many or most people are farmers producing largely for their families and neighbours, it may be more important to know how much and what variety of food they grow than what they actually earn. Most Europeans have to buy all or nearly all of their food, and even European farmers buy a large part of it; but this is not necessarily the case in West Africa, where the same money income will therefore buy more of what has to be bought. Even in Calabria money incomes are above the world average, though the standard of living may be slightly below. On the West African coast it is the other way round.

†The division between agriculture, manufacturing industry, and services has an honoured place in Common Market and world statistics. It is, however, rather artificial and misleading,

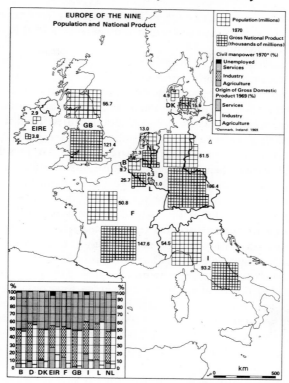

Fig. 2. Europe of the Nine: population and national product. (European Communities Information Service, London).

first because some manufacturing industries are directly linked with farming and fishing (food processing and production of agricultural equipment, etc.), and, secondly, because the services sector is very wide and includes nearly everybody who does not work on a farm, on a fishing boat, in a factory, or down a mine. Many of those involved in it are in fact providing services for farmers and their workers and dependants, and must therefore be considered as part of the "agricultural interest" in the same way as those who are making tractors or converting milk into butter or cheese. Thirdly, on the Continent and in Scotland and Ireland, if not in England, many people are at the same time growing food and doing something else (e.g. running a café or a small filling station). Hence, though farmers and farm workers as such are a minority everywhere, the "agricultural interest" certainly amounts to a majority in Ireland, probably also in Italy, and it is a very substantial minority in most of the other member-states.

Several countries publish statistics which show the breakdown between those living in rural districts and in small towns, and those living in larger towns and cities. These may be more relevant than the conventional division between the primary, secondary, and tertiary sectors. As a rough guide, those who live in open country, in villages, or in towns with a population of under 5000 (and in some countries, such as Italy, even 10,000) may be regarded as forming part of the agricultural interest. This is only a rule of thumb, which allows, on the one hand for miners and factory workers living in villages, and, on the other, for people in larger towns which live largely by providing services for farmers.

them is a parliamentary democracy with a multi-party system, whatever the method of electing MPs and the number of parties, and this is, indeed, a condition of membership.

Without these common factors the Common Market could not exist because it can only function on the basis that all the member-states have compatible economies and a comparable way of life (a state where average wages were £5 a week could not be fitted in: either its industries would undercut those of all the rest or its workers would all migrate to the more prosperous countries), and that some decisions are taken jointly through the Council, while others, taken at national level, tend to run on similar lines and are often the subject of informal discussion between the ministers of the nine states.

Once the decisions have been taken, it is the states that apply them, and their co-operation is essential to the whole process. In most cases each state is responsible for implementing the agreed Community policy on its own territory: in some instances (reception and, if necessary, training of migrant workers, educational arrangements for their children, and social welfare for their families) two states, e.g. West Germany and Italy, have to work out the details together. It is also on the member-states that the Community as a whole depends for information as to how the various policies are working out: its own "Civil Service" is very small considering the size and population of the Common Market, with under 14,000 staff, of whom only 2500 are in the administrative grade, for 255,000,000 people, and very few of them stationed anywhere other than Brussels, Luxemburg, and the research centres.

If the Community survives at all it is not because it can depend on the European will of the European people—not at present anyway—but because the nine states, as states, want to go on working together. It will only progress as far as they want it to progress, and only so long as they feel they can generally trust one another.

CHAPTER 3

The Institutions of the Community

This chapter is only intended to give an outline picture of the Common Market institutions in non-technical language. It is not in any sense an exhaustive survey.

The Common Market staff numbers 13,688 and by far the largest of its institutions is the Commission in the broader sense, that is, taking the thirteen commissioners together with their personal staff and supporting "Civil Service". It employs 10,182 people of whom 2157 are administrative grade officials, 1147 are interpreters or translators, 1754 are research scientists mainly at the Joint Research Centre, with a few working on other projects financed by the Community. The rest are mainly secretaries and typists. A few hundred more may be found working with the Commission at any given time as freelance interpreters, executive trainees (*stagiaires*), and advisers of one kind or another.*

Its main functions are to prepare policy decisions for the Council, to implement these decisions in co-operation with the member-states, and to manage the Regional Fund, the Social Fund, the Customs Union, and various aspects of European agriculture. It has inherited the ECSC High Authority's overall responsibility for the production of steel and for the production and purchase of its raw materials, coal, iron, and scrap: together with the European Court of Justice it also does its best to ensure compliance with the rules laid down in the ECSC, EEC, and Euratom treaties, or made on the basis of these treaties (regulations, directives, and decisions). The division of labour between the two institutions implies that the Commission

*By way of comparison the Council employs 1505 persons, the Assembly (European Parliament) employs 1404 (of whom 127 are temporary, mainly attached to the political groups), the Economic and Social Committee 302, and the Court 244. Another 35, paid from the Council budget, keep track of the Community's finances. Up to 200 freelance interpreters may also be present at any given time, mainly in Brussels, with a few in Luxemburg. This depends on the number of meetings on any particular day. The Commission, Council, and Economic and Social Committee between them have 40 conference rooms in Brussels; the Commission, Parliament, and Court together have another 10–12 in Luxemburg, and the Parliament has a few more in Brussels for its committees. Including groups for which simultaneous interpretation is not required, it is possible to hold over 60 Common Market meetings at the same time.

acts first by finding that a government or a firm is doing something unauthorized and telling it to stop. This is usually enough, but where it is not the offender may be reported to the Court, which then gives a ruling. National courts will generally back up the decisions of the Court if the offender is a firm. If it is a government this may be difficult or impossible, but in practice such disputes are nearly always settled by a political compromise at Council level rather than by legal proceedings: well over 90% of the cases in which the Court has to intervene involve firms rather than national or local authorities.

The Commission in the narrow sense consists of thirteen named individuals, appointed by the Council as a whole on the recommendation of the nine governments. Each of the larger states (France, Germany, Italy, United Kingdom), has two commissioners; the rest have one apiece. Most of them are not former civil servants but have a political, diplomatic, or academic background. They take an oath to serve the Community alone and to accept no instructions from their national governments or any other outside body, but they are expected to maintain contact with political and other leaders in their own countries and return home frequently for a few days at a time. This prevents the Brussels bureaucracy from becoming too isolated in its ivory tower (in fact cement and star-shaped) and concocting impractical schemes that would have no chance of being approved by the member-states nor, therefore, by the Council.

Each of the commissioners is assisted by a chief of staff, normally of his own nationality, and by a personal staff (usually also of his own nationality), who help him work out the aspects of policy for which he is responsible and to process the draft regulations, memoranda, etc., which come up from his department as well as to arrive at an opinion on matters which come before the Commission as a body. Unlike other EEC officials they are appointed by him at his discretion and leave with him. This arrangement was taken over from French Government practice, each minister having a personal staff of this type who come and go with him: in the United Kingdom the Prime Minister alone has a similar group at his disposal.

The Commission in the broader sense consists of the above together with twenty administrative departments each headed by a director-general, and a few specialized services (Statistics, Legal Service, Spokesman's Group). While the Commissioner may in United Kingdom terms be compared to a minister (except that he is more independent and much harder to get rid of), the Director-General is more similar, in his status and functions, to a permanent secretary.

These departments, or directorates-general, vary considerably in size depending on the work they do. By far the largest is DG VI (Agriculture and Fisheries) which spends over 80% of the Community's budget and includes 8 directorates and 91 divisions. The reason for its size is that it has to administer FEOGA (the European Agricultural Guidance and Guarantee Fund), operate the complex system of levies, interventions, and refunds, and run all the management boards: in principle all the main policy decisions in the sphere which it controls are taken at Community rather than national level. On the other hand, DG XII (Research, Science, and Education) and DG XVI (Regional Policy) are very small—no larger than some of the individual directorates in DG VI—because their task is to co-ordinate and support work already being done by national governments and by regional and local authorities.

The administrative set-up may best be understood by looking at the largest of these departments. The Commissioner for Agriculture is traditionally a Dutchman: the present Director-General is a Frenchman and will in due course most probably be replaced by another Frenchman. The reason is that every country is entitled to a certain number of senior posts. When a DG retires he must normally be replaced by someone of his own nationality, otherwise his country will be one down. At director level this is less important because it is quite likely that two or three of them will retire or be promoted at about the same time; a German may then be succeeded by an Italian, an Italian by a Belgian, and a Belgian by a German, and the proportions will still be right. The Agricultural DG's closest colleagues (three deputy DGs and two assistants) include, at the time of writing, an Italian, an Englishman, two Germans, and another Frenchman.*

The eight directorates are concerned with:

(1) international affairs connected with agriculture (e.g. the activities of the FAO and the participation of the Community as such and of its member-states in these activities);
(2) the organization of markets in cereals;
(3) the organization of markets in livestock products;
(4) the organization of markets in other products;
(5) agricultural structures and the agricultural environment (this includes such things as the size of farms one should encourage and the organization of marketing co-operatives);
(6) the Guidance and Guarantee Fund;
(7) agricultural economics;
(8) agricultural legislation.

The eight directors are all of different nationalities. If we look more closely at one of the directorates (Livestock Products), we shall see that it has a Dane as its director with an Italian, an Irishman, and a Dutchman as its three heads of divisions. The Italian is responsible for meat and live cattle, the Irishman for dairy products, and the Dutchman for eggs and poultry. Each of those three controls, among other things, one of the management committees described in the next chapter.

*The Commissioner for Agriculture (since 1 January 1977) is now a Dane, but the general principle remains unaffected.

DG IX (Personnel and Administration) is even bigger because it includes all the translators and interpreters on the Commission staff (the Council has its own translators but "borrows" its interpreters from the Commission). It makes no policy, however: it is there purely to enable the rest of the Commission to do its work. Again it includes citizens of all nine member-states.

In principle the Commission is the body which holds "Europe" together while the Council ensures that it goes on consisting of nations and does not lose its distinctive character as the result of too much "harmonization". The Council can do nothing without the Commission apart from holding general discussion (and even these are often based on Commission reports and memoranda), because it would have no proposals to work on if they did not emerge from the star-shaped building after a great deal of consideration and reconsideration. The Commission cannot do much without the Council apart from setting the price of products (within narrow limits, themselves set by the Council) and preventing undesirable mergers, monopolies, and commercial agreements. Even this is only possible in so far as the national governments co-operate and provided the Council votes the budget which enables the Commission to carry on. The two bodies are in fact indispensable to each other however much they may disagree or appear to disagree at times.

The Council

Most people think of "the Council" as consisting of the nine foreign ministers, and this is usually the case when the most important decisions have to be taken. But it may equally well consist of the nine ministers of agriculture (and often does) or of the finance ministers, or (less frequently) of the ministers responsible for scientific research, for instance. In some cases there may be two cabinet ministers from each member-state, or from some of them. This would be the case if overseas development were on the agenda. Britain and France, as former imperial powers, each have a cabinet minister who is specifically responsible for this very important field, but the United Kingdom Foreign Secretary and the French Minister for Foreign Affairs both take a serious interest as well. In Germany, Belgium, and Holland it comes under a junior minister at the Foreign Office: in the remaining countries it falls within the general responsibilities of the Foreign Minister. Hence a meeting of the Council to discuss overseas development would involve the nine foreign ministers, the specialist cabinet ministers, and junior ministers from the states which have them, and probably also a number of senior civil servants. Since all the foreign ministers would be there, it would almost certainly find time to discuss other matters as well.

While the Council of Ministers does not consist of named individuals in the same way as the Commission, its supporting body, COREPER, does— these individuals being the nine permanent representatives who have a diplomatic or senior Civil Service background and are the "ambassadors" of the member-states to the Community as a whole. Except in rare emergencies, no Commission proposal goes to the Council without being first considered by COREPER or by CSA, which consists of the agricultural specialists attached to each Permanent Delegation. Each COREPER member has a staff of national experts (usually civil servants) stationed in Brussels with him, covering the main fields in which the Council is expected to take decisions. Hence a COREPER meeting, like a Council meeting, will not consist of nine people only, but of fifty or more, including other civil servants, scientists, etc., sent out, as circumstances require, by their governments. Only the Minister or Permanent Representative, however, may claim the right to speak, but, having been given the floor he may ask one of his colleagues to put a particular point.

Ministers, permanent representatives, and their staff are appointed directly by the nine governments. In addition, however, the Council itself, through its Secretary-General, recruits and employs several hundred officials, translators, secretaries, etc., to help it in its work of processing the Commission's proposals before they are adopted as directives, regulations, decisions, or non-binding resolutions. They are organized in directorates-general, directorates, and divisions in much the same way as the Commission Services, but each of these units is far smaller than its Commission counterpart.

The Presidency of the Council rotates at six-month intervals in approximate order of car identification plates, but Britain sits as UK, not GB, and DK (Denmark) comes before D (Germany).* New states, as and when they join, are fitted into their place in this scheme; thus Spain (E) will sit between Germany and France if and when she joins, Greece after France, Portugal after the Netherlands, and Scotland, in the event of becoming independent, after Portugal. During a country's term of office it provides the chairman for all meetings of the Council of Ministers, COREPER, CSA, and the Council study groups whose work is described in the next chapter. It also acts as host to the European Council (the President of the French Republic and the nine prime ministers, who meet in its capital once during this period (there are in fact three meetings of this body each year. Each of the two countries holding the Council Presidency gets one of them, and the third normally takes place in Brussels.)

An important part of the Council set-up is the Committee of Jurists-Linguists, which goes through directives and regulations with a fine-tooth-comb after they have been approved by the ministers but before they take

*The order is in fact that of the countries' names in their own language.

effect, to ensure that they mean exactly the same things in each of the Community's six languages. They have the status of officials rather than translators, and are lawyers trained in administrative drafting. Serious consequences would follow if they failed to do their work properly; if a regulation does not mean the same thing in all languages it may be found out of order by the European Court. All the arrangements made on the basis of that regulation will then be invalid and somebody may lose millions of pounds.

The Assembly (European Parliament)

One peculiarity of this body is that it has two names. It is called the Assembly in the Treaty of Rome and the Council always refers to it thus. It is therefore mentioned under the name in regulations and directives when they are published. But it calls itself the European Parliament and is known by that name to the Commission, the Press, and the general public in so far as the general public knows of its existence. Strictly speaking, the Council is right because the Assembly is not elected (though in principle it will be as from 1978), levies no taxes, and enacts no laws. It consists of delegates from the parliaments of the nine member-states, appointed by their governments but in approximate ratio to the strength of the various parties and after consultation with these parties. It is an advisory body, but its advice carries considerable weight and it is being given an increasing say in determining how the Community is to spend part (but not all) of its budget.

The Assembly (or Parliament) itself consists of 36 members each from France, West Germany, Italy, and Britain, 14 each from Belgium and the Netherlands, 10 each from Denmark and Ireland, and 6 from Luxemburg. It will be enlarged at the same time as it becomes a directly elected body, and the four large member-states will then have 81 members each. These members, and the political groups which they form, are backed up by research, language, and secretarial services which are normally housed on the Kirchberg, just outside Luxemburg City, but move to Strasbourg whenever the Parliament meets there.

This rather wasteful procedure, which involves carting some 50 tons of documents back and forth, is necessary because France insists on having one of the institutions at least some of the time. The Assembly therefore holds most of its plenary sessions in the Council of Europe building, together with a few in Luxemburg. In addition, however, it has a dozen committees which normally meet in Brussels. Each of these committees includes members of all the political groups, coming from most though not necessarily all of the member-states, and every member of the Assembly is expected to join one or two of them and take a regular part in its work.

The Assembly's main task is to give an opinion on all proposals (draft directives, regulations, and major policy decisions or statements) submitted by the Commission to the Council: such proposals are considered in turn by the relevant committees (e.g. Agriculture, Legal, Regional Policy), by the political groups (Socialist, Conservative, Christian Democratic, Liberals, etc.), and by the plenary session. But it also serves as a forum for general discussion and criticism, much as the United Kingdom Parliament does, and the commissioners appear before it, or its committees and groups, to answer questions, defend their policy, and explain what they are doing or planning to do. It also plays an important part in maintaining links between the Community and the many developing countries now associated with it; this is done through meetings taking place in Brussels or in the capitals of these countries.

The Economic and Social Committee

This body has *functions* similar to those of the Assembly, but without *powers,* and in a narrower field: it is about two-thirds of the Assembly's size. Its members are appointed in much the same way, i.e. by the governments of their respective countries and after consultation with various bodies; these bodies, however, are not political parties, and the committee members, as a rule, are not politicians. One-third of them represent the employers' side of industry, including nationalized undertakings, and one-third represent trades unions, these two groups together being known as the "Social Partners". Group III is a very mixed bag, including farmers, doctors, shop-keepers, and "consumers". The Economic and Social Committee is divided, like the Assembly, into a number of committees including members of all three groups, while the groups themselves meet in much the same way as the Assembly's political parties. But its work attracts less attention, except in specialist circles (e.g. farmers' organizations), and its meetings are not reported in the Press. Its permanent staff is very small compared with the other institutions.

The European Court of Justice

This is a far more important institution, located on the outskirts of Luxemburg City, across the road from the Assembly. Its task, as we have seen, is to ensure compliance with the treaties and with the Community's own legislation (directives, regulations, and decisions).

In some cases it acts on a complaint from the Commission or from a member-state against another member-state or more usually a firm. This complaint may, for instance, allege payment of unlawful subsidies or the collection of unlawful taxes (if a state is involved) and various unlawful trading practices (monopolies, market-sharing agreements, etc.) where the offender is a firm.

In other instances the Court may be asked for a "preliminary ruling" by a judge who is already trying a case in one of the member-states. This is in fact a more frequent occurrence than action on a direct complaint from the Commission or one of the nine governments because it is the only way in which an ordinary firm can normally get a decision from the European Court either against its own government or a rival firm.

The Court also deals with disputes between institutions (e.g. the Commission and the Council). One such case occurred in 1973: the Commission, under pressure from its staff, agreed to give them a 10% increase, backdated eight months. The Council, under pressure from the nine governments (which were all trying to hold down inflation in their respective countries), refused to make the money available. After a strike lasting several days the matter was referred to the Court, which ultimately found in favour of the Commission.

Finally, it deals with disputes between the other institutions and their employees over such matters as wrongful dismissal, refusal of promotion opportunities, and transfer from one of the Community's establishments to another: some cases of this type have been known to drag on for years.

The Court consists at present of nine judges, one from each member-state, plus two advocates-general, whose main task is to prepare draft opinion for their colleagues. Britain has two legal systems and only one of them could be represented: at the time of writing (1975) Scotland has a place on the Bench while England has one of the two advocates-general, the other being a Frenchman.

Like the other institutions the Court has its own permanent staff, but this is relatively small: it borrows its interpreters from the Assembly as the Council borrows them from the Commission.

(The European Investment Bank is sometimes regarded as one of the Community institutions: it is, however, quite different in kind from the others since it plays no direct part in the preparation, taking or implementation of Community decisions. It is therefore described separately in Chapter 13.)

CHAPTER 4

The Decision-making Processes of the Community

Within the fields covered by the Community treaties the general rule is that the Commission proposes, the Assembly and the Economic and Social Committee advise, the Council disposes, and the Commission comes in again to implement any decisions that may be taken. The Court only intervenes if difficulties arise, i.e. if somebody (a government or a firm) disregards these decisions or claims that they are invalid because they are inconsistent with one of the treaties or with a regulation which is already in force and has not been amended or repealed.

Every such decision (a term which covers directives, regulations, and "decisions" in the narrow sense) must refer to the appropriate treaty (ECSC, EEC, or Euratom) and to one or more of its articles. This is not a mere formality: it is done in order to ensure that the Common Market authorities do not legislate on something which does not fall within their competence. They could not, for instance, make a regulation to establish the same school-leaving age throughout the EEC because the Treaty of Rome does not give them any such power. On the other hand, they can and do make rules about trade within the Community, trade between Community states and the outside world, subsidies, and other government aids to industry, farming, transport, and much else besides.

The first step in the decision-making process is that *somebody* asks for action of some kind to be taken. This "somebody" is likely to be the Council at the request of one of the member-states, or it may be a meeting of the thirteen commissioners or of their chiefs of staff, or the Assembly in the course of a general debate. The Regional Policy, which is of some interest to nearly everybody in Scotland and Ireland, and to millions of people in most of the other EEC countries, was called for by a meeting of the European Council held in Paris shortly after Norway had voted not to join the Community and just before Britain, Denmark, and Ireland did join: Norway's decision to stay out was largely due to the absence of such a policy at the time and to fear that farmers and fishermen might suffer in consequence from the Community's centralizing tendencies. The same meeting also called for a start on the Environment Policy and for greater activity in the field of Social Policy.

The next step is that a few people in the Commission get down to writing a first draft. Who these people are depends on the subject-matter, but they almost always belong to three or four different countries, and generally produce their working paper in French, less often in English or German. It is always translated into the other two main languages, sometimes also into Italian and Dutch, hardly ever into Danish, and then comes up for discussion by one or more study groups. These consist mainly of national civil servants and experts, with a Commission official as chairman and another Commission official, perhaps even two, presenting, explaining, and defending the draft proposal.

How many study groups are involved will depend on just how complex the proposal is; it may, for instance, have public health and industrial safety aspects, requiring two quite distinct sets of experts—doctors in one case and engineers in the other—along with civil servants from different ministries. At this stage they are helping the Commission to arrive at something that will be more or less acceptable to all nine governments. A few months later, however, these same people may reappear as a Council working group, under instructions from their governments, to say whether or not the proposal is in fact acceptable, and if not, what is wrong with it.

This "committee stage" will normally last anything from three months to a year or more, depending on how detailed the draft proposal is, and how often the civil servants and experts can meet: once they have done their work, senior officials of the Commission produce a final draft which is then put to the commissioners themselves through their chiefs of staff. If it is a routine matter and unlikely to be very controversial, each Chief of Staff *may* discuss it individually with his Commissioner, and it is then submitted to the Council when all thirteen have approved it. Anything which is of considerable importance, however, must go before the Commission as a body. The normal procedure is that, if nobody on a Commissioner's personal staff queries a particular draft regulation, directive, or decision, the approval of the whole body will simply be assumed. If there are queries, or if the matter is obviously of more than routine significance, each Chief of Staff *will* probably discuss it with his Commissioner, but it may not be necessary for the whole of the Commission to discuss it. Nobody could possibly expect the commissioners to read or even glance through every one of the 3000 or more administrative measures and draft policy items which go through the mill in the course of a year.

The proposal, once formally approved by the Commission, does not go straight to the nine ministers except in rare emergencies such as the West African drought. It is received by the Council Secretariat and distributed to the nine member-states through their permanent representatives. At the same time it is sent to the Assembly and possibly to the Economic and Social Committee for their opinion. The nine governments look at it, or more probably get some of their civil servants to look at it, and send in their comments through their representatives on the Council working groups mentioned above: one of these, belonging to the country which holds the Presidency for the time being, chairs the group. As a rule, this procedure is not as time-consuming as at Commission level, since the proposal can no longer be amended until it reaches the ministers' table. All the experts are doing is getting together as a body, listening to what the Commission has to say, putting their official point of view (whereas in the Commission groups they were speaking as individuals) and advising their ministers when they get home.

Meanwhile the Assembly (or "European Parliament") and the Economic and Social Committee are preparing their advisory opinions, which are not binding but are taken very seriously because anything which is unacceptable to the Assembly will probably be unacceptable to several of the national parliaments, while anything which does not get past the ESC is likely to be rejected by some at least of the national employers' organizations and trades unions. The ministers are well aware of the difficulties this could cause when they get back home and will therefore turn down the proposal or demand extensive amendments.

The procedure in the Assembly is that the Commission's proposal is considered in turn by the appropriate Committee (e.g. Agriculture, Regional Policy, and Transport, Social Affairs, and Employment) by the various political groups and by the plenary session, but what really matters is the draft opinion submitted to the plenary by one of the committees, since this is usually accepted as it stands or with minor amendments. In every case a member of the committee (which consists of 25–35 members) acts as "rapporteur" and writes a pre-draft opinion which is considered by the whole committee and passed on as a draft opinion to the political groups and the plenary.

This procedure is also followed in the Economic and Social Committee, but with Group I (Employers), Group II (Trade Unions), and Group III (Others) taking the place of the Assembly's political groups.

As often as not, the real decision is taken at a meeting of COREPER, the nine "ambassadors" of the member-states to the Community as a whole, acting on instructions from home and often phoning their ministers for further instructions. If they reject a proposal it obviously does not stand a chance and the Commission may then withdraw it. If they accept it unanimously, the ministers usually approve it without any further discussion, since it is they who told the "ambassadors" to let it through. If they only accept it by a majority, amendments will probably be required and a discussion at the Council table is certain. What then happens is that the Commission sends two of its members (usually its President and the Commissioner who is responsible for the particular matter under discussion (e.g. agriculture, industry, foreign trade), and these two have delegated powers from their colleagues to make any amendments that may be necessary within reason.

The final product will generally be a directive, a regulation, or a decision. These three ''acts'' of the Community are quite distinct.

A directive sets out an objective to be achieved, e.g. uniform safety standards for commercial vehicles, or aid for underpopulated or poverty-stricken regions; but the member-states then have to enact national legislation to achieve this objective. It only comes into force once the states have had reasonable time to take this action.

A regulation becomes law throughout the Community (and as it stands) as soon as it has been published in the *Official Journal* (generally a few days or weeks after it has been approved by the Council of Ministers, depending on the time taken to have it processed by the jurists–linguists and printed by the Council's printers). The member-states, however, have to apply it through their own officials, police, courts, etc., and in some cases they do not get round to it.

A decision settles a particular issue, often of some urgency. For instance, one member-state may have too much wine, or too many eggs, and may try to stop another member-state from selling it any more. This is contrary to Common Market rules, but the alternative could be violence—French farmers barricading the road from Italy or English farmers smashing up lorry-loads of French eggs. Every state is responsible for the maintenance of public order on its own territory, and the easiest way to maintain it is to prohibit the offending imports. The ministers of agriculture then get together, the Commission puts up a proposal, and the probable outcome is that one country agrees not to export so much, but to turn the eggs into egg powder or the wine into alcohol for medical and industrial uses, while the other agrees not to stop imports, and the Community as a whole agrees to make funds available for processing the eggs or the wine as the case may be. The emergency aid to West Africa was approved by the same procedure. On such occasions the routine of first drafts, working papers, and second drafts is cut out, and the Economic and Social Committee is not involved, nor, as a rule, the Assembly.

The decision procedure, in a somewhat modified form, is also used for the admission of new member-states. In these cases the application to join the Community is sent to the Council in the first instance, but the Commission is expected to give an opinion on the country's suitability for membership (it could be unsuitable because it does not have a democratic form of government or because its economy is not sufficiently developed. This would lead to problems in the state concerned and probably in the Community as a whole.) In order to arrive at an opinion the Commission holds preliminary talks with representatives of the applicant state. It then submits its opinion to the Council, which is not bound to abide by it, though in practice a state considered as insufficiently developed, or as undemocratic, would be unacceptable to several of the existing member-states, if not to all.

Thereafter the member-states negotiate with the applicant state at COREPER and Council level, but at the same time they negotiate to some extent with one another, since a wide variety of national interests are involved, first when one considers whether the state should be admitted at all, and secondly, in deciding what terms it should be offered, (e.g. how many years it should have to adjust external duties to the Common Customs Tariff, and to abolish duties and quota restrictions on imports from the existing member-states; how quickly it should be required to apply regulations which may affect its agriculture and industries). A small country, whose need for special concessions will not have much effect on the economy of the Community as a whole, is likely to have a much easier passage than a larger one; thus Ireland's accession raised fewer problems than Britain's, and Portugal would probably have an easier time getting in than Spain, once both are politically acceptable.

Three main aspects have to be considered: the basic political decision on whether to accept the country at all; the terms it should be offered, and in some cases also special arrangements to protect the interests of existing member-states (e.g. to prevent seriously excessive production of olive oil within the Community—which would be damaging to Italy—if and when Portugal joins); and, finally, the re-allocation of financial obligations, voting rights, and senior Commission and Council posts following from the enlargement of the Community.

While the first step is to consider whether the state is acceptable in principle, the decision to admit is only taken after both parties—the applicant state and the existing Community—have agreed on terms and concessions. Voting rights and financial obligations are settled at the same time, but call for relatively little argument since they are based on the applicant state's population and gross national product, both of which are known, and to some extent on existing precedents. Thus, if Norway were to have second thoughts she would most probably have the same rights and obligations as Denmark, and so would Scotland in the event of becoming independent and acceding to the Community as a member-state in her own right. Portugal might have the same voting entitlement as Denmark, but this is not certain: her population is appreciably larger but her GNP considerably less, which means she would contribute less both in agricultural levies (since she cannot afford and does not need to import much food) and from the proceeds of customs duties and

VAT. In her case, equality of voting rights with Denmark would seem a typical EEC compromise between considerations of population and of economic status. Spain, on the other hand, would almost certainly go in as a major member-state with the same voting rights as Italy, and two commissioners. The redistribution of senior posts, on the other hand, is among the loose ends that are tied up after the decision to admit has been made.

This decision has to be unanimous and can only take effect when it has been ratified by the parliaments of all the existing member-states. At the same time, the decision to join must, of course, be ratified by the Parliament of the applicant state, and may involve a referendum, as it did in Denmark and Ireland (which joined) and Norway (which stayed out).

The Commission on its own may also take decisions (e.g. to prohibit an undesirable merger between two firms) and make regulations or issue directives. Commission regulations fill out some of the details of a Council Regulation adopted by the complicated procedure set up above. They follow the same routine up to the point where the Commission approves them, and are then published in the *Official Journal* and become Community law. Before this happens, however, any member-state may demand that they be considered by the Council, usually because it feels the Commission has gone beyond its remit and is making new policy rather than applying existing policy.

The relationship between Council and Commission regulations is similar in British terms to the relationship between Acts of Parliaments and the regulations which ministers are authorized to make under these Acts. The former are more important; the latter more numerous, and United Kingdom ministerial regulations may be challenged in Parliament by a procedure quaintly known as a "prayer" in much the same way as Commission regulations may be challenged before the Council by one of the member-states. In both cases this has to be done within a certain time-limit. In round numbers, the Council may enact 500 directives, regulations, and decisions in the course of a year: the Commission may churn out well over 3000, but several hundred of these are price-setting decisions of the Agricultural Policy Management Committees, which only remain in force for a week or a month at a time.

The Commission also runs the Customs Union and the Common Agricultural Policy through a number of management committees, each with a Commission official as convener and a delegation from each of the member-states. These delegations are there essentially to give advice; at the end of the day it is the Commission that actually decides, but if it decides against the advice of the majority (a very rare occurrence), the matter comes up before the Council. Management committees can only act within very narrow limits, and in many cases their action follows automatically from the price of live cattle, wheat, etc., recorded on a number of markets and averaged out according to predetermined rules. What they do, having worked out the necessary sums, is to decide what "intervention price" is to be paid to farmers, what levy is to be collected on imports (or on exports in times of scarcity), or what refund is to be paid on exports. If they tried to do more (e.g. to fix an intervention price for a product which does not have one under the regulations in force at the time), they would quickly be called to order by the Council.

An important Community tradition, which operates at all Council and Commission meetings where the member-states are represented (ministers, COREPER, management committees, study groups, etc.) is the *tour de table* procedure. The nine delegations sit around the table and each is called in turn on every point as it comes up, going clockwise or counter-clockwise at the chairman's discretion. Any delegation which tries to discuss Article 2 before everybody has had a chance to comment on Article 1 will quickly be called to order. This ensures that everybody has time to think and a chance to speak, and (given a strong chairman) it generally prevents one or two countries from dominating the whole discussion. Of course, some delegations will say more and others will say less, or nothing at all: Luxemburg has no fishermen, while Denmark and Ireland produce no wine, so they take little interest in some of the debates: what matters is that everybody gets the opportunity, and this encourages a spirit of give-and-take, as do the voting arrangements described below.

Any major Council decision must, in general, be taken by a unanimous vote unless a member-state which is opposed to it agrees to let itself be out-voted. This sometimes happens because the Minister concerned recognizes that it is necessary but, in order to satisfy his colleagues and MPs back home, feels he must be on record as having voted against it. If there is a majority decision, however, this is taken by a "weighted" majority, which means that Britain, France, West Germany, and Italy have 10 votes each, Belgium and Holland 5 each, Denmark and Ireland 3 each, and Luxemburg 2, making a total of 58 votes. A total of 41 votes from five states or more are required for a majority decision; Norway would have had 3 votes if she had joined, and the weighted majority would then have been 43 votes from six states or more. This rule makes it impossible for the four large states to dictate to the rest.

It is because no state is ever *compelled* to give way, where its vital interests as it sees them are at stake, that the whole system can work at all. Some regard these arrangements as "undemocratic", in that the will of the majority does not automatically prevail, but the Common Market would have broken up a long time ago if any serious attempt had been made to run it like a parliamentary democracy. Indeed, it could never have been formed at all if the member-states had not been able to claim this particular safeguard because the Treaty of Rome would not have been ratified by their parliaments or approved by the people in a referendum where the Constitution made this necessary. The system may not work ideally, but it does work, whereas a number of more ambitious unions (e.g. Egypt–Syria, Egypt–Libya, Libya–Tunisia) either failed completely after a trial run or never got off the ground.

The essential point to bear in mind, when we look at the Community's decision-making processes, is that they are in general very slow, and involve a great deal of consultation all along the line. There is no automatic majority as there normally has been in the British Parliament and often in the French National Assembly. When the Commission submits a proposal to the Council it is by no means certain of getting it through, and fully expects important amendments to be made. If a United Kingdom Bill is rejected, or if it is substantially amended against the Cabinet's wishes, the Prime Minister normally has to resign or call an election, and as MPs on the government side are reluctant to face an election, especially when the Government are unpopular, they usually let the Bill through even if they do not like it. But the Commission does not resign in a similar situation, and the Council cannot be dissolved: both have to soldier on. Individual commissioners do resign, however, not because they have to, but because they find the whole process too frustrating.

In an emergency what usually happens—unless the crisis directly concerns the Community as a whole—is that the national government which has to cope with the immediate situation does so, and informs the Commission, which in turn puts the matter before the Council if necessary. In many cases this is not necessary because the emergency measure only remains in force for a few days or weeks.

Otherwise any of the following may happen:

  (i) The Council may approve the emergency measure.
 (ii) It may give the member-state concerned a temporary exemption from one or other of the Community's rules (e.g. Article 93 of the Treaty of Rome which restricts the right of member-states to grant subsidies of various kinds).
(iii) The state concerned withdraws the measure but the Council as a whole takes other steps to deal with the situation (e.g. the wine and egg surpluses mentioned above).
 (iv) The emergency measure is ruled out of order. If the state which took it does not withdraw it, the Commission or another member-state may ultimately raise the matter before the European Court. This in practice is extremely rare because all the member-states want the system to work and know it can only work on a basis of co-operation and mutual confidence, and because they are aware that they might themselves have to take emergency measures at some future date. The Commission and the Council therefore bend over backwards to avoid

making life difficult for any state which already has difficulties, and the usual solution is therefore the second or the third—a temporary exemption or agreement to replace the national measure by a Community one.

The other way to handle a crisis when the whole of the Community is involved from the start, is to convene an emergency meeting of the Council or put an emergency item on the agenda of a meeting which has already been arranged. Either can be done at a few hours' notice: the state which holds the Presidency for the time being makes the necessary arrangements and the Commission puts up a proposal. Whether or not the crisis can be handled effectively depends on whether there is any vital conflict of interests between the member-states or some of them.

It is worth noting that the Commission and Council do not spend their whole time resolving crises or making Community law. Some of their most useful work consists of getting member-states individually to take the same or similar decisions and to follow compatible policies. This process is known as "harmonization" or "co-ordination" and is mainly carried on by Commission and Council study groups, and in the course of informal discussion, by the ministers. In some cases states which are not members of the Community but are linked with it by various agreements (e.g. the remaining members of EFTA—Norway, Sweden, Austria, Switzerland, and Portugal) take part in this work by sending experts and contributing discussion papers.

At the end of the day there is no effective means by which the Community can enforce its decisions on a reluctant member-state because it has no army or police of its own, and the judgements of the European Court can only be put into effect through national courts which may or may not co-operate. In theory the other eight states could refuse to trade with the odd man out, whoever that might be: in practice this would seriously disrupt their economy as well, and has never been done or attempted. But the whole thing holds together because every member-state stands more to lose from a break-up of the Common Market than it stands to gain from being able to do exactly what it likes.

CHAPTER 5

The Common Agricultural Policy

Though the Commission and Council are concerned with many other matters, agriculture is generally recognized as one of the most important.

In the first place we cannot live without food. Secondly, though every one of the member-states has its own Ministry of Agriculture, nearly all the major decisions in this sector are now taken by the EEC authorities. Thirdly, the Common Agricultural Policy is generally helpful to France, on balance the most powerful and certainly the most self-sufficient of the member-states. Without it the Community would fall apart.

The basic principles of this policy are set out in Article 39 of the Treaty of Rome. They include:

(i) increased productivity through technical progress and the best use of all the factors of production, in particular manpower;
(ii) a fair income for the farming population;
(iii) the stabilization of markets; *NB: Imports.*
(iv) security of supply;
(v) reasonable prices to consumers.

In practice the fourth of these principles has so far been given the highest priority, which means budgeting for some surplus production and mopping it up, if necessary, through the intervention procedures described below, thus ensuring that western Europe never starves and never becomes dependent on imports from sources which may be cut off or from suppliers who may suddenly raise their prices, as the oil sheiks did in 1973.

Security of supply is impossible unless the farmers can get a fair income and unless they know roughly at what price they can be certain of selling their produce; hence the fourth principle cannot be implemented without the second and third.

How far the fifth principle can be implemented depends on what one considers as a "reasonable price". Those who live in the country or in small towns with strong farming connections, and who know that milk comes from a cow, and that the cow as well as the farmer must be fed, may not have the same views as those who live in cities and who think milk comes from a bottle.

What is certain, however, is that the CAP can and does prevent prices from rising as high within the Community as they may sometimes rise on the world market. This is achieved by restricting exports when circumstances require it, much as in Britain under the Corn Laws before 1846: in fact the whole system is similar to that of the Corn Laws, both in its aims and in its methods, though more extensive (it covers well over 90% of all agricultural production) and far more sophisticated. It seeks to maintain prices within a certain range and protects producers under normal conditions and consumers in times of scarcity; it works on the basis of import levies and export bounties (technically known as refunds or "restitutions") normally and export levies with import subsidies in the event of a shortage; under extreme conditions there may be a straight prohibition on imports or exports as the case may be.

The first principle—increased productivity—has given rise to considerable argument. Increased productivity is not the same thing as increased production. It means more food produced by each person engaged in agriculture (as a full-time farmer, part-time crofter, or farm worker)* rather than more food altogether, and involves phasing out many if not most of the smaller operators (Fig. 3). The leading exponent of this policy is Dr. Sicco Mansholt, formerly Commissioner for Agriculture and for a brief period President of the Commission. One of its leading critics is Dr. Otto von Habsburg, head of the House of Austria. He feels that, with a large number of small farmers one can, in an emergency, produce considerably more than with a smaller number of large farmers, and points to the example of his own country which recovered from the Second World War and abolished rationing considerably faster than Britain.

A further point is that by phasing out small farmers, one alters the balance of population between the countryside, small towns, and cities. This may lead to a waste of the existing infrastructure of roads, houses, schools, and medical services, to deterioration of the land,† to heavier burdens on the Welfare State (and therefore higher taxation), and to an increase in the number of people who vote for left-wing parties. The governments of the member-states, and the regional authorities which may in some countries

---

*Because of the importance of part-time crofting in some areas, and of the part-time work done by members of the farmer's household, the Commission uses the concept of "man-days" in assessing productivity. Thus a farmer may contribute seven "man-days" a week, his wife another four, and his two children another three days between them.

†The importance of this aspect is now recognized by the Common Market authorities. Not only may the soil deteriorate where farms are abandoned, but this may have adverse affects on rivers passing through such areas and lead to severe damage further downstream. Moreover, hill farms, though uneconomic in themselves, may supply essential breeding stock to more profitable lowland farms. The recreational value of the land may also suffer; tourists feel happier where there is some sort of permanent population, places to stay, garages in case they break down, etc. A Hill Farming Directive has therefore been adopted in order to help small farms which would not otherwise be viable to remain in production (Fig. 4).

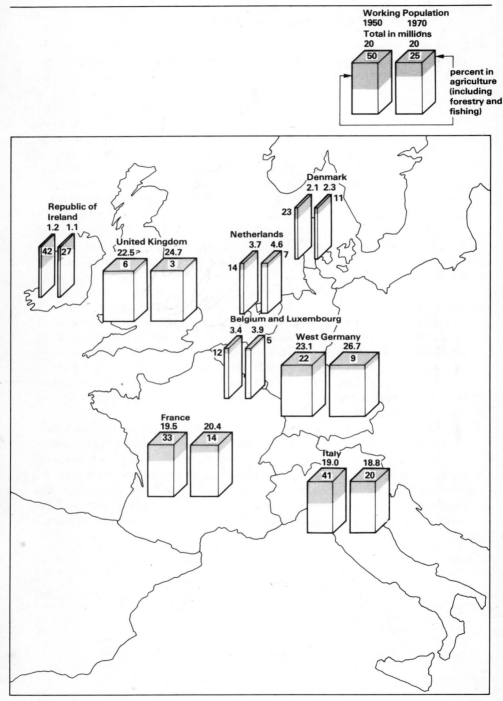

Fig. 3.   The decline of the agricultural workforce. (European Communities Information
Service, London)

share the responsibility for implementing some aspects of the CAP, are not necessarily in favour of this, and Dr. Mansholt resigned partly because of their lack of enthusiasm for his ideas.

The Treaty of Rome has relatively little to say about agriculture considering its importance to the European economy and, indeed, to the survival of western Europe. It lays down basic aims in Article 39 and specifies some of the methods to be used in arriving at these results, but the CAP consists essentially of directives and regulations enacted by the Council since 1960 and of "implementing regulations"made by the Commission within the framework established by the two institutions together. It cannot be found in a single document. As the whole set-up is extremely complex, what follows can only be a very simplified outline.

In the first place the Council, on the Commission's advice, sets what is variously known as a target or guide price for most products. This is the price which farmers should in principle get on the open market, and it fluctuates slightly according to the time of year.

For products which are or may be imported into the Community, the Council also sets a threshold, reference, or sluice-gate price (three names for approximately the same thing). This is the price at which these products should come into the EEC so as not to undercut European farmers, and if possible give them a slight preferential margin. Some products (e.g. fresh milk) are seldom if ever imported, while others (e.g. bananas) are not grown within the Community, and for them there is no threshold price.

The Commission then observes the prices at which imported products actually come in and sets import levies, if necessary, to bring them up to the threshold price. On the other hand, if prices within the Community rise well above the target price due to a European or world shortage, it can help consumers first by abolishing import levies and export refunds, then by granting import subsidies, then by imposing export levies, and, in the last resort, by prohibiting the export of a scarce product.

The intervention price is usually about 90% of the target or guide price. If market prices fall below this level, farmers have the option of selling the product involved (e.g. wheat, beef, or butter) to intervention boards, operated by the nine member-states but financed by the Community as a whole through FEOGA (the European Agricultural Guidance and Guarantee Fund), which itself receives the proceeds of import levies, exceptional surcharges, etc. In practice, farmers do not always take up this option because they have to bear the cost of getting their product to the nearest intervention buying centre which may be many miles away.

Products bought by intervention boards are then kept off the ordinary channels of trade for a while to avoid upsetting market prices. Depending on their nature (some deteriorate faster than others) they may be held back until prices rise and then sold in the normal way, processed to become animal feed instead of human food, sold at a concessionary price to various special customers (old age pensioners, mothers of large families, schools, hospitals, children's homes), turned over to industrial uses (alcohol distilled from surplus wine), used for emergency food relief, or disposed of on the world market with the help of export subsidies.

In many instances strings of some kind are attached. Thus farmers may be restricted in the planting of new vines or they may only be given the intervention price for a fixed quantity of sugar-beet. Without these conditions it could easily become profitable for them to produce indiscriminately for the intervention boards rather than for the real market, and the Community would then become impossibly expensive to run.

Apart from being very costly, this kind of overproduction would be damaging to the long-term interests of European agriculture, which is at present heavily dependent on imported fertilizers, imported cattle feed, and imported fuel to run tractors and other machinery.

One problem which has arisen over the years is that of fluctuating currencies and a higher rate of inflation in some countries than in others. Target, threshold, and intervention prices are set in "units of account", one UA being the same as the American dollar before 1971 but now worth somewhat more. The UA may on a given day be worth 3 Deutschmarks or 60 pence, but on the next day the mark may have risen and the pound fallen, so that it is worth 2.97DM and 63p. This is inconvenient for those who have to work out the prices payable to farmers, so that there is in fact a fixed and artificial rate of exchange between the UA as used for farming transactions and national currencies.

This arrangement, however, puts farmers at an advantage in some countries and at a disadvantage in others, thus distorting agricultural competition. In order to even this out, "compensatory amounts" may be paid or collected by the Community on produce crossing its internal frontiers, e.g. the Channel, the Rhine, and the Alps, and this is one of several reasons why customs officials may still be seen at these frontiers.

Compensatory amounts are really a political compromise, and the Commission does not like them since they make Europe look and feel less united and act as a brake on product specialization (e.g. wheat to be grown in France, beef in Ireland and the United Kingdom, fruit and vegetables in Italy) which some of its officials would like to see; but the system could not at present work without them. In any event it is not certain—bearing in mind the need to conserve lorry fuel and the risk of a bad session in one country one year and in another country the next—that product specialization is really desirable even if it saves money. From the standpoint of security of supply (which is, as we have seen, the most important objective of the CAP or has been treated as such up till now), there is a strong case for continuing

to grow a bit of everything in most of the member-states so far as the climate will allow.

An important part of the Commission's work is aid for the modernization of farms. The involves two main aspects:

(a) getting excessively small farms up to a viable size by encouraging older farmers to retire and helping younger farmers to buy up their holdings;
(b) helping these younger farmers to reorganize and improve their production, e.g. by mechanization or by switching over from dairy to beef cattle:

Financial aid is provided by national governments and in some cases by regional authorities, with FEOGA backing (grants and cheap loans), but only on certain conditions:

(i) those receiving Community aid must be full-time farmers or nearly full-time;
(ii) they must be competent farmers;
(iii) they must submit a development plan, get it approved by their national or regional authorities, and keep accounts throughout the period when it is being implemented;
(iv) once the plan has been carried through, the farm must provide them with an adequate income on a level with the average income of non-agricultural workers in the same area. Hence it must be of adequate size either from the start or when they have taken up land released by the retirement of elderly farmers and by others who leave agriculture for industry.

This policy of modernization is not being carried out uniformly. British agriculture was generally "modernized" before the United Kingdom joined the Common Market, and the same is largely true of Denmark and of Holland. Hence relatively little remains to be done along those lines, and in parts of Britain it might well be desirable to have more people on the land.

In Italy, and especially in the south, the main problem is lack of education. Few farmers would be able to draw up a development plan or keep detailed accounts for six years. At the same time the very small and "uneconomic" farmers, who must be induced to clear out if the policy is to work, are so numerous that very serious problems would arise if they all went. It is better for them to be poor and underemployed on their own land (often with the possibility of seasonal work in the building trade, etc., to supplement their incomes) than desperately poor and wholly unemployed in the cities.

In West Germany there are other considerations: the need to maintain a reasonably large population in districts close to the East German frontier, where industry is often reluctant to invest, and a feeling—in Catholic Bavaria especially—that there is something beautiful and worthwhile in farming as such, and that one does not want to reduce the number of people engaged in it.

At the time of writing, widespread unemployment makes it difficult to press the Mansholt Plan very hard: if one encourages small farmers to leave the land they will either draw pensions or go on the dole, depending on their age, and this will place an additional strain on the Welfare State. Before the current recession, however, there was a steady decline in the number of people working on the land in Common Market countries, which has nearly halved since the war. This trend was already well on the way a long time before the EEC did anything to encourage modernization, and the main reason for it was that the average industrial worker made more money than the average small farmer and considerably more than the average farm worker. For younger people especially, industrial work meant a real wage and the amenities of urban life instead of pocket money from their fathers and very little to spend it on anyway. With unemployment often running at less than 1% (mostly layabouts and people changing their jobs) the security which farming provides had become a less powerful consideration than it was before the war or is at the present time.

An interesting aspect of the CAP is the very small number of people directly involved in running it—no more than fifty senior officials including the Commissioner and the Director-General, and about 1000 EEC staff altogether with secretaries, typists, and a proportional share of the linguists who serve the Community as a whole, but may spend about one-third of their working hours interpreting at meetings of management committees and farm experts or translating agricultural policy documents. This for a sector which spends about £2000 million a year from EEC funds (over 70% of the Community budget), and is concerned with the livelihood of 11 million farmers, crofters, and farm workers, and the survival of 258 million inhabitants of western Europe, not to mention Africans and others who may receive food aid in an emergency. There can hardly be a government department in the world which handles so much business with so few officials.

This is only possible because, as we have seen, much of the "committee stage" of decision making is undertaken by groups mainly consisting of national officials and experts, while most of the administrative work, once the major decisions have been prepared by the Commission and taken by the Council, falls to national, regional, and local authorities, farmers' organizations, and various specialist bodies whose staff do not appear on the Community payroll, any more than the customs officers who collect the duties of the Common Tariff once they have been set. Every one of the member-states has its own Ministry of Agriculture, usually combined with Fisheries, and each of these ministries, except in little Luxemburg, employs more staff than DG VI (and, in the larger states, more than the Commission as a whole).

The agricultural policy illustrates, perhaps better than any other, the inevitable conflicts which occur between the European interest, represented by the Commission, and national interests, represented by the ministers at the Council table. The European interest, at least as seen by the Commission, is to rationalize output so that each country or region produces what it is best fitted to produce by its climate, soil, and other geographical factors. The national interest is to keep production diversified and in some cases to diversify it further, so as to keep transport costs down and retain the goodwill of farmers who do not want to change their arrangements—perhaps also as a re-insurance if the whole Common Market structure should ever break down. Party interests are also involved. Non-socialist parties form the Government or part of the Government, in most of the member-states. These parties are largely dependent on the votes of farmers and of people in small towns. Anything that weakens *their* national agriculture or reduces the number of farmers and of those who live by providing various services for the farmers, is liable to weaken their prospects of remaining in office.

Nevertheless, all these governments agree that the Common Market must continue, and cannot now function without a Common Agricultural Policy, so a compromise solution is usually found even if it means an all-night debate. These marathon sessions—incidentally less frequent than is widely believed —may themselves be intended largely to impress the people back home and to show them that their ministers are standing up for them: the ministers themselves probably start with a fair idea of the outcome they are going to achieve.

Whether or not one accepts the way in which it works as ideal—and many would like to see intervention arrangements reformed so that consumers may get the benefit of lower prices when surpluses occur*—there is general agreement that the policy itself is valid. Western Europe suffered a considerable shock in 1973 when it realized just how dependent it was on imported oil and how insecure its supplies were and still are. Food is even more necessary than oil, and nobody can now doubt that security of supply must have absolute priority, especially with the population of the world increasing all the time.

*This would imply operating the intervention boards in much the same way as the United Kingdom marketing boards before Britain joined the Community. They would buy from the farmers at a guaranteed price and sell to the trade, their losses—if any—being made up as at present from import levies, etc. Up till now this procedure has been regarded as intolerably expensive because agriculture forms a much larger slice of the Common Market economy as a whole than of the British economy on its own. But it could probably work now, combined with the existing system of levies, which Britain did not have pre-1973, so long as one does not attempt to make food as cheap, relative to the overall cost of living, as it was in the United Kingdom before we joined the Community. The Common Market works on the assumption that people pay for their food at the grocer's and the butcher's rather than at the tobacconist's or the petrol pump, and that it cannot be systematically supported out of general taxation. Britain accepted this principle when she joined: there can be no question of going back on it now.

CHAPTER 6

The Rules of Competition

There cannot be a Common Market without some common rules as to what firms may or may not do in order to make and sell their products, and what national governments and regional authorities may or may not do in order to help them. The reasons for this are quite obvious.

In the absence of such rules, the firms which are subject to fewest regulations as regards wages, hours, working conditions, safety standards, pollution, and publicity will inevitably have a considerable advantage unless they are so bad that they cannot find workers or that their products fall apart. Governments which in the public interest impose relatively strict standards will then have to take counter-measures, and these counter-measures will in some way restrict the free flow of trade. Hence there will be no Common Market even if there is a customs union.

Again, if firms can make agreements to carve up the market so that certain products are sold in Britain but not in France, or so that German products coming into Belgium shall not be sold cheaper than similar products already available there, customers will not get the full benefit of the single West European economy. Agreements of this type are prohibited by Article 85 of the Treaty of Rome, and all such agreements are declared to be void,* while Article 86 prohibits firms which already enjoy "a dominant position in the Common Market or in substantial parts thereof" from making unfair use of this position.

As regards subsidies (Articles 92–94) these could frustrate the Treaty's objectives in two ways:

(i) by making it difficult for the produce of one country (e.g. West Germany) to be sold in another (e.g. Italy) whose Government grants various aids to its own industries;

*Subject to certain exemptions which may be obtained from the Commission. Thus if an agreement between two firms (for joint research and development services, for instance) is likely to promote technological progress and to make European industry as a whole more competitive, it will probably be approved. Another case for an exemption arises when a patent is involved and the new product is being manufactured under licence from the patent-holder by different firms in different countries. These firms have paid a fee for the right to use the invention and naturally expect to make something out of it.

(ii) by helping firms in one EEC to sell its products in another (export premiums, tax rebates, preferential freight rates for exports, etc.).

Again there are legitimate as well as unlawful subsidies, just as there are legitimate as well as unlawful agreements.

Three types of aid are recognized by the Treaty as legitimate in any event:

(i) "social aids to individual consumers, not linked with the origin of products": examples include cheap travel and food vouchers issued to old age pensioners and similar concessions to large families;

(ii) emergency aids following on damage caused by storms, floods, earthquakes, forest fires, severe riots, etc.;

(iii) special aids granted by the West German Government to help West Berlin and border districts along the Iron Curtain.

Various other subsidies, especially those in favour of underpopulated and other disadvantaged areas, may be considered as legitimate subject to approval by the Commission alone or by the Commission and Council together. Some of these aids may in fact be supplemented from Community funds under the Regional and Social policies.

To begin with the problem of unfair advantages enjoyed by firms subject to fewest national regulations, the Common Market authorities are working, slowly but successfully, along several lines. One is to encourage trade unionists in the nine member-states to get together, through their own organizations and in the Economic and Social Committee. They have a natural interest in levelling wages and working conditions upwards so long as they do not price themselves out of a job. Another line is to try and harmonize national legislation on safety standards and on protection of the environment, again by levelling upwards. This is done informally through several study groups and formally through the adoption of directives which will then have to be "translated" into national legislation.

Unlawful agreements (Article 85) can be quite tricky to deal with, the first difficulty being to establish that they exist. If a German businessman invites his main French and Belgian competitors to a quiet lunch in Luxemburg City and they arrive at some unwritten understanding over their coffee, liqueurs, and cigars, nobody need hear about it for years to come. In practice the Commission does not get to know unless and until somebody complains— another and smaller manufacturer who cannot sell his products, or a merchant who cannot buy the supplies he wants at a reasonable price. The Commission then investigates, and this can be difficult, as DG IV, which deals with such matters, is very small, while the field in which it may have to act is very large.

Assuming, however, that it finds the complaint justified, the Commission will send the offending firms a letter asking them to stop. This is often enough; if not, the next stage is an official "opinion with reasons", which is in effect a formal warning. If that does not suffice the Commission takes up the matter with the European Court; the final problem is to get the Court's ruling (usually in favour of the Commission) obeyed in the member-states, but this has not proved too difficult so far except where the offending firm is itself a state or semi-state body.

"Abuse of a dominant position" (Article 86) also raises problems, the first again being that of identification. What is a "dominant position", and what is "a substantial part of the Common Market"?

If a firm has a 50% share of a given market, that is quite clearly a dominant position. A 30% share, on the other hand, is considered "dominant" if the next largest firm has only 5% but not if the runner-up has 25%, with a third competitor holding over 20%. In other words the test is: can anybody stand up to that particular firm in that particular field? The Commission and the Court may also want to know whether the firm's share of the market is increasing, steady, or declining.

Each of the major member-states is considered "a substantial part of the Common Market" on its own; so are the three Benelux states taken together, but not separately. On the other hand, if it could be proved that a firm had a dominant position in Scotland or Bavaria, or in a small area including part of two or three states (e.g. a twenty-mile radius around Aachen), the Commission would not feel unduly concerned.

The mere fact of having a dominant position is not an offence in itself, as it is in America (but some people think this should be changed); the next step, therefore, is to show that it is being abused. This is easier than to prove unlawful agreements: the Treaty itself lays down that certain practices are to be considered as abuses, in particular:

(i) *unfair purchase or selling prices* imposed by the dominant firm rather than negotiated between it and its clients (dominant firms tend to be major producers dealing with the trade rather than with the general public);

(ii) *restrictions on production, outlets, or technological development*;

(iii) *unequal conditions* (special terms for special clients);

(iv) *irrelevant additional conditions*. An obvious example of this would be a large firm, making both jam and soup, which only allowed shops to sell its jams on condition they did not sell any other firm's soup packets. But there could be other less obvious examples where the irrelevant condition might not be commercial so much as political or religious, e.g. an Arab-owned oil firm requiring client garages not to employ Jews.

The procedure, once a breach of Article 86 has been established, is much the same as in the case of unlawful agreements, but the sanctions are different.

An agreement may be declared void by the Court of Justice, but an outsize firm cannot at present be broken up: the penalty is therefore a substantial fine.

As regards subsidies, the Common Market authorities tend to be more lenient than where unfair trading practices are concerned. The last word rests with the Council, whose members are national ministers, and all national governments wish to grant subsidies of one kind or another, regularly or from time to time; moreover, many of the aids which might be challenged are unlikely to affect the economy of the Common Market as a whole because the areas concerned are too small or too remote from the heartland of the Community.

In principle, states should inform the Commission before granting any aids other than those specifically authorized by the Council (social, emergency, and German border): in practice they tend to act first and then inform the Commission. In many instances, if not most, it then finds the aid reasonably justified, especially if it is only intended to be temporary. If not, it will raise the matter before the Council, or another member-state may do so because its own interests are adversely affected. The matter is then usually resolved by a political compromise.

The Commission may also take the offending state before the European Court after an official warning, as in the case of unlawful agreements and abuses of a dominant position, but this is not the usual way if only because the Court decision could not be enforced on a reluctant government.

One political difficulty up till now has been the existence of state monopolies in France and Italy. The most important of these involved the sale of cigarettes and tobacco in both countries, and of salt in Italy alone. These monopolies provided the Government with revenue that would otherwise have to come from taxation, and also enabled it to help war widows, disabled people, and others by appointing them as tobacconists, also licensed to sell stamps.

These people are not civil servants but privileged shopkeepers, entitled to sell something which many or most people want and which no one else is allowed to sell, and protected against competition, like taxi-drivers, by the fact that the authorities only issue a limited number of licences. Until recently they were only allowed to stock government-produced cigarettes and tobacco. This, of course, was an infringement of Common Market rules since it meant that British and Belgian cigarettes, though manufactured within the Community, could not be sold in two of its most important member-states together having just over 40% of potential consumers. The Commission stepped in, and both countries now have to make other cigarettes, matches, etc., available to their consumers through these licensed shops, while the Italian salt monopoly has simply been abandoned.

The basic purpose of the competition policy is to help consumers by giving them the widest possible choice as well as by keeping prices down, whereas the agricultural policy is mainly intended to help producers—though it also protects consumers in times of scarcity. Its main weaknesses are that it is difficult to enforce because the Commission does not have anything like adequate manpower for this purpose (in particular it does not have field inspectors in the member-states who would be essential in order to keep track of unlawful agreements and practices), and that it was set up at a time when there was plenty of work available (and therefore little point in keeping "lame ducks" alive), while fuel (and therefore transport) was cheaper than it has since become. It makes quite good sense to argue that, in present circumstances, it is essential to maintain employment and to cut down on fuel consumption and that, on both counts, small firms producing mainly for a local, regional, or national market should be encouraged rather than discouraged. Ministers may be reluctant to say this at the Council table since it goes against the whole spirit of the Common Market as well as the letter of the Treaty, but they probably think along those lines, and many MPs of all nationalities and of all parties certainly do. Hence the Commission cannot expect a great deal of help from them in its efforts to break up market-sharing agreements, and those which it uncovers are only the tip of the iceberg anyway. Where subsidies are concerned, one often gets the impression that some governments at least are trying to see how much they can get away with, and finding new loopholes as fast as the existing ones are closed. In this cat-and-mouse game the mice have a built-in advantage because there are nine of them, but only one cat, and because the cat is never allowed to eat them even if he catches them.

Another aspect of competition policy is the right of firms throughout the Community to tender for public contracts (government and regional authority) to be awarded anywhere from Shetland to Sicily. In theory all contracts above a certain value (at present 100,000 UA) should be widely advertised, with a reasonable period for replying, and should then be awarded to the lowest reliable bidder regardless of nationality. In practice things do not work out that way.

For a start advertising is expensive and time is also money. A Scottish authority, such as Cumbernauld District, or an Irish one, like County Cork, may have a contract worth £500,000 to award, this being well above the minimum level at which these rules apply. It is most unlikely to advertise in *Die Welt* or *La Stampa*, let alone the *Official Journal of the European Communities,* nor will it wait for replies from German or Italian firms even if their bosses read Irish or Scottish papers.

If inquiries do come from abroad, however, the continental firms will probably not be invited to tender, and even if they are their offers are not likely to be considered very seriously. The Germans might stand a chance because everybody knows their workmanship is sound and they keep to their delivery dates, but the Italians will not get very far unless they are the acknowledged specialists in the particular branch of engineering that is involved. In practice the Scottish contract will almost certainly go to a Scottish firm (because Cumbernauld District is Nationalist-controlled, but another authority might place it in England), while the Irish contract will probably go to an Irish firm, possibly to a British firm.

Even at government level, where contracts tend to involve much larger sums and where the cost of advertising is therefore relatively less significant, well over 90% of them are placed with national firms and so are most of the sub-contracts arising from them. The reasons for this are mainly political—a government must be seen to provide work for its own people, from whom it gets all of its votes and most of its revenue—but also practical. Many contracts involve maintenance work or repeat orders, and it saves bother to have a bridge repaired by those who originally designed and built it, and to buy goods from one's regular suppliers. Even where an entirely new job is being done, governments often find it convenient to do business with firms they already know.

A further point is that strict enforcement of the competition policy, where public contracts are involved, could frustrate the objectives of the social and regional policies described in the next two chapters, and possibly also of the environment policy. It will generally place large engineering firms in the heartland of the Community at a considerable advantage over medium-sized and smaller firms in Scotland, Denmark, western France, central and southern Italy, Bavaria, etc. Congestion, pollution, and reliance on foreign labour will increase in areas where these are already very serious problems; conversely, there will be more unemployment, underemployment, depopulation, deterioration of amenities, and waste of the existing infrastructure in the outlying parts of the Community. It may be safer to leave well alone, even at some sacrifice of principle.

CHAPTER 7

The Social Policy of the Community

Social policy, as the Community understands it, is rather an elusive concept. The ground which it covers overlaps with three other fields at least—agricultural policy, regional policy, and the rules of competition. Let us take an example from each.

The measures which the Community and the member-states are taking in order to improve agricultural productivity involve helping some farmers to transfer to other occupations—which means retraining—and others to retire early. They are in effect no different from similar measures to help industrial workers hit by mass redundancies, or to encourage early retirement so that young people can find jobs, and they could well be regarded as social policy. But they are considered and financed as agricultural policy because DG VI can spend about four times as much money as the rest of the Commission put together.

Action taken to create new jobs in areas with too little industry or with too large a share of declining industries, generally comes under the heading of regional policy. But this is not invariably the case especially if the declining industries happen to be coal and steel, and it may be that new factories will be partly financed out of the Regional Fund (and mainly by the member-states concerned), while the Social Fund helps to pay for retraining and to pay the people who are being retrained: in some instances, where wages in their new job are lower than in the old, it makes them up to the old level for three years.

Finally, some rules which contribute to the health and safety of workers are made enforceable throughout the Community in order to prevent unfair competition. An obvious case in point is the use of the tachygraph on lorries (a device which records speeds, distances continuously driven, and stopping times) coupled with the rule that long-distance drivers may not cover more than 280 miles in one day. Without this rule, states which do not protect their workers adequately would have an obvious advantage in transport costs; without the tachygraph the rule could not be enforced. It is part of the Community's social policy—and, indeed, an essential part—that work should be made healthier and safer, but the object in this instance is achieved through a competition policy directive.

In general terms, however, the Social Policy helps people to find work; it seeks to improve their working conditions, wages, and fringe benefits; and it does something for them if their job is threatened or disappears. At the same time it seeks to protect the interests of their dependants, of those who for various reasons do not work or cannot work, and of those who cannot compete on equal terms with other workers—the disabled, the mentally handicapped, mothers with young children, etc.

These responsibilities are based partly on the ECSC, EEC, and Euratom Treaties (the ECSC Treaty especially) and largely on the decision of the European Council (including the prime ministers of the new member-states) held in Paris in October 1972, a few weeks before the Community was formally enlarged from six states to nine, but at a time when the running-in process was already well under way and the new commissioners were already in Brussels organizing their work, recruiting their personal staff, and generally preparing for their new functions.

At Community level most of the work in this field is done by the Commission and by the Economic and Social Committee, which exists largely for this purpose. The Council discusses the proposals which are then put up by the Commission, but the actual decisions are then taken by the member-states—so far as possible on similar lines—rather than by the Community as such.

What the Commission and the ESC do first of all is to organize an exchange of information between governments, civil servants, employers, and trade unionists. This enables the nine states to learn from one another and is, in itself, very useful. In some cases Community financial support may then be forthcoming in order to expand a service which is already being provided. Thus Italy is the main "exporter" of labour within the Community, and Germany a bigger "importer" than the other eight combined. The two states have made arrangements to exchange Ministry of Labour officials, so that Italians who are thinking of working in Germany can find German civil servants at their employment exchange, and obtain from them most of the information they need, not only on jobs, wages, and working conditions, but on climate, food, the cost of living, etc. On arrival in Germany they will find Italian civil servants who help them to settle in. The Commission has decided to support this scheme.

Secondly, the Commission carries out its own surveys as a preliminary to various "actions" which are intended to achieve the objectives set out in the Paris Declaration of October 1972 and subsequent Council resolutions, e.g. *full* and *better* employment in the Community, improved living and working conditions, greater involvement of management and workers in the economic and social decisions of the Community, and of workers in the running of firms and of nationalized undertakings.

In general these "actions" are to be carried out mainly by national governments and by industry, with some financial help from the Social Fund and some co-ordination provided by the Commission's services. In a few cases, however, directives may be required (equal pay and job opportunities for women; legislation on mass redundancies) or it may be necessary to set up new bodies working under the Commission, e.g. the European general safety committee; the European Foundation for the improvement of the environment and of living and working conditions. Sometimes rules already exist (e.g. for the exchange of information between national employment services) and it is simply a matter of making greater use of them.

A brief outline may be given here of some of these actions. One of the most important concerns vocational training, which is very good in some parts of the Community but virtually non-existent in others. Most of the work on this project is to be done by the member-states but a "European Centre for Vocational Training" will be set up to keep track of what is going on, organize pilot schemes for training instructors and some highly skilled workers, and improve the situation in areas which are particularly backward in this field (e.g. southern Italy). This centre will be financed mainly from the Community budget.

Another important "action" concerns the maintenance of income while workers are being retrained and seeking new jobs. If this can be arranged, mass redundancies may in some cases be avoided because workers can be encouraged to leave a firm which is obviously "over-manned" and therefore unable to pay its way; as a result it will be able to stay in production instead of suddenly folding up and throwing thousands of people on the dole. Under the ECSC Treaty the Commission itself, as the supreme managing body of the coal, iron, and steel industries in the Community, can take care of this problem where workers in those three industries are concerned, but the intention is to extend this scheme to other industries and to have it financed nationally with Community support.

The Community, as we have seen, is concerned with equal job opportunities as well as equal pay for women—the latter being required by the Treaty of Rome. One problem here is that equal pay is in fact an obstacle to equal job opportunities. Women, on an average, are off sick a little more often than men, and are much more likely to take time off due to their children being ill; their careers are liable to be interrupted by marriage and child-bearing, and in some countries, the United Kingdom among them, they may (but need not) retire a few years earlier, so their firms do not have the use of their knowledge and experience quite as long. This being so, most employers will naturally prefer to employ men if they have to pay the same wage or salary, and this especially in jobs involving some responsibility. Moreover, especially during a recession, when many men as well as women are applying unsuccessfully, it is very difficult for a woman to prove that she did not get the job *because* she was a woman (similar considerations apply to coloured workers), so it is largely a matter of trying to change the attitude of employers and of male workers where, as often happens, they do not want women around doing what they regard as their work. It may be mentioned in passing that the Commission's record in this field is not altogether exemplary: it has no women Commissioner (out of 13), no woman DG (out of 20), and very few women directors, though one of those few runs the very important Interpreting and Conference Service, and therefore has more subordinates than anyone else of equivalent rank. But this is largely the fault of the member-states rather than of the Commission itself, since the upper echelons are still mainly staffed by people who were originally recruited in the Civil Service of their own country: in the middle and junior administrative grades the proportion of women is higher than in most of the member-states though probably lower than in Denmark or Britain.

A very important aspect of social policy, in several countries (West Germany, Belgium, Luxemburg, France) is the position of migrant workers three-quarters of whom are from outside the Community. Those from the Community itself are mainly Italians and take much the same jobs as the citizens of their "host countries". They are now well integrated and, under Community law, they must be treated on exactly the same basis as citizens of the host country; language apart, a north Italian in south Germany or Belgium will have fewer problems than a Sicilian or a Calabrian in north Italy because he has moved from one industrialized society to another, whereas the southerner has moved into modern Europe from an area which is educationally and economically well behind some parts of Africa.

Foreign (i.e. non-Community) workers, on the other hand, are in a very different situation. They are often illiterate and language is, in any event, a tremendous handicap; they are obviously foreign to look at; they have the worst jobs and the worst housing; many if not most have left their families behind and are often desperately lonely, and the local people dislike, distrust, and despise them, but use them as hewers of wood and drawers of water (or carriers of bricks and oilers of machines). They are often terrorized by an imported underworld for which they provide the necessary cover. As a rule they are the first to be made redundant and cannot then move around the Community in search of work, but have to return home as their permits expire or are taken from them. A substantial proportion, in France and Belgium especially, have no permits anyway. They cannot therefore declare their existence or claim their rights if they are paid a grossly substandard wage, unfairly dismissed, or fleeced by their landlords. If they make themselves known to the authorities they are liable to arrest and immediate expulsion.

It is Commission policy that these foreign workers should be employed on the same terms as Community citizens, that they should be able to count their periods of employment in various member-states together for insurance purposes, and that they should be free to transfer their social security benefits from one member-state to another (thus a Turk who works in Belgium but has his family in Germany should be able to have their family allowances paid to them there) or back home. The Commission is also anxious to see an improvement in reception arrangements for these workers and for their families, including language and general adaptation courses, and in training facilities. How far this is likely to be accepted by the member-states is another matter. Germany will not have Arabs (other than diplomats and visiting oil sheiks) at any price; France has enough North Africans and West Africans, under bilateral arrangements which follow from her old colonial responsibilities, and will not accept Turks or Yugoslavs; Italy has a chronic unemployment problem and therefore will not take foreigners anyway. The present trend (1975) is to get rid of the foreign workers who are already in the Community and to admit no more; but it is possible that, once their overall number has been substantially reduced, more will be done for those who remain: many of them will be at least semi-skilled and they will have had some years to adapt to their host countries.

Industrial safety is a "grey" area in which social and competition policy merge. This is an advantage from the Commission's standpoint, since competition is a field in which it can propose rules to the Council or make them on its own, whereas social policy is one in which it advises the member-states but cannot, in general, lay down the law.

Other things being equal it pays firms to take risks at the expense of the workers, if the unions let them get away with it, because safety measures are costly and do not add a great deal to productivity, when they do not actually reduce it. Hence it is not enough to research and advise—though the Commission does both—one must also legislate, and individual states will not put themselves at a disadvantage by making more stringent rules, and thus adding to their industrial costs, if the others do not keep in step with them.

Directives, if not binding regulations, will therefore most probably be required in this area: meanwhile the Commission is bringing employers, workers, and government officials together to investigate problems and discuss improvements, and it is carrying out a number of studies through its own services assisted by national experts.

The Commission is also interested in eliminating pockets of self-perpetuating poverty which exist in various parts of the Community, e.g. south Italy, Clydeside, and some backward rural areas of France. Very often the people concerned are of below-average health and intelligence and are not aware of their rights under existing national and Community law. In some cases their rights are themselves less than those enjoyed by the population at large because they have not worked continuously or because they earned so little that they could not pay insurance contributions. For the moment the Commission is only at the stage of finding out what the situation really is in order to have some idea of what would and should be done. It will probably be a matter of recommending national measures which will have Community financial backing through the Social Fund.

The Social Policy is not concerned exclusively with those who work: one must also consider pensioners, widows, divorced and unmarried mothers with young children, the severely disabled, etc. As real wages rise* their benefits usually rise, but not in the same proportion nor to the same extent (a 20% rise on a £50-a-week wage is £10; the same proportionate rise on a £10 pension is £2). It follows that they cannot get their hands on as many of the things they need or would like to buy because those who have work and a rising income are at an increasing advantage over them. The fact of being old, for instance, is a far greater disadvantage now than it was at the turn of the century. If a man had survived to the age of 70 in 1900 (which was generally less likely than at present) he was quite likely to be still working, though probably at a lighter and less well-paid job than his 45-year-old son. He had probably saved something, and in those days money held its value far better (it declined less from 1800 to 1900 than from 1972 to 1975). There were fewer consumer goods around, so he would not felt left behind in the race to consume them, and his family probably took more notice of him then than they would now.

In an effort to redress the balance to some extent, the Community seeks to achieve the "dynamization of social security benefits". This means, in the simplest terms, that non-earners should continue to have about the same slice

---

Money wages may rise while *real* wages fall because everything costs more. Real wages may be calculated roughly by considering how many hours of work are required in order to buy various things which most people have or might reasonably want to have. Thus if a worker only needs to put in three hours to earn the weekly rent of his council house, or thirty hours to buy a TV set, his real wages (other things being equal) are probably higher than those of another man in a different industry or country who needs four hours and forty hours respectively. This method is in any event valid for comparing real wages between countries with a Western-type economy. It is less valid for comparing Western and Communist countries. The reason it is less valid is that, in these countries, food tends to be cheaper in terms of man-hours than in the West, while housing and commuter transport are much cheaper; on the other hand, consumer goods in general are far more expensive, and some are not available at all, or only to privileged individuals (e.g. party officials) or after a very long wait. The best one can do therefore is to arrive at an approximate comparison of the standard of living.

of the Community cake, if the cake starts growing again, and that workers*
should not be allowed to race ahead of them. Whether this can be achieved is
another matter, one problem being that the number and proportion of non-
earners are both likely to increase because those reaching pensionable age
now were born at a time when the birth rate was much higher altogether and
was still adapted to the high death rate of earlier years. This means that, in
any given year, more people are reaching retirement age than are reaching
earning age, a state of affairs which is likely to continue until the year 2000 or
thereabouts. At that point the new pensioners will be people born in the
1930s, when the birth rate was generally low because of the Great Depression,
while those born between 1945 and 1955, when it was quite high, will still be
working, and most of today's pensioners will have died. But there could
again be serious difficulties around 2015, when those born in 1950 retire. We
cannot be certain, because it is possible that the stresses of modern life will
mean that fewer people reach retirement age.

Another difficulty is that, again because of a greatly reduced death rate,
the number of disabled people is far higher than it was. At the same time their
disability (or mental handicap) is a greater drawback from the standpoint of
employment. Formerly there were many simple and useful but lowly paid
jobs which they could do, and which have been phased out, either by
automation or by scaling down certain services while increasing wages. Thus
the Post Office delivered letters much faster and more often in 1900 or 1930
than it does now, and the railways, then privately owned, served many more
stations. Both provided much of this "non-demanding" work.

There is, incidentally, a considerable difference in the proportion of
"workers" to "non-workers" from one country to another, and still more
between regions. In Denmark "non-workers" are barely half the
population, in Italy two-thirds, in parts of south Italy perhaps as many as
four-fifths. Moreover, the proportion of "workers" has shown a tendency to
increase in Denmark and to a lesser extent in Belgium and Luxemburg, while
there has been no appreciable change in France, and a decline everywhere
else. All this may make "dynamization" very difficult to achieve, at least on
a Community scale.

---

*Workers, in this context, refers to the so-called civilian labour force (thus described in EEC
statistics), that is including salaried employees as well as wage-earners, and the self-employed as
well as those working for others, but excluding those below working age, pensioners, "non-
working" housewives, single mothers living on social security, disabled people who cannot
work, and soldiers. It *does,* however, include those who should normally be working but
happen to be unemployed. Some marginal cases are difficult to place, e.g. elderly people and
women in south Italy living mainly on remittances from Belgium or Germany but also
cultivating a small plot of land. The Italian authorities seem to class them as "non-workers"
while the French authorities may take a different line as regards elderly peasant farmers
drawing a pension but still growing most of their own food.

The Commission has recently shown a considerable interest in the problems of unemployed school-leavers, elderly workers, and women re-entering or trying to re-enter paid employment after some years spent in bringing up their families. At the moment it is mainly collecting and comparing information, with the co-operation of national experts, but these categories can be assisted to some extent from the Social Fund and Community projects, in addition to national ones, may be set up to help them in finding suitable work.

These three categories have been, to some extent, the victims of social and economic progress and specifically of higher wages, improved fringe benefits (whether gained by the unions or enforced by the state) and the rationalization which has made it possible to pay those wages and fringe benefits. There is a considerable pressure on firms to employ as few people as they can, not only to save on wages but to save on insurance contributions, etc., which are often a fixed per capita charge and do not come down if workers are put on short time, but only if they are made redundant. If a firm has to reduce its work force or refrain from enlarging it, it will naturally start by not taking on people (boys, girls, and married women returning to industry) rather than by getting rid of those it already has. If it must get rid of people it will probably start with those who would be retiring fairly soon anyway. For married women, with husbands to support them, the hardship may not be as great as for the other two groups, but it is depressing for young people to get into the habit of not working, and perhaps even worse for men of 55 to be thrown on the scrapheap and to feel that nobody wants to know them and that twenty bleak years lie ahead.

The problem is less severe—if it exists at all—in the Communist states of eastern Europe, where industry and the Government are two sides of the same outfit. East Germany, with a standard of living roughly equal to that of Ireland and higher than in south Italy, is probably the easiest of those states to compare with the present Community because it is far and away the most industrialized. What happens there is that industry, though state-owned, is in other respects more "conservative" in its structure than in western Europe. It pays lower wages and employs more people to get through the same amount of work. There is, of course, no company taxation, since there are no companies, nor is there an employer's share of social security contributions and a worker's share as in Britain. The state pays wages as an employer and family allowances, etc., as a state, and lives very largely by selling its products to its own citizens and to the outside world, rather than by collecting taxes. More people work (including 80% of married women) than in the West, and it is, indeed, an offence to be deliberately out of work. They earn less than in any of the industrial areas of western Europe, but the gap between the standard of living of non-earners and earners is also considerably less, and there is certainly no juvenile or pre-retirement unemployment among those in normal health. Though the whole social and political set-up is very different, it is possible that the Community might have something to learn from informal contact with the East Germans and with the Poles, who did have the problem of placing a very large number of young people in employment a few years ago due to the post-war surge in their birth rate.

Two other important actions are concerned with job enrichment (getting rid of some of the drudgery of industrial work and making the workers feel more involved in what their firm is doing) and with health protection against pollution and environmental hazards—an area in which social and environment policy overlap. At the moment these actions are still at the stage of research: the Commission brings together employers, trade unionists, and scientific experts, and helps to finance what is being done by industry and by universities in the member-states. An interesting feature of these projects is that they often involve co-operation with states which are not members of the Community, e.g. Sweden (where there have been interesting experiments in job enrichment, notably in the automobile industry) and Switzerland. The Community is also working on proposals to improve the protection of workers in nuclear power stations and of the general population in the neighbourhood. This is a matter of increasing urgency, as it is expected that most of Europe's electricity (including the power to run factories) will come from those stations before the turn of the century. Community legislation will be required because this protection is expensive (like conventional industrial safety measures, and probably more so) and because any accident could affect people in several member-states. Thus a reactor exploding near Dunkirk would certainly kill people in Belgium as well as France; depending on how the wind blew, it could also cause radiation sickness and leukemia in Holland, West Germany, Luxemburg, and England.

Finally, it may be worth noting the Commission's plans for an expansion of its housing activities. Under the ECSC Treaty it can already provide houses for miners and steel workers, and help to rehouse as well as retrain them if they move to other industries. It is now envisaged that it may also build new houses or modernize and reconvert old houses for the benefit of migrant workers, handicapped people, and others in special need.*

*There could be some criticism of special housing for migrant workers on the basis that they should be encouraged to mix with the existing local population rather than live in ghettoes. But it seems clear that they prefer to live among their own kind and that the "natives" are happier that way. If they have to live in ghettoes it is better that these should be decent and comfortable ghettoes rather than decaying slum property as is often the case. Present conditions are bad enough in English "immigrant" areas; they can be even worse in Germany. Part of the difficulty in West Germany is that there is relatively little in the way of council housing. The United Kingdom and France, the other main "importers" of migrant workers, are better off in this respect; but local authorities tend, for political reasons, to favour the "natives". Another problem, as we have seen, is that the immigrants are often unaware of their rights and afraid to complain against landlords who are as likely as not to be fellow countrymen.

At the moment there is a great deal more in preparation than has actually been accomplished. This is inevitable bearing in mind that the Community has only become seriously active in this field quite recently apart from its specialized tasks under the ECSC Treaty. Its interest was due to a very widespread feeling that, while most people were increasingly prosperous, various minorities (pensioners, the disabled, lower-paid and especially migrant workers, some peasant farmers) were getting left behind and suffering not only from their own poverty but, in an envious and competitive society, from the prosperity of the others. But the Commission has been set to work on these projects—all of them worthwhile and some of them rather costly—at a time when growth came to a sudden stop and when everybody was trying hard not to fall back. One can only hope that the resources will be there when the plans are ready.

CHAPTER 8

The Regional Policy

The need for a Community Regional Policy was first officially recognized by the Conference of Heads of State and Government in 1972; but though it became more urgent with the accession of the new member-states, all having large and relatively underdeveloped regions on the edge of the Common Market, it existed before, and this mainly for three reasons.

In the first place, the income gap between affluent areas such as the Paris basin, Hamburg, and the Ruhr, and less affluent ones such as southern Italy and parts of west central France (fig. 5), was already too large and was still growing as wealth attracts wealth and poverty tends to get worse, a fact already observed by Jesus of Nazareth nearly 2000 years ago, when the Roman "common market" was at the height of its prosperity: "to him that hath, there shall be added; from him that hath not, there shall be taken away even the little that he hath." This trend reversed during the Dark Ages and the early Middle Ages (AD 400–1000 approximately) when life was precarious everywhere and the economy was essentially local; but it got under way again as trade revived and living standards began to rise at the time of the Crusades, and has been fairly continuous since the Industrial Revolution.* The establishment of the Common Market speeded it up by making it easier for men and money to move around: at the same time people in the poorer and

---

*Between 1850 and about 1960, however, the gap widened mainly through some areas growing faster than others. Thus average income might rise from £100 to £200 in one area, and from £150 to £1000 in another. The more prosperous region would then be five times as well off, instead of only 50% ahead of the other, though both would have improved if the increase was at constant money values. Since 1960 the poorer areas have actually lost ground in some cases if one thinks in terms of what money will buy rather than nominal wages, salaries, etc. It should also be borne in mind that "average income" is calculated per head of population rather than per individual actually earning, and that in areas with a low standard of living one tends to find at the same time lower wages and more old people, non-working wives, and young children than in more prosperous areas. If an average wage of £1000 a year has to support six people, per capita average income will be just over £160. On the other hand, if an average wage of £1500 has to support 2.5 people, average income will be £600, and if an average wage of £2000 only has to support two people, average income will be £1000, and this third area will not be twice but six times more prosperous than the first one mentioned. The difference between Hamburg and Calabria is in fact nearly of this order, while the proportion of 16%, 40%, and 50% working population just about represent the average and extreme figures for the Community.

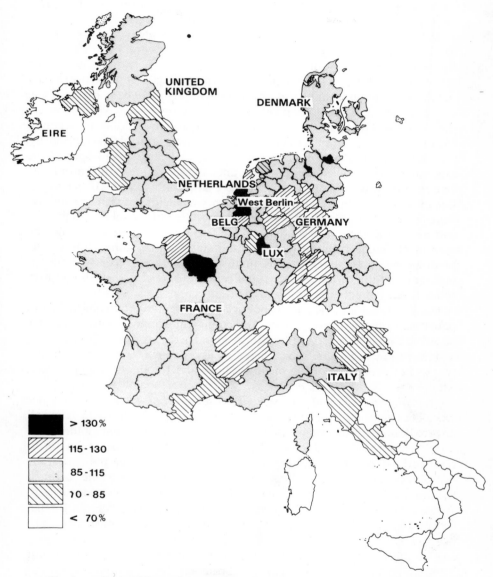

Fig. 5.   Regional inequalities in the Community, 1974. Gross domestic product at
market prices per inhabitant in relation to the Community average expressed in purchasing
power parities as of 1970. (This means that allowance has been made for differences in
purchasing power in 1970. Thus £1 at the time would have bought 140 Belgian francs. But £1 in
England would have bought the same there as 180–200 francs in Belgium; currently £1 is worth
65 francs but buys much the same in England as 100 or even 120 francs in Belgium.)

more outlying areas have become increasingly aware of the wealth existing elsewhere, and therefore increasingly resentful.

Secondly, some of the measures which European states could take, if they so wished, in order to correct these inequalities were contrary to the Treaty of Rome or restricted by some of its provisions. In theory at least some could no longer be used, while others could not be used as effectively as before or only subject to Community approval which might or might not be available. Thus, if France chose to limit investments in one of her own overdeveloped areas, there was nothing to stop a Paris industrialist from expanding in Belgium, 150 miles away, rather than in Brittany or the Massif Central, 300 miles away.

Thirdly, some of the existing Community policies worked against the interests of underdeveloped regions, thus aggravating existing problems. One example was (and still is) the fact that a large share of FEOGA payments is made to farmers in cereal growing and dairying regions of the Community, which tend to be fairly prosperous already, while little is done to help olive and citrus-fruit growers in south Italy who on the contrary suffer through the agreements made between the EEC and states on the other side of the Mediterranean. In general terms there has been until recently little co-ordination of the various sectorial policies to ensure that they should help rather than hinder the development of problem regions.

These inequalities were and are politically unacceptable in themselves, and potentially very dangerous, since they could lead to local violence (as has occurred both in Italy and southern France) and to the growth of Communism and the resurgence of Fascism. They were also liable to create or aggravate two sets of problems for the member-states and for the Community as a whole.

(i) *Problems due to an excessively high standard of living in a particular area.* The first thing that happens is that too many people move in. They all have to be housed somewhere. Schools have to be built for their children and hospitals for the sick and elderly. Very often (as is now happening in north-east Scotland) the added wealth is mainly to be found in a few industries; the rest cannot get local workers because they cannot offer the same wages or because working conditions are naturally unattractive whatever one tries to do about them. In that case they wilt away or become dependent on foreign labour. Crime, pollution, mental health, heart disease, and cancer all tend to increase as a result of overcrowding and overindustrialization. There may also be political dangers due to the fact that, although the local standard of living is high, pockets of severe poverty appear and deepen among immigrants and others who have been left behind in the rat-race; this, for instance, has happened in France and West Germany.

(ii) *Problems due to an inadequate standard of living in a particular area.* In the first place people move away, and this is a waste of the existing infrastructure of schools, medical services, roads, public transport, etc., and the first to move are those whose wages and salaries, through local taxation, would help to support this infrastructure. Secondly, these services themselves begin to deteriorate. Small schools are closed down, doctors who retire are not replaced, buses are taken off the road, branch railway lines are axed. More people still then move away. Thirdly, the land may deteriorate because the only farmers who remain behind are elderly people living mainly on social security benefits and from what their children send them rather than from agriculture as such, and they cannot take adequate care of their fields.

In the past some governments tended to let things drift, while others tried to do something with varying success, but this was a national rather than a European problem. With the emergence of the Common Market, and still more with its enlargement and the commitment to an Economic and Monetary Union (EMU),* the responsibility of one became the concern of all. While the Treaty of Rome does provide for freedom of movement and freedom to seek and take up work anywhere, it is not in the interest of western Europe as a whole that too many people should take advantage of this possibility, and still less that they should be economically compelled to do so. To take an extreme example: it would be disastrous for Italy, France, and Germany if 5 million people moved from the Mezzogiorno to the Ruhr and another 5 million to the Paris region. Even 2 million leaving Italy, with 1 million going to France and 1 million to West Germany, would aggravate quite considerably the problems existing in all three countries. It is better for Europe, for the individual member-states, and for their regions, that people should be able to make an adequate living where they belong, and most of them will be happier that way.

The need for a Regional Policy having been accepted, together with the general principle that it should be based on encouraging people to stay more or less where they were, the next step was to decide on the measures to be taken, the regions most in need of help, and the resources to be used for this purpose.

The measures could be taken either by the member-states or by the Community: in the former case it was essentially a matter of allowing the states greater scope and restoring to them, by general agreement, some of the freedom of action that had been taken away from them by the Treaty of Rome, and specifically by Articles 92 and 94. No actual change in the rules

---

*The Community's EMU tends at present to resemble its Australian namesake, a large heavy bird which runs around in circles and never gets off the ground. For this reason some people, especially in West Germany, have suggested that the Regional Policy was not really necessary. Even without EMU, however, the Common Market has a natural centralizing effect, due to the free movement of capital, goods, and people, and to restrictions on what the member-states can do to help problem regions, and it is necessary to counteract this effect by measures taken at Community as well as national level.

was required; simply an understanding that the Commission would not intervene where state aids were obviously useful to regions in need of help and unlikely to affect the economy of the Common Market as a whole. The Treaty already stated that such aids *could* be regarded as legitimate: all that was necessary was to agree that they normally *would* be so regarded within reasonable limits.

The regions themselves were defined in the first place by the Commission, which produced a report illustrated by a large map. The Council accepted the general principles of the Report but discarded the map, replacing it by another.* Some of these regions were at a disadvantage because they were too. remote or isolated; others because of excessive dependence on agriculture (lack of alternative employment tends to drive younger people away, especially if they have no prospect of inheriting a viable-sized farm) or on declining industries, leading both to depopulation and to a high level of unemployment; others again, including small areas not amounting to a "region" because they were close to an internal frontier (e.g. Belgium–Germany) or to the external frontier of the Community itself. South Italy, most of Ireland, and much of Scotland suffered both from remoteness and from excessive dependence on agriculture.

The map showed:

(1) How much aid could be given to industrial investments from national and Community sources *combined,* the total being 20% in what might be called the "inner" areas of the Community (with a few exceptions in favour of areas suffering from serious industrial decline; 30% in areas with some problems but not severe ones; 40% in areas with more severe problems; and no definite limit in a few areas with exceptional difficulties. The rule in these exceptional areas is that the Government may go on doing what it has been doing up till now but no more. If aid is up to 80% it may remain at that level, but the ceiling cannot be raised from 80% to 90%, or 60% to 80%.

(2) Where aid could be given from the Regional Fund, to be created once the Council had approved the map and decided how much money could be made available. The Regional Fund is not the only source of Community aid which may also be provided through FEOGA, the Social Fund, and, where miners and steel workers are involved, under the ECSC Treaty (Fig. 6).

In general, aid from the Regional Fund was only to be available in areas

---

*The Council decided to provide Community regional aid to all regions already receiving national aid, and to those only. As a result, for instance, all the Iron Curtain frontier districts in West Germany were included (some, e.g. around Lübeck and Wolfsburg, had been left out of the Commission map because they were already quite well off); on the other hand, various mountain areas in north Italy, which satisfied the Thomson Report's criteria of depopulation and excessive dependence on agriculture, were struck off because Italy had taken a political decision to concentrate regional aid in the south. These Alpine areas, however, receive FEOGA aid in accordance with the Hill Farming Directives.

photocopy

Fig. 6. Regional aid zones of members of the EEC (European Community Commission, Brussels). (This map differs in minor respects from the final map by the Council of the EEC)

where the total ceiling was 30% or above, and only for quite substantial projects. The Fund itself was originally endowed with £150 million approximately for its first year of operation (1975) and £250 million for each of the two succeeding years: it was only given a "life" of three years in the first instance, but on the understanding that it would be renewed thereafter, an important point as most countries organize their development planning on a four-year or five-year basis. It is administered by the Commission, like the Social Fund, FEOGA, and ECSC aid, and works roughly as follows.

In the first place all applications must come from member-states, not from regional or local authorities or from firms wishing to set up or expand in a region which qualifies for aid. (These authorities and firms may, however, apply for loans from the European Investment Bank and most EIB loans are, in fact, made for projects in these Community "development regions".) This is an important point because governments have their own political reasons for choosing to support projects in one area rather than another; for instance, they may not do much for people who are going to vote for them or against them, whatever happens, and may be more interested in helping those whose support could make the vital difference in a general election. If a national government decides that a particular region should be abandoned to sheep and summer visitors, there is nothing the local people can do about it under present Community rules. This is possibly the most serious weakness in the existing arrangement, but anything which gave the Commission greater powers would have been unacceptable to several of the member-states and, therefore, to the Council.

Secondly, Regional Fund aid may only be sought for projects in areas which already receive regional aid from the national governments concerned, and in general for projects which are themselves to receive aid from the Government or from other public authorities, regional or local.

Thirdly, every project for which aid is sought must cost at least £25,000 approximately and must either create ten new jobs or maintain a number of jobs which would otherwise disappear. Preference is given under the regulation which sets up the Fund to projects which apply to both.

A fourth rule is that there must be some proportion between the Community aid to be given and the jobs to be created or maintained. If somebody wanted to build a factory costing £5 million but employing only twenty people, it is quite likely that the Commission would refuse to finance the project, but even if it agreed (e.g. because the factory was likely to help other industries locally, and so maintain more jobs), only £1 million of the investment would qualify for aid, and the maximum available from Community funds would be 20% of that sum. On the other hand, if it were to employ 200 people, or even 100, the whole project would be eligible for aid (and far more likely to be accepted), and the Community could then contribute £1 million.

Once the project has been submitted, it is assessed by Commission officials with special reference to the following criteria.

(1) *Whether it seems useful to the region concerned.* In some cases it may provide employment but be of no other obvious use (thus the Commission would be most unlikely to approve aid for a chain of bingo halls each providing two jobs), and in rare instances it may actually be damaging because of its effect on other local industries. But the national government is unlikely to sponsor such projects in the first place.

(2) *Whether it is consistent with the Community's programmes or objectives.* There are three main cases of possible inconsistency:

(i) An industry, e.g. textiles, may already have serious difficulties in selling its products, and it may not be desirable to increase its production capacity. But that is already covered by the next criterion, financial viability.

(ii) It is not desirable that any given region should be too heavily dependent on one type of industry.

(iii) The project may have undesirable side-effects, e.g. increased pollution in an area where this is already a serious problem.

(3) *Whether it is economically worthwhile.* The Commission does not encourage member-states to breed lame ducks which then require continuing aid. Difficulty in selling the product is not the only reason why an investment may not be worthwhile. Another is that it may be intolerably expensive to bring the necessary raw materials or component parts to the factory or that the right type of labour force does not exist locally, and that it would then be necessary to try and attract a large number of workers from elsewhere. They might not want to come, and even if they did they might get on badly with the local people or find the climate and amenities did not suit them and leave after a year or two.

(4) *Whether the projected development is to take place on or near one of the Community's internal frontiers.* This may be a point in its favour if it compensates for the disadvantages which a small area suffers through being just across the border from another state which does more for its own industries, or if two states jointly apply for aid to a project which they are jointly financing. But it may be a point against if the new industry is going to make it harder for others just across the border to hold their own.

(5) *What other Community aid is being given to the region concerned.* Regional Fund aid may be given for infrastructure projects (e.g. roads, canals) provided they will help other activities which also qualify for aid, and for new factories, craft workshops, tourist developments, and similar projects. Hill and mountain farming activities do not receive aid directly from the Regional Fund but from FEOGA; on the other hand, roads serving hilly and mountainous areas may qualify. In some areas where the main problem is dependence on traditional declining industries, ECSC aid may be available for retraining and the creation of alternative employment. Since the resources of the Regional Fund as such are limited, the Commission may wish to consider what other ways exist of helping a particular area.

Every member-state submits a programme showing all the projects for which it is seeking aid from the Regional Fund. These national programmes as a whole, and some major individual projects, have to be considered by the Regional Policy Committee described below: smaller projects are assessed by Commission officials and by the Regional Fund Committee.

The Regional Policy Committee is made up in much the same way as the various management committees which operate the Common Agricultural Policy, but the national and Commission officials involved tend to be of higher rank (thus its chairman is not a director, but the Director-General for Regional Policy, whereas the Fund Committee is on the same administrative level as the management committee). Its procedures are similar; that is to say, it discusses and votes, but its advice is not binding. If, however, the Commission disregards this advice, its own decision does not take immediate effect, and is reviewed by the Council, which may amend or reverse it. The Committee reports direct to both institutions.

What the Committee does, apart from assessing national programmes and individual major projects, is to see how far the regional policies of the various member-states are consistent with each other and with the regional policy of the Community as a whole, and how far national and Community policies have been successful. It also looks at the combined effects of several Community policies, e.g. Regional, Social, Agricultural, on the regions which qualify for aid; the effects on these regions of Community taxation and levies and of FEOGA payments and what, if anything, is being done to discourage investment in overdeveloped regions. These disincentive measures, however, may themselves have undesirable results, e.g. severe unemployment among young black people in the London area, and among North Africans in Paris, and one might have to think of providing enough work for those who already live in such areas, while discouraging others from moving in. The most effective way might be the issue of city residential permits, as in Russia (people not already resident in Moscow or Leningrad cannot, generally, move in), but this would be contrary to one of the basic principles of the Treaty of Rome, so the Community will have to think of something else.

One problem in working out and implementing a Community Regional Policy is that there is, in general, no one minister responsible for regional policy at national level; it falls to several ministers in charge of planning, trade and industry, agriculture, transport, and possibly also social welfare, education, housing, and health. In some member-states, elected regional assemblies or parliaments, and governments or councils responsible to them, may have taken over much or most of the work (e.g. in the German *Länder*, the Italian autonomous regions, and Greenland). It is therefore very difficult to bring together at Council level all the people who take the relevant decisions. At present this does not matter a great deal because regional policy is something which each state handles as it sees fit, and the Community only has a co-ordinating and supporting role. A very different situation could arise if and when "economic and monetary union" is achieved, which implies that the Common Market would have a single economy and that individual states could no longer do anything to prevent too much money going out or too much coming in. It would then become very much harder for them to plan their own budgets or to take adequate steps to cope with over-development and underdevelopment: decisions which are now taken and mainly financed by national authorities would have to be taken and financed by the Community as a whole.

Another and more immediate problem is that the Community authorities cannot take effective steps to ensure that Regional Fund aid is used in accordance with Community policy, i.e. to supplement the aid which is already being given by the member-states and enable them to do more. Some governments at least simply recoup themselves from Community funds for the aid which they are giving anyway, and regard it as a general subsidy rather than as a contribution to specific projects. The Commission does not like this nor do the people of the regions concerned.

The future of the Regional Policy depends on the way the Common Market itself develops, that is to say, on whether there is a further transfer of resources and responsibilities from the member-states to the Community as a whole or, on the contrary, a tendency to hand back to the states, in practice if not in theory, some of the powers taken from them by the Treaty of Rome. If the Community evolves towards a federation, even without actually becoming one, it will be necessary to enlarge the Fund very considerably; when one bears in mind that over 100 million people live in areas which qualify for regional aid, and that several million of them have an annual income which is less than half the Community average, the present sum of £250 million a year (1976) is nowhere near adequate. It will also be necessary to allow regional and local authorities, and even firms, to go straight to the Commission for help. If, on the other hand, the Common Market is going to remain the kind of organization it is now, and if anything slightly less centralizing in outlook and tendency than it was before the new member-states came in, the Regional Policy in its present form is approximately right. It recognizes the principle that we cannot allow wealth to go on attracting wealth and draining away the substance of those who are less well off, and it also recognizes the fact that, with the Community as it is, the member-states are best placed to do the actual work of helping their regions, while the essential task of the Commission and of the Council is to see that they do not get in each other's way and that other policies (e.g. Agriculture, Competition) do not prevent them from doing what their resources allow.

CHAPTER 9

Industry and Technology

Nobody can expect an uninterrupted record of success, and the field covered by this chapter is one in which the Community, and specifically the Commission, often gives the impression that it has bitten off more than it can chew. Perhaps it would be fairer to say that it has bitten off more than it is being allowed to chew, the opposition to its efforts coming both from governments and from business interests. This chapter therefore mainly gives an indication of what the Community is trying to achieve than of what has actually been achieved, and lays some stress on the difficulties which have been encountered up till now.

An essential objective of the Industry and Technology Policy, in so far as it exists, is to make the Community more competitive, especially with the United States and Japan, and create, to that end, a single industrial base. This involves, in particular:

(i)   getting rid of anything which breaks up the internal European market;
(ii) encouraging the creation of "European companies";
(iii) encouraging co-operation between companies which do not wish to merge but merely to work together in research and development or sales promotion, for instance: this is the one really successful aspect of the Commission's efforts so far;
(iv) encouraging the development of high-technology industries (computer and aerospace in particular);
(v)   modernizing certain traditional industries (shipbuilding, paper, textiles);
(vi) opening up contracts for public works. As we have already seen, these still tend to be awarded on an essentially national basis, though local authorities close to a border may place contracts on the other side where this is obviously convenient.

Other aspects of the Industry and Technology Policy include efforts to evolve a common approach to multinational firms (both American and European) and to the problems which they can create by their very considerable economic power—some of them have a larger budget than several

Plate 1. The signing of the Treaty of Rome, 25 March 1957. (By courtesy of the Information Office, EEC, Brussels)

Plate 2. The first formal meeting of the Council after the enlargement of the EEC, 15 January 1973. (By courtesy of the Information Office, EEC, Brussels)

Plate 3.   The signing of the Lomé Convention, 23 February 1975. (By courtesy of the Information Office, EEC, Brussels)

Plate 4.   Water-hole with modern equipment in the Sahel Region of West Africa (a project financed by the EEC). (By courtesy of the Information Office, EEC, Brussels)

Plate 5. A school in West Africa. (By courtesy of the Information Office, EEC, Brussels)

Plate 6. A group of nine pupils at the European School in Brussels (one from each member-state). (By courtesy of the Information Office, EEC, Brussels)

Plate 7.   The farmers' demonstration in May 1971 (three cows were brought into the meeting of the Council of Agricultural Ministers by farmers protesting against pricing policy). (By courtesy of the Information Office, EEC, Brussels)

Plate 8.   The Rt. Hon. Roy Jenkins, President of the Commission, at a Press Conference.

Plate 9. ISPRA, the principal research centre in the EEC. (La Communauté Européenne, Information Office, Paris)

Plate 10.   A plenary session of the European Parliament at Strasbourg. (By courtesy of the Information Office, EEC, Brussels)

Plate 11.   Meeting of the new Commission. (By courtesy of the Information Office, EEC, Brussels)

member-states—and, at the other end of the scale, to find ways of making small and medium-size firms and craft industries more viable. Contrary to popular belief, the Commission is not trying to get rid of these smaller undertakings; they have an important part to play, especially in helping to achieve the objectives of the Regional Policy; there is something typically European about them; their labour relations are often much better than in larger firms and they often promote useful developments because of their more flexible structure. But they are difficult to fit into a Community economic system as they tend to produce mainly for a local or national market. Their sales department is not very highly developed, and sometimes consists essentially of the boss making phone calls and dictating letters to his secretary. The Commission is investigating the possibility of finding them more work in subcontracting.

This and other forms of co-operation are being promoted through the Business Co-operation Centre, a small but useful liaison office operated by the Commission at its Brussels headquarters. The Centre has a threefold remit. In the first place it provides firms with information on Community regulations and on national regulations in the other member-states. Secondly, it puts firms in contact with each other; it is then up to them to decide whether and how far they can co-operate. Thirdly, it provides the Community (and the Commission in the first instance) with information on existing obstacles to co-operation. It received over 1200 requests in its first six months of operation (642 for information on Community and national regulations; 617 for possible partners). This tempo has been maintained, though Italian firms have so far shown less interest than those in other countries.

There is also a programme to promote research into data processing and to encourage its industrial development and application. Work on this is to be done by the member-states with some Community financing where the Community as a whole is likely to benefit.

At the same time the Commission is studying the problems which might arise in supplying the Community with raw materials, especially non-ferrous metals (iron and steel are taken care of separately, since in that sector the Commission is operating as the ECSC High Authority, with powers of decision as well as co-ordination).

A very interesting *Industry and Society* symposium was organized in Venice in 1972 with the participation of 120 industrialists and trade union leaders as well as Commissioner Spinelli and several senior EEC officials. The area which it covered included several distinct policy fields: industrial, environment, regional, and social. Its main themes were:

(i) industrial development and the reduction of social and regional disparities;

    (ii) industrial development, public relations, and the quality of life;
    (iii) the Community's place in the world.

These were further subdivided into subject themes, e.g. industrial development in the Community, its problems and prospects; man's role and status; the necessary conditions for an increased flow of investments towards less-developed regions—there being ten subjects altogether. On each of these, three reports were read, one by an industrialist, one by a trade-union representative, and one by an independent expert.

The Commission has also considered the problems involved in setting up a European aerospace industry, making the Community competitive with the United States. Here America has a tremendous start both in the production of airliners and where light aircraft are concerned. This is due to the fact that, with a higher standard of living and a lower population density, many more Americans than west Europeans fly, though the Community's population is larger (258 million against 213 million). For distances of less than 300 miles it is usually more satisfactory to drive or take a train than to fly, once allowance has been made for time spent at airports and in getting to them, and inter-city travel in the Community, more often than not, involves distances of 100–300 miles, whereas in America one is usually going further. The home market base in the United States is therefore much stronger, and always will be; but in the Community there is not even a home market base in the accepted sense. The Commission is trying to set one up.

As part of its industrial policy, the Community is taking measures both to restructure its textile industries (some of which still use obsolete plant) and to protect them by means of negotiated quotas against excessive competition by low-wage countries and city-states (Pakistan, India, Singapore, Hong-Kong, Taiwan, and South Korea). It is also taking steps to help the paper pulp, paper, and board industry. This involves the encouragement of forestry and recycling, financial help with anti-pollution measures, which are necessary in themselves, but whose cost could otherwise put firms out of business, often in regions which already have serious employment problems, and co-operation with non-member-states which export wood pulp, paper, and newsprint (essentially Finland, Sweden, Norway, and Canada).

The difficulties which the Commission has encountered in its efforts to develop an Industry and Technology Policy comparable with, say, the External Trade Policy or the Common Agricultural Policy, are mainly political. Governments feel obliged to do something for their own people, and therefore continue to award contracts on a national basis. Thus engines for the Belgian railways are still made in Belgium, although France, the United Kingdom, and West Germany are all much bigger producers. It is always possible to find technical reasons for placing the work in one's own country, for instance reliability, delivery dates, greater facility in maintaining contact as the work progresses, but the simple fact is that no government likes to miss an opportunity of keeping down its own unemployment figures.

Again, there is a well-entrenched tradition of "over-manning" in some countries, especially Italy and the United Kingdom, for social reasons. Workers were prepared to accept relatively low wages, combined with a cost of living appreciably lower that in high-wage countries such as Switzerland, West Germany, and Sweden, in return for an easier pace, and felt it would be selfish of 300 men to hog the work and wages that could be spread out between 500. Industry was geared to these arrangements, which did no real harm so long as the cost of living could be kept down, since the total wage bill for producing 1000 cars, for instance, was not necessarily higher in countries with lower wages and lower productivity than in those with higher wages and higher productivity. They could even be advantageous since, with the British system, there was a certain amount of slack that could be taken up in a crisis. Thus, if 20% of the men were off sick, the others could work overtime or simply work a little harder and production would hardly suffer. The same thing happening at Volkswagen or Volvo would be more serious.

The trouble has come with British workers expecting something like German wages while retaining their British habits and practices. This has led to serious difficulties at a time when industry already had to face other problems due to the general recession and the high price of oil. Governments have to follow policies which are acceptable to their own people in the short term or in the medium term (depending on the date of the next General Election). They cannot work on a long term basis unless they are dictatorships or permanent coalitions (as in Switzerland). This has made it impracticable for them to arrive at a common industrial strategy.

Yet another problem is the rooted dislike of large firms, and of "capitalism" in general, in several countries. This has so far made it impossible to set up the sort of firms that could stand up to American competition in the aircraft and data-processing industries in particular.

Economic nationalism also plays a part in other fields than the award of public contracts. Each country wants to get in its own supply of scarce raw materials and other requirements, and this makes the agreed allocation of basic supplies impossible except where the Commission is acting as the ECSC High Authority and has the power to decide. Several countries wish to maintain their own aircraft industries for defence and prestige reasons, and subsidize them heavily: defence, and any industrial production directly connected with defence, fall outside the scope of the EEC Treaty in any event, and many important firms are engaged both in defence and in other industrial work. There is also a general reluctance to integrate in case something goes wrong in one of the member-states and everybody is left without cars, for instance, or without TV sets. The British are unfortunately notorious for unpredictable strikes with quite trivial causes, such as a foreman swearing at a worker, or cats making a smell in an assembly shop; while the Italians have less trivial but more prolonged disputes, so this reluctance is not altogether unjustified. Each of the major states likes to be approximately self-sufficient in what it regards as vital industries.

A further difficulty arises through the need to take into account the interests of developing countries. They would like a bigger share of the market for labour-intensive, low-technology industries (e.g. textiles and footwear); but the Community states are reluctant to concede this, since it would throw very large numbers of their people out of work and further increase European dependence on outside sources of supply.

These problems are largely insoluble in the absence of a European Government with quite considerable powers; this itself is politically not on in present circumstances and difficult to envisage in the foreseeable future.

(The coal, iron, and steel industries, falling within the scope of a different Treaty, which confers greater powers on the Commission, are dealt with separately in the next chapter.)

CHAPTER 10

Coal and Steel

While the European Coal and Steel Community no longer exists as a distinct organization, its activities are still carried on under the ECSC Treaty, whose rules are quite different from those of the Treaty of Rome. Several commissioners and directors-general are responsible for these activities (the bulk of the work, however, being done by those in charge of Energy, Industry, and Social Affairs), but the Commission itself, when it functions as the High Authority of the ECSC, has greater powers than in its normal capacity as the EEC Commission. The Council has correspondingly less power, and a specialist body, the Consultative Committee, has the same sort of remit as the Economic and Social Committee in EEC and Euratom matters. It consists in equal numbers of producers' (nationalized under-takings and private firms) representatives, trade unionists, and users' representatives, and meets in Luxemburg City: ECOSOC, which meets in Brussels and is much larger, is not consulted in this field. Another important difference is that the Commission, acting as the ECSC High Authority, has a relatively much larger disposable income than it does in its more usual capacity when one bears in mind the fact that much of the normal expenditure of the EEC consists of intervention payments to farmers, to which they are automatically entitled when prices fall below a certain level, and that the ECSC sector is quite small, employing something under 2% of the total work force in the Common Market. This income, moreover, consists entirely of "own resources", essentially levies and interest from loans, further to which the High Authority (in other words the Commission acting under the Treaty of Paris rules) has borrowing powers, but only in order to make loans. In the circumstances it seems appropriate to make this sector the subject of a separate chapter even though it does not have a Commissioner to itself.

The legal and institutional framework, as we have seen, is provided by the Treaty of Paris (1951) as amended by the Merger Treaty (1965) which took effect in 1969. The preamble is more dynamic and "Europeanist" altogether than that of the Treaty of Rome, and worth quoting in full:

"Considering that world peace can be safeguarded only by creative efforts commensurate with the dangers that threaten it;

"Convinced that the contribution which an organized and vital Europe can make to civilization is indispensable to the maintenance of peaceful relations;

"Recognizing that Europe can be built only through practical achievements which will first of all create real solidarity, and through the establishment of common bases for economic development;

"Anxious to help, by expanding their basic production, to raise the standard of living and further the works of peace;

"Resolved to substitute, for age-old rivalries, the merging of their essential interests; to create, by establishing an economic community, the basis for a broader and deeper community among peoples long divided by bloody conflicts; to lay the foundations for institution which will give direction to a destiny henceforward shared;

"Have decided to create a European Coal and Steel Community and to this end have designated as their plenipotentiaries . . ."

(The signatures of the six foreign ministers follow: Adenauer signed in this capacity, though he was at the same time Chancellor and therefore head of the West German Government.)

The Treaty creates a common market in the products which it is intended to cover,* and the ECSC institutions are mandated to ensure an orderly supply to this market taking into account the needs of third countries; to ensure equal access to sources of production for all comparably placed consumers at the lowest prices consistent with stability of prices; maintain conditions which will encourage undertakings to expand and improve their production potential and at the same time promote a policy of using natural resources rationally and avoiding their unconsidered exhaustion; promote improved working conditions and improved standards of living for the workers in each of the industries for which they are responsible; promote growth and international trade and ensure that equitable limits are observed in export pricing; promote orderly expansion and modernization of production and improvement of quality.

---

*The list of these products is given in an annex. At first sight it looks rather arbitrary, but on closer investigation makes sense. It *includes:*
  (a) coal but not (except for statistical purposes) brown coal, which is useless for making steel;
  (b) iron ore but not iron pyrites, again useless for making steel;
  (c) pig iron, iron bars, etc.;
  (d) manganese ore, mainly used for making steel;
  (e) steel as such, as well as rails, fishplates, and wire (normally made in a steelworks and consisting wholly of steel).
It *excludes* cars, refrigerators, and many other products, mainly or wholly made of steel, but not in a steelworks. The one unexpected omission is tungsten (wolfram), but this is only used to a very limited extent by the steel industry. On the other hand, scrap (iron and steel) is included.
  Statistics for brown coal are needed because if more of it is used as a fuel, more black coal becomes available for making steel.

Article 4 lists a number of prohibited practices and state measures, substantially the same as those mentioned in Articles 85, 92, and 94 of the EEC Treaty; but the ECSC Treaty is more restrictive as regards possible exemptions from these rules: it also prohibits the creation of "dominant positions", whereas the EEC Treaty (Article 86) merely seeks to prevent their abuse.

The Community's essential tasks are specified in Article 5:

(a) to provide guidance and assistance for all parties concerned (producers, workers, users) by obtaining information, organizing consultation, and laying down general objectives;

(b) to place financial resources at the disposal of undertakings for their investments and bear part of the cost of readaptation;

(c) to ensure the establishment, maintenance, and observance of normal competitive conditions, and exert direct influence upon production or upon the market only when circumstances so require;

(d) to publish reasons for its action and take the necessary measures to ensure the observance of the rules laid down in the Treaty.

Article 7 sets up the Community institutions:

(i) The *High Authority* (later merged with the Commission), assisted by the *Consultative Committee* (still functioning);

(ii) the *Special Council of Ministers*, whose functions were "inherited" by the Council of Ministers under the Merger Treaty. In ECSC matters, however, it acts mainly as an advisory rather than as a decision-making body, though its approval is required for some purposes (e.g. budgetary increases);

(iii) the *Common Assembly*, whose remit was subsequently broadened so that its members also became the EEC Assembly (European Parliament);

(iv) the *Court of Justice* (which became the EEC Court in the same way).

Article 8 empowers the High Authority to implement the Treaty:

"It shall be the duty of the High Authority to ensure that the objectives set out in this Treaty are attained in accordance with the provisions thereof."

Articles 9–13 were repealed by the Merger Treaty. They specified, *inter alia,* how the members of the High Authority were to be appointed and how long they were to hold office. Eight were to be appointed by the six governments, no state having more than two: the ninth member was to be co-opted, and this possibility could, for instance, be used in order to bring in a trade unionist. The Commission does not have this power of co-option.

In accordance with Article 14 the High Authority (Commission) does its work by taking *decisions,* making *recommendations,* and issuing *opinions.* ECSC decisions correspond to EEC regulations and decisions, and are immediately binding as they stand. ECSC recommendations correspond to EEC directives; they are binding as to the objectives to be attained, but the member-states translate them into national legislation and regulations. ECSC opinions correspond to EEC recommendations and opinions: they are not binding in themselves but further actions may be taken if they are ignored. Reasons must be given in every case.

The duties and functions of the High Authority (Commission) include the following:

(a) it consults with governments, public undertakings, firms, workers, dealers, and consumers, and with associations (e.g. of producers or of consumers), and may present suggestions and observations;

(b) it conducts a permanent study of the market and of price trends, and periodically draws up programmes with forecasts;

(c) it sets out general objectives as regards modernization, etc.;

(d) it takes part in studying the possibility of re-employing, in ECSC industries or otherwise, workers made redundant by market developments or technical changes;

(e) it obtains any information it requires in order to assess the possibility of improving working conditions and living standards for workers in the coal and steel industries;

(f) it *must* publish its general objectives and programmes after submitting them to the Consultative Committee, and *may* publish the studies and information mentioned above.

It has a *right* to any information it requires for these purposes, but is bound by the obligation of professional secrecy where confidential information is involved.

Its *income*, as stated above, is derived mainly from levies on all transactions in the industries which it supervises and interest on loans made over the years. It also takes loans and may receive gifts (but in practice never does). Its *expenditure,* in addition to administrative costs, includes the following main items:

(i) loans for investment programmes and for "works and installations" which contribute directly and primarily to increasing production, reducing production costs or facilitating sales;

(ii) the promotion of technical and economic research relating to production and increased use of coal and steel or to occupational health and safety;

(iii) assistance with the financing of programmes for the creation of new and economically sound activities, capable of reabsorbing redundant workers into production and employment. This assistance also includes "tideover" allowances (change of employment often involves loss of wages), resettlement allowances, and financial as, for instance, with retraining. The state in which investments are made, or workers are retrained as above, is normally required to make a matching grant on a fifty-fifty basis. It also helps workers who move about within the industries which it supervises (e.g. when a pit is closed down) and may, for instance, provide housing loans at a very low rate of interest.

All ECSC activities were originally run from Luxemburg City, the seat of the old High Authority. As a result of the Merger Treaty, work was dispersed to some considerable extent, not only between several Commission Departments but between Luxemburg and Brussels. The general picture is now as follows: the Commission normally meets in Brussels but can meet in Luxemburg when the Council does so (March, June, and October). The Consultative Committee meets in Luxemburg, where it maintains a small secretariat; the health and safety aspects, including research and study groups, are run from Luxemburg, but other research and social programmes (retraining, housing, tideover aid) are organized from Brussels. The research itself, however, both on the health and safety and on the economic and technical side, is essentially carried out in the member-states by industry and by specialized institutes. The rules of competition are enforced from Brussels by means of fines and quite substantial *per diem* penalties, which continue as long as the rules are infringed by a particular firm or public undertaking.

The merger, carried out for essentially political reasons, seems to have led to some loss of efficiency and sense of purpose. One complaint that is sometimes heard is that the Commission, accustomed to proposing draft regulations, directives, and decisions which the Council may or may not accept in due course, find it hard to behave in a more authoritative manner when acting as the High Authority, which furthermore consisted of people specifically appointed to run coal and steel, whereas they are a general-purpose policy-making and administrative body.

The research side covers a wide field: improvement of measurement and analysis techniques; automation; the use of computers and lasers in monitoring the quality of steel being produced at any given moment; ways of making steel more suitable for specific purposes; corrosion and how to prevent it; metal fatigue and creep; new uses for steel; alternative sources of energy in the steel industry; injection of natural gas instead of carbon gas. There is some co-operation with other steel-producing countries in western Europe, in particular Sweden, Austria, and Spain.

The ECSC's work on the health and safety side (including protection of the environment against pollution arising from mining and steel-making activities) has also been quite extensive. Again, it involves co-operation with other countries. It includes study of the effects on health and safety of such technical developments as:

more rapid progression of coal faces;
the greater concentration of mining operations in relatively few mines;
faster drilling and possibly the use of heavier explosive charges;
increased use of diesel engines underground;
the use of high-powered compressed air equipment underground.

Efforts are being made to develop or improve equipment for such purposes as the measurement of noxious gases and of ventilation, reducing the emission of noxious gases by diesel engines, elimination of dust and more effective ventilation. The Commission is assisted for this purpose by a Standing Committee which consists of government, employers' and workers' representatives, and has the Commissioner for Social Affairs as its chairman. This body deals with mining operations only (including oil and gas drilling and non-ferrous mining (copper, zinc, tin, etc.)). It has set up a number of study groups mainly staffed by outside experts, usually with a remit extending over several years. Some of these groups are concerned with the prevention of individual accidents and major disasters, others with the better organization of rescue work in an emergency, others again with the general improvement of working conditions in mines. Between them they meet about sixty times a year, an average of five or six times for each group. A similar body helps to co-ordinate health and safety work in the steel industry; it is peculiar in bringing together producers and workers without the intervention of government representatives. It drew up, soon after its establishment in 1964–5, an inventory of health and safety questions arising in the industry. Unfortunately, there were more of them than the Commission could handle, and a few only could be selected as priority subjects for specialist groups. These included, for instance, the organization of accident prevention (the group investigating this drew up an interesting list of principles, the most important being that safety should be the responsibility of *everybody* in management rather than of a Safety Department, enjoying little prestige and likely to be constantly overruled by the production side); safety training; first-aid and rescue work; gas pipes; oxygen pipes.

While the steel industry is in itself less dangerous for its workers than coal-mining, it is more liable to impair the environment and create public health problems (though the Aberfan disaster, caused by the collapse of an unstable tip on a primary school, was considerably worse than any one "outside" accident attributable to steel-making). A substantial part of the ECSC's research budget (between 20% and 29%) is therefore spent on environment projects. The most important problems, so far as the general public are concerned, are the elimination of waste gases (sulphur and brown fumes in particular) and the neutralization of slurry to prevent water pollution. New problems have also arisen through the establishment of large coastal steelworks (e.g. Scunthorpe, Dunkirk, Fos) using imported rather than home-produced coal and iron ore. Unlike the traditional (and generally declining) industries of Lorraine, the Ruhr and the Scottish and English Midlands, these tend to be in areas where the tourist trade is of some significance, and they may give rise to marine pollution and damage or destroy fishing grounds. Moreover, they are much bigger than traditional steel mills, and if anything goes wrong there it could go very seriously wrong.

The Consultative Committee, already mentioned, served as the "prototype" for the EEC Economic and Social Committee, but is smaller and more specialized. Its members are appointed by the Council by the following procedures:

(i) producers (= employers) and workers. The Council decides which organizations are to be invited to send members and how many each organization will have. The organizations then propose twice as many candidates as there are seats allocated to them, and the Council selects from the names submitted to it.
(ii) Users (including dealers). Each of the following sectors is entitled to one representative, appointed by the Council with due regard to national distribution of seats: the import–export trade, the chemical industry, the railways, metal-using industries, electricity, energy, domestic consumption, the coal trade, coal users, mechanical engineering, metal engineering, shipbuilding, the scrap trade, steel merchants, coke producers, and the cement industry.

The ECSC Treaty prescribes twenty-five purposes for which the Committee must be convened, either to receive information or to give an opinion. One of them is "whenever the High Authority (Commission) thinks fit". The others include consideration of the general objectives and programmes, information on investment activities and on action regarding (illicit) agreements and (undesirable) concentrations; discussion of non-refundable aids to re-employment of workers displaced by technical progress; manifest crisis or serious shortage; establishment of maximum and minimum prices; export restrictions; a fall in the standard of living of workers; consideration of major research projects; any event not foreseen by the Treaty. There is enough to keep the Committee, its three groups (producers, workers, users and dealers) and its various sub-committees active, the more so as it has the right to request an exchange of views at any time.

CHAPTER 11

The Community and its Environment; Consumer Protection; Transport

The three subjects covered in this chapter are closely linked by their very nature. Consumer protection and the defence of the environment are two aspects of the same thing, which is to ensure that everyday life remains tolerable (Figs. 7 and 8); transport policy and the environment are connected first because much of the pollution which we have to fight is due to various forms of transport, as are some of the "nuisances" against which the environment policy of national governments and of the Community is also directed. Another reason is that efficient transport makes it possible to provide a better environment by keeping small towns and villages inhabited, and by using the infrastructure created when society was more rural than it is today, while preventing urban sprawl.

Before we go further it may be worth noting the essential difference between pollution and nuisances. The former is almost always more dangerous than the latter. Nuisances (loud noises and unpleasant smells) disappear of their own accord after a while and are in general less dangerous to health. They are unpleasant *because one notices them,* and can always be noticed. Pollution is at its most dangerous when it is hardest to detect, and often cannot be detected without scientific apparatus. It may build up in the human body over a period of time, and may be carried over considerable distances by the wind and by rivers and marine currents. It includes, for instance, lead and sulphur fumes, untreated sewage, and various chemicals discharged into water or absorbed into food. Very severe nuisances, e.g. the noise suffered by people who live directly under the flight path of incoming aircraft, may be more harmful than moderate pollution (e.g. the air found over the greater part of London, excluding busy thoroughfares), and in such cases it may be legitimate to speak of noise pollution. But in general the distinction holds: fumes, waterborne chemicals, and contaminated food may kill; noises and smells merely annoy and are far easier to get rid of.

Fig. 7.   Cartoon (La Communauté Européenne, Information Office, European Communities, Paris)

Some experts also speak of thermal pollution, i.e. the unnatural rise in the temperature of rivers and small lakes caused by power stations taking in cold water for cooling purposes and then discharging it as warm or hot water. But it is not clear that this increase is always harmful. This depends on what else is already in the water. In some cases a higher temperature may lead to the multiplication of dangerous germs, or of plants which take up too much oxygen and kill off all other life. In other cases the main effect will be that different fishes will live in it, for instance carp instead of trout. This cannot be regarded as bad except by fishermen whose tastes may differ. There may even be advantages for shipping (no ice in winter) and riverside farmers (a longer growing and grazing season).

The European Community needs an environment policy because of its free trade and competition policies as well as for other reasons. If this is left

Fig. 8.   Cartoon (La Communauté Européenne, Information Office, European Communities, Paris)

entirely to the member-states, countries which tolerate pollution will be at a financial advantage because they will be able to produce and therefore sell their goods cheaper. This will distort the conditions of competition as understood by the countries which do not tolerate it, and they will then defend their environment and their industries by excluding products which themselves *create pollution* (e.g. cars with unsatisfactory exhaust systems) and possibly also products which are *made by methods that allow more pollution* and thus place their own more strictly supervised industries at a disadvantage, in exactly the same way as the Community protects its own textile industries by restricting imports from Asian countries where wages are far lower and children start work younger. This, of course, will go against Community free trade; obstacles of this type—mainly safety standards of which dozens, if not hundreds, still vary from state to state—are known as "technical hindrances" or "non-tariff barriers". If EEC countries are to compete on equal terms in a genuinely common market, uniform standards are essential in this field.

An environment policy is also required because pollution spreads across inter-community frontiers, especially down the Rhine, and indeed across the external frontier, in both directions, for instance between the two Germanies.

There is incidentally an important link between the environment policy in the narrow sense of keeping down pollution and nuisances, and the energy policy described in the next chapter. If you conserve energy you do not need to produce so much of it in the first place, and this reduces pollution. Thus proper insulation of houses in winter, as in Scandinavia, also means cleaner air. Secondly it is desirable to produce energy by methods which keep pollution down—from hydroelectricity and from the sun, where the climate makes this possible, rather than by using up coal and oil. These cleaner methods have the added advantage that the water is still there after it has gone through the turbines, and the sun is also still there after giant reflectors have captured and focused a little of its heat: these resources are used but not consumed in the same way as fossil fuels.

The Community Environment Policy, however, is not concerned with pollution and nuisances alone, important though these are. It has several other aspects, among them the conservation of resources, both those which are "non-renewable" and therefore must ultimately run out in any event, and those which are renewable but tend to run out if used faster than they can be replaced, or to deteriorate if misused, e.g. air, land, forests, and water. It also covers town and country planning and the "working environment" (factories and offices for instance). Transport is closely linked with the environment, though a special policy is being worked out for it, and the same Commissioner is responsible for both.

The Community as such began to take a serious interest in the environment during Dr. Mansholt's brief term of office as President of the Commission. He was among the first to see that the Treaty objective of ever-continuing growth could not, in fact, be sustained indefinitely as originally conceived, and that one should think in terms of greater happiness and a better quality of life rather than increasing material wealth and higher consumption. The decision that there should be an Environment Policy was taken by the Heads of State and Government in October 1972, at the Paris Conference which also decided that there should be a Regional Policy. The Commission was asked to submit a programme within eight months, and beat this deadline by a few weeks. The main points of the programme were as follows:

In the first place the policy should aim at:

(1) "preventing, reducing and so far as possible abolishing the harmful effects of pollution and nuisances on the environment";

(2) "ensuring the sound management of natural resources, the balance of ecological systems and the protection of the biosphere";*

(3) "guiding development in accordance with the requirements of quality, by the improvement of working conditions and the setting of life";

(4) "planning the geographical distribution of activities, housing and transport conditions, so as to curb in particular the harmful consequences of the increasing concentration of people in the towns" (this ties up with the Regional Policy);

(5) "organizing co-operation with states outside the Community in order to find common solutions to the environment problems caused by economic and industrial development".

A dozen principles were set out in this document: only the most important are quoted here. In the first place, the best protection of the environment consists in preventing at source the creation of pollution or nuisances rather than trying to counteract their effects. Secondly, the effects of any new development on the environment should be taken into account as early as possible in all the technical processes of planning and decision making. Otherwise too much national prestige, or too large an investment may be involved, and it may then be politically impossible to cancel an undesirable project or intolerably expensive to reshape it. Thirdly, all exploitation of

*The biosphere includes the earth's surface, the sea (which covers seven-tenths of it), the atmosphere, and everything that lives and grows. Damage to any part of it may have incalculable effects on the rest. Thus pollution at sea may poison fish (later eaten by people) or kill off plankton (thus starving the fish). If too many forests are cut down, the world may run out of oxygen. Cutting down hedgerows to have bigger fields (more convenient for machinery) means fewer birds to kill insects, hence more pesticides are needed, and they leave dangerous residues. It may also lead to more erosion, so that the same acreage of land will grow less food or will require more fertilizers (a non-renewable resource in so far as phosphates instead of natural manure are now used) to grow the same amount. Many more examples could be given.

resources and of the natural environment causing significant damage to the ecological balance must be banned.

A very important principle is that the cost of preventing and abolishing nuisances must be borne by the polluter (generally an industrial firm or a public undertaking) with exceptions to be defined at Community level. These exceptions might arise, for instance, where the cost of making the necessary changes would put a large firm out of business, causing massive unemployment, or where the only remedy is closure of the factory concerned, and the question of compensation and retraining then arises, with thousands of workers involved. In such cases the Community might also give the firm a longer period to get rid of the pollution if this enabled it to stay in business.

Another important principle is that care should be taken to ensure that activities carried out in one member-state do not cause any degradation of the environment in another state, whether or not a member of the Community. The main problem in this connection arises along the Rhine: the Germans, the French, the Swiss, and the Dutch frequently get together on this, and some improvement has already been achieved. But there have also been discussions between the East and West Germans and between the various states around the Baltic Sea, two of which (Denmark and West Germany) are members of the Community, while two are neutral (Sweden and Finland) and three are Communist (East Germany, Poland, and the Soviet Union).

Finally, environment protection is a matter for all Community citizens who should be made aware of its importance, and environment policies should be harmonized in the Community, while national programmes on the environment should be co-ordinated with each other and with the Community programmes on the basis of a long-term plan.

In general the action to be taken by the Community as such will mainly involve information which the Commission will get from the member-states, piece together, and make available to all, and co-ordination of national research projects and policies, but regulations and directives may also be used within the context of the Competition Policy, for instance to set common safety and pollution standards for vehicles.

The Earth has only one atmosphere and all the seas, in the last analysis, are one; hence co-operation with other international bodies (UN and its subsidiaries, the Council of Europe, OECD), and with non-member-states individually, is an important part of the Community's work in this field. The work itself consists largely of establishing which are the most harmful forms of pollution, arriving at common methods of establishing standards (otherwise some states will continue to be stricter or more lenient with polluters than others), exchanging information, as stated above, and arriving at a common method of calculating the cost of the fight against pollution, bearing in mind that anti-pollution measures may cost jobs as well as money, and that some states, left to themselves, might only count the cost while others would also consider the saving made by having less bronchitis and less cancer, or fewer houses and public buildings falling to bits, due to erosion caused by pollution. Some states might go further still and consider that while money is being saved through fewer people being ill, it is also being spent through more people living longer. All these sums are extremely complex, and if one cannot agree on a way of working them out, the final result will be that some countries decide it is too expensive to make any real effort, while others consider it worth while, but their efforts and expense are largely wasted through pollution spilling over from their neighbours.

The Commission document also pointed out that the object should be to *improve* as well as *protect* the environment. Hence there should be aids in favour of hill and other marginal farming to keep the countryside inhabited and because good farming in marginal areas is helpful to farmers in more productive areas: streams and rivers reach these areas in better shape and so do store cattle for fattening. Measures should also be taken to help forestry, to improve the working environment, and to make towns healthier and more pleasant to live in.

A number of *priority actions* were suggested. In the first place it would be necessary to investigate *particularly harmful substances,* such as lead, phosphorus, sulphur, carbon monoxide, asbestos, mercury, and some derivatives of crude oil (hydrocarbons). Health standards should be established at Community level, e.g. how much in the way of harmful substances may be contained in a product in direct contact with man (for instance food, drink, tins and other containers of food or drink, cooking vessels, clothing, bed linen). There should be Community directives, forming part of the machinery for eliminating trade barriers, and specifying:

   (i) the maximum amount of lead and other additives in fuels;
  (ii) the maximum amount of lead in crockery;
 (iii) the maximum amount of harmful substances in domestic heating oils;
 (iv) the toxic substances which may be contained in detergents and in electrical appliances, paints, and varnishes;
  (v) maximum permitted noise levels for motor vehicles and engineering equipment (bulldozers, pneumatic drills, compressors, etc.)

Another priority action would be to investigate pollution problems and measures already being taken or needing to be taken, first of all in the paper and pulp industry, which uses and pollutes a great deal of water, and in the iron and steel industry, which releases a great deal of pollution in the atmosphere. Next would come such industries as the production of nitrate and phosphate fertilizers, petrochemicals, and leather; also the canning, sugar-refining, potato starch, and corn starch industries, and wool combing, washing, and carding. Most of these industries are dirtier in themselves than the paper, iron and steel industries, but on a smaller scale and therefore creating less total pollution. The canning industry was included at this level of priority because it is the part of the food industry in which the greatest dangers are likely to arise, either due to additives or to badly sealed tins; the rest of the food industry was to be investigated later, along with metals other than iron and steel (they are all produced on a smaller scale, though some of the processes are more dangerous, involving the use of highly toxic substances such as cyanide) and textile industry processes other than wool combing, washing, and carding, which are the dirtiest and involve some risk from diseases such as anthrax.

The Commission also indicated that it would take action on wastes and residues. The first step would be to find out what they are and how dangerous they are, and the next to investigate the problems involved in getting rid of them, starting with particularly harmful metals and minerals, such as mercury and cadmium, as well as certain plastics; these would be followed by residual oil and residues containing petrol and tar, bulky scrap (discarded cars, refrigerators, and washing machines for instance), non bio-degradable (plastic and glass) packagings for consumer products, and animal wastes from slaughterhouses and factory farms.

The Community action to be taken, once the facts have been ascertained, would include the harmonization of regulations (some countries are at present much stricter than others), an exchange of information and the promotion of new techniques which generate fewer residues or get rid of them more efficiently. This could be done under the headings of industrial policy and research policy. One might also consider the establishment of an information agency on wastes and their disposal, and of a European treatment plant (some processing is very expensive). This would be particularly useful in areas where several frontiers meet, for instance around Aachen and Luxemburg City. Special problems would arise in connection with radioactive wastes, some of which are extremely long-lived, and these would require further study.

Further action would be up to the member-states. To ensure that it is taken, the Commission would publish, in an annual report on the state of the environment in the Community, the information it obtained on what was being done in each country. It would then appear that some were doing more than others, and this would influence public opinion. Finally, the Commission would take defaulting states to the European Court where it seemed that actual Community laws were being infringed.

As regards the *conservation of resources*, the Commission would undertake a survey of non-renewable resources and of the rate at which they are now being depleted: it would then make a forecast of the future rate of depletion and of the effect on their price and on the economy in general, and follow up with recommendations as to what could be done to conserve and recycle them. It would also investigate water resources; these, as we have seen, are renewable, but only if one does not use them up too fast.

As regards *town and country planning* one should try to reverse excessive concentration where it has occurred, and to maintain "areas in which the natural or cultural environment has hitherto been fairly well preserved" (these include, for instance, much of Scotland, the French and Italian Alps, and quite large areas of Germany), since their unspoilt character attracts people and new activities. One should also fight against the deterioration of town centres and seek to improve the working environment: this goes beyond safety measures as such and includes anything which makes factories and offices more pleasant: better lighting; working methods which give people a greater sense of involvement in what they are doing; flexible working hours where practicable—they have, for instance, been introduced in some of the Common Market offices.

In general the Commission does its work by calling on national experts to provide the information and discuss what should be done: it then makes their recommendations its own. The work of implementing these recommendations thereafter falls almost entirely to the member-states, to regional and local authorities, and to industry. The Community only intervenes where competition policy and the internal market are involved, and where directives and regulations may therefore be issued, or where existing rules are broken and the European Court may therefore act.

Consumer protection, where safety standards are concerned, covers exactly the same ground as environment policy, but it also includes the right to know what one is buying and what one is paying for it. On both points, but especially the first, Community rules exist or are being created. The best known, probably, is that wine must be what the Community has decided it is, the fermented juice of grapes, with an alcoholic content not below 8% nor above 18% and only such additives as the Council has decided to allow, e.g. sugar in German and Luxemburg wines. If it is not made from grapes, or if it contains too little alcohol, it may taste delightful, and may be very good for you, but it is not wine, and cannot be sold under that name. If it contains too many additives, or unauthorized ones, it is not wine and cannot be sold at all. To be sold as *quality wine* it must conform to some added specifications; thus it must be made in a particular place, from a particular kind of grapes, it must generally be bottled there, it must not be blended with any other wine (e.g. Beaujolais with Algerian or Bordeaux with Spanish), and there is usually a limitation on the quantity that may be produced from a given acreage. There are strict rules about the size of labels, not only on wine bottles, but for many other products, and about the information these labels have to carry.

The Commission is also working on rules against misleading sales literature and undesirable sales practices (e.g. sending out unsolicited goods and then demanding money from those who have received them unless they return the goods at their own expense). Such rules already exist in most of the member-states, but they are not the same, and problems might arise where, for instance, a German firm sends goods through the post to Denmark or a Dutch firms sends misleading literature to Britain. Consumer credit raises the issue of national discrimination; thus Belgian firms may charge higher HP interest rates to non-Belgians because they could disappear back home, and some British firms will not transact this kind of business with foreigners at all, even though they are Community citizens.

Transport policy is a field in which there has been far more in the way of discussion than of actual proposals, and where the Commission has proposed far more than the Council has actually decided. The member-states are extremely reluctant to give up what they regard as satisfactory arrangements from their own standpoint, and two important aspects—sea and air transport—have not so far been brought within the competence of the Common Market authorities except in an incidental way. Thus it would be a breach of the Treaty for a member-state to insist that its products should be exported on its own ships only to the exclusion of ships from other member-states, or to require its officials to fly by its national airline only. But the Commission cannot propose, and the Council cannot enact directives or regulations in these two fields at present. What the Commission is trying to achieve includes:

(i) *A more uniform method of charging for the use of the infrastructure.* The railways have to pay both for the fuel which they use and for the maintenance of their track, embankments, cuttings, bridges, and tunnels, and this is reflected in their costs and in their passenger and freight charges. Road transport undertakings do not have to pay directly for the maintenance of the road or for the much greater pollution which they create, as compared with the railways: they pay indirectly but only in the course of paying for their fuel.

(ii) *More uniform working conditions for those working in transport.* This includes, for instance, a uniform limit on the hours and distances to be driven by lorry crews in one day. The drivers themselves are not always in favour of this because they may have organized their private lives around a traditional run (e.g. London–Glasgow) which they cover at a single stretch, with some sort of a home at either end. To keep within Community law they would now have to stay at Penrith or Northampton on their way, and this does not suit them. On present showing Britain will probably refuse to apply this rule unless an exception can be made to cover such cases.

(iii) *Uniform qualifications for transport operators and drivers,* enabling a German, for instance, to be sure that he can set up in France, or a Dutchman in Italy. At present, rules vary quite considerably and may not be the same for "own-account" operators (e.g. farmers and industrialists who deliver or collect with their own vehicles) and professional carriers, being in general more flexible for the former, even though you are just as dead if you are run over by somebody who is carrying his own goods as if you are hit by a container lorry. It is true that the "own-account" operators tend to have lighter and slower vehicles than the professionals, but the TIR men with their juggernauts are also more experienced and possibly more careful about maintenance.

(iv) *Uniform conditions for those taking part in international road transport.* At the moment rules vary from country to country and are again more liberal for "own-account" operators than for professionals, though this is not always the case. They are also more liberal for local international transport (e.g. Aachen–Eupen, Strasbourg–Offenburg) than for the real thing (e.g. Paris–Cologne, London–Milan) which is subject to a system of quotas, so many journeys in each direction being allowed for vehicles from either country in the course of a year. The Dutch feel this is particularly unfair, since it cuts them out of the profitable Franco–German trade, contrary to the spirit of the Treaty. The Commission would like these bilateral arrangements replaced by overall control of transport capacity, giving all Community operators the right to take part in this international trade so long as there are not too many vehicles on the road. It would also like similar arrangements for the control of river and canal transport capacity.

(v) *More rational financial arrangements between railway undertakings and the member-states.* All the major railway systems are now nationalized, and all operate at a loss, but there are also some smaller undertakings, owned by private companies or local authorities, and usually subsidized to some extent. The state does more or less for its railways, not only by subsidizing them but in some cases by prohibiting competitive traffic along the routes which they serve. This distorts the conditions of competition in general through its effect on industrial and commercial costs. In some cases these are lower because firms have to use the railways and cannot send their goods or obtain their supplies by road.

(vi) *Uniform taxation of road transport vehicles and fuel.* Lack of uniformity again distorts the conditions of competition, putting Luxemburg in particular at a considerable advantage. This is not a very important matter as the country is so small, but appreciable differences also exist between the major member-states.

(vii) *Action on the pollution and congestion caused by transport*, especially in urban areas. Everybody recognizes this as desirable; the problem here is that it is expensive and that, in several of the member-states, a majority of the population either own a car or have one in the family. Some of the most effective measures would be politically impracticable. In any event this is more a matter for the member-states.

The Commission, with the help of national experts, is also carrying out a number of interesting studies, for instance into the possibilities offered by new modes of transport, such as hovercraft.

CHAPTER 12

Energy Policy

The same Commissioner is at present responsible for *energy* and for *taxation and financial institutions,* and this is a reasonable arrangement in order to equalize work loads within the Commission. However, these subjects do not really belong together and are therefore separated in this book.

The essential objectives of Community policy in this field are:

(i) to slow down the growth in *total energy consumption* without affecting economic growth in general;

(ii) to reduce the amount of *imported energy* especially from politically unreliable sources, or brought along routes which are easily threatened;

(iii) to reduce the Community's *dependence on imported energy* as a percentage of its total consumption.

This will, incidentally, save us a lot of money because several of the countries which supply us with energy do not take much else in return. Kuwait has about the same population of Edinburgh; some of the emirates along the Gulf have populations more comparable to those of Limerick or Cambridge; hence they are not very useful consumers of Europe's products. In the long term it may also be in the interest of the oil-producing states themselves since, with their small populations and limited needs they do not want to get rid of all their oil at once. When it is gone they will have nothing left except people, sand, and investments, which will not be worth a great deal to them if our economy is still dependent on oil and can therefore no longer function.

Another useful byproduct of this policy should be a decline in pollution because the new sources of energy (e.g. nuclear, solar) and the new methods of using existing sources of energy (e.g. producing more electricity from coal rather than directly using the coal as fuel), will tend to cause less pollution.

On the other hand, there will be three very serious problems in connection with the increased use of nuclear energy, which is expected to produce 50% of the Community's electricity by AD 2000.

(a) *Getting rid of dangerous and often very long-lived wastes.* Some of

119

these products will still cause serious illness and death, often after prolonged suffering, 250,000 years from now. This is an almost unimaginable span of years when one thinks that the Pyramids are about 4000 years old, that Jericho, the longest continuously inhabited settlement at present known, goes back 10,000 years, and that we are only 30,000 years away from the cave artists of Altamira and Lascaux.

The quantity of these wastes, which will have to be buried in a very safe place and guarded by the next 8000 generations, will increase year by year, and we cannot tell how long civilization will remain at the level which makes it possible to look after them properly.

(b) Preventing these wastes, which could be used for poisoning water supplies, and fissile materials (*intended* for producing energy, but *capable* of being used for making bombs) from falling into the hands of hostile governments, terrorists, or madmen.

The security measures involved would be very expensive if they are to be adequate. They would also involve severe restrictions on the personal freedom of people who work with these materials, transport them, or even live near the places where they are produced, used, or stored after disposal. These restrictions might not be politically acceptable, and even if we were prepared to accept them, they would involve the creation of small, semi-Fascist "states-within-a-state" around these places, so that the rest of us could enjoy Western democracy together with a high standard of living. The people who formed these mini-states would develop a distinctive outlook and a very strong *esprit de corps,* as well as a dangerous awareness of their own power.

(c) *Preventing nuclear accidents.* In principle, anything which *can* go wrong *will* go wrong, sooner or later, no matter what precautions are taken. Up till now, however, no major accident has occurred, though there have been minor incidents, making locally produced milk unsafe for some weeks, and involving the shut-down of a reactor until the core could be extracted and replaced. The risk will inevitably increase as more nuclear power stations are set up, and one will then have to consider whether it is better to have a considerable number of small reactors, in which case the risk of an accident will be greater (simply because there are more places where it can happen) but the casualties could be kept down to a few hundred if one of them blows up provided it is suitably isolated; or a few large ones, in which case it may be a long time before anything disastrous happens, but a million people might die when it does.

Table 1 (taken from a Commission document) shows how the pattern of energy consumption has developed over the past few years in the Community. In the first place, the total consumption of coal as a source of energy has declined quite considerably, both in actual tonnage and as a percentage of all

TABLE 1. *Total Primary Energy Needs in 1985(a)—Community*

	1973 estimates		1985 initial forecasts		1985 objectives	
	Million tonnes	%	Million tonnes	%	Million tonnes	%
Solid fuels	227	22.6	175	10	250	17
Oil	617	61.4	1160	64	600–650	41–44
Natural gas	117	11.6	265	15	340–290	23–20
Hydroelectric and geothermic power	30	3.0	40	2	43	3
Nuclear energy	14	1.4	160	9	242	16
Total	1005	100	1800	100	1475	100

(a) Internal consumption + exports + bunkers.
Source: Projects of primary energy demand in the Community (1975–1980–1985) (doc. SEC (72) 3283 final), and an additional estimate made in January 1973 for the new member states (doc. SEC (73) 128).

consumption. Secondly, the consumption of oil has increased very considerably on both counts. Thirdly, the degree of dependence on imported energy has also gone up, mainly because we use more oil, but also because much of our coal now comes from abroad, especially the United States, East Germany (brown coal), and Poland. A fourth point is that imports of energy now cost us considerably more than they did twelve years ago (when we still relied largely on coal) or five years ago (when imports of oil were very cheap). Finally, though this does not appear from the table but is mentioned in the document itself, the economy of several regions in the Community has suffered, more or less severely, through the decline of coal production and of local coal-consuming industries. This happened in the following way: the steel industry was generally located where there was iron ore and coal could be brought in, or where there was coal and iron could be brought in, or ideally where both were found close to each other. Other industries then gathered where steel, their essential raw material, was readily available.

The present member-states of the Community generally became dependent on imported iron when they were still self-sufficient as regards coal. However, when coal ceased to be the main source of energy and became important mainly as one of the major components of steel, which is an alloy of carbon, iron, and (in generally small quantities) other metals such as tungsten, it was often more profitable to import the coal and have the steelworks close to the sea. Areas such as the Scottish Midlands, southern Belgium, and Lorraine then began to have serious problems, not only because it was less profitable to make steel there, but because their steel-consuming industries also suffered in two ways: their raw material was now more expensive, and greater use was being made of plastics, themselves a byproduct of the oil industry. All this was due to an incorrect strategic decision made when Middle East oil became plentifully available; to go for cheapness and hope for the best rather than give precedence (as in agriculture) to security of supply, and accept a slower rate of growth with a standard of living that could be sustained. The Communist countries did not make this mistake; but their leaders did not depend on popular votes and could therefore afford to take a longer view.

The Community has now recognized that it cannot allow this state of affairs to continue: on 17 December 1974 the Council approved the targets proposed by the Commission, that is a reduction of dependence on imported energy from the 61% recorded in 1973 to 50% and ideally 40% by 1985. With 60% self-sufficiency (40% dependence) the Community could always ride out a crisis by emergency measures: moreover, 40% dependence would mean that we could get most if not all of our imports from politically reliable countries such as the United States, Canada, and Australia, and the rest from countries which, though having different political systems, would suffer quite serious economic damage if they suddenly stopped trading with us (e.g. Poland, East Germany, and Algeria).

Our total requirements in energy would then be satisfied as follows:

> *solid fuel* (essentially coal): 17% instead of 10% in 1973
> *oil:* at most 49%, ideally 41% instead of 64%
> *natural gas:* at least 18%, ideally 23% instead of 15%
> *hydroelectric and geothermic power:* 3% instead of 2%
> *nuclear energy;* 13–16% instead of 9%.

At the same time, *expected energy consumption* in 1985 should be reduced by 15% in comparison to earlier forecasts for that year, though it would still be some way above the 1973 level (Fig. 9).

If we look more closely at these targets we shall see that they also involve a considerable reduction in the Community's dependence on *politically unreliable countries.* Thus most of our coal would be produced in western Europe and most of the rest would come from the United States; some of our reduced oil consumption could also be met from European sources, and quite a lot of it from Algeria and Nigeria (both unlikely to stop trading with us abruptly). Natural gas is a mainly European resource, with the rest coming largely from Algeria. Hydroelectricity (river and possibly tidal), and geothermic power (a very minor component) would be wholly European resources. This leaves nuclear power: the necessary fissile material can be imported entirely from politically reliable countries, including one or two in Africa which have a better record of stable government than several in Europe.

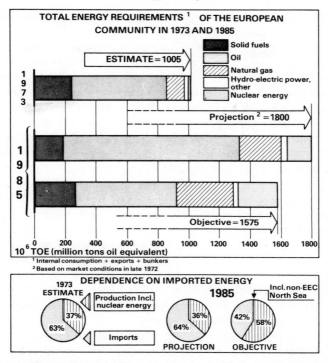

Fig. 9.   Energy policy (*Bulletin of the European Communities,* Supplement 4/74, Luxemburg)

The objectives mentioned on p. 119 would be achieved as follows:

(1) *Slowing down growth in energy consumption.* This can be pursued by various methods, all of them useful and some of them also tending to improve the environment and the overall quality of life: smaller cars, higher taxation on petrol and on large cars, better insulation of houses, better heating systems, spreading out working hours by the use of "flexi-time" and shifts (factories and offices have to be heated all the time and it is a waste to leave them empty sixteen hours a day); but the advantages of flexi-time and shifts depend on the relative cost of heating and of lighting. As a general rule, people like flexi-time and dislike shift-work; both conserve heat by making it possible for more people to use less working space. They also save fuel by making it possible to run buses and trains in a more rational way, and reduce rush-hour pollution, but they consume more electric light. There are other possibilities of slowing down growth in consumption, including some fairly unconventional ones like allowing people to do more of their office work in their homes (which have to be heated anyway). The Community authorities

help by bringing experts together, by co-ordinating national policies, and to some extent by financing research.

(2) *Reduction in the amount of imported energy.* To some extent this follows automatically from (1) in so far as one saves on oil, almost all of which has at present to be imported. But more has to be done to achieve this aim. In the first place more energy should be produced from *sources within the Community*: British and German coal; North Sea oil and natural gas; hydroelectricity from the Alps and Scotland; eventually tidal and geothermal energy from various places and solar energy from Italy and southern France, though these are not expected to become more than minor but useful additional sources. This (and especially the reactivation of the coal-mining industry) will incidentally create more employment within the Community, much of it in regions where this is particularly desirable.

In so far as one must import, it is cheaper to import small quantities of uranium ore than lakes of oil; it is also cheaper and safer to import coal from America (the Community's best customer) than oil from tiny countries which only take our money and could live on their investments and cut off supplies for a while if they chose. Again, the Community helps to finance research and development which will allow more energy to be produced within its territory, but, as in the case of energy-saving projects, most of the work is undertaken by the member-states.

(3) *Reduction in percentage dependence on imported energy.* This should follow automatically from the steps mentioned above. In addition, however, it is essential that the Community should at all times carry adequate reserve stocks of oil, coal, and nuclear fuel. This has already been organized so far as oil is concerned: all member-states must now have 90 days' supply in hand, not counting any quantities that may already be on their way to Europe by sea. These are sometimes quite considerable, tankers being ordered to slow down when storage capacity at the refineries is fully taken up or nearly so.

With adequate stocks in hand, the Community is better placed to take any additional measures that may be needed in a crisis: petrol rationing, stepping up the extraction of coal, placing further orders in America and elsewhere, and switching over from one method of producing electricity to another.

An important aspect of the Community's energy policy is the encouragement (and the enforcement by national authorities) of a more rational way of using the various kinds of energy that are available. Thus it is wasteful to produce electricity from oil when it can also be produced from any of the other sources of energy mentioned above—coal, nuclear fuel, natural gas, running water, and to a limited extent the heat from the sun and from the centre of the earth. It is also wasteful to make extensive use of natural gas for this purpose, since gas will also provide heat, and may be used to propel cars. On the other hand, nuclear fuel, which will provide electricity, cannot be used for anything else, except to propel ships (essentially submarines and other warships, in view of the risks involved). It is therefore sensible to use it in power stations, and to design most new power stations to use it, subject, of course, to finding some way of keeping the various hazards under control (leakage, explosion, theft of fissile material, and danger from radio-active wastes).

At the same time it is undesirable to become exclusively dependent on any one source for any one purpose because supplies may run out or become temporarily difficult to obtain, and because this places excessive power in the hand of a small number of people (e.g. those who know how to run nuclear power stations). Hence it is not envisaged that *all* power stations should be nuclear.

There are difficulties in getting all the member-states to play their part in operating the energy policy, which cannot work unless they do so. National interests conflict to some extent, depending on what sources of energy, if any, they control, and on their relationship with oil-producing countries which can in the meantime supply them with all they need. One serious problem is the risk that oil-producing countries could suddenly halve their prices, thus making it apparently unprofitable to invest heavily in North Sea oil and alternative sources (coal, nuclear, etc.). This could make it essential to establish a system of import levies similar to those used in the Common Agricultural Policy, and indeed to operate the whole policy on much the same lines as the CAP, all the major decisions being taken by the Council and implemented by the Commission, through an Oil Management Committee, a Nuclear Power Management Committee, etc. Otherwise member-states which import temporarily cheap oil could be at an unfair advantage over those which stick to the agreed line, in Europe's long-term interest as well as their own.

An energy policy as centralized as the CAP, however, could give rise to other difficulties, one of them being the fact that any states which are themselves oil producers, or think they can become such, may have very different views on how to run it from those of member-states which are purely consumers. They might, for instance, want to extract the oil slowly and keep the supply going as long as possible, while the consumer states might prefer to use it up fairly quickly to maintain their standard of living and find an alternative (e.g. a cheaper and safer form of nuclear energy) before it runs out. In this sense the CAP is easier to run, because all the member-states grow food, all except Britain grow most of their own food (and even Britain can do it at a pinch) and everybody knows we cannot live without it. Europeans have been farming for thousands of years: they have only been using coal on a large scale for a few generations, and electricity and oil for a few decades. The use of nuclear energy is more recent still, and we do not know as yet just how much can safely be done with it. This makes it harder for people to agree on objectives and methods, and stick to what they have agreed. With their economic survival in the balance, the member-states may be reluctant to let anyone else take their decisions for them: if every proposal is going to run into a veto it is perhaps better that the Community authorities should stick to their present co-ordinating role.

Nuclear research and development (Fig. 10), and the use of nuclear energy, are governed by a separate treaty (Rome II) signed at the same time as the main EEC Treaty. However, the institutions which run this side of the Community's work have always been the same as those responsible for the Common Market as a whole, and their activities in the nuclear field are best described here and in Chapter 15 (Education, Science, and Research).

The Euratom Treaty mentions the following as the objectives of the Community in this field:

(i) to promote research and ensure the dissemination of technical information;

(ii) to establish uniform safety standards;

(iii) to facilitate investment and ensure the establishment of the necessary basic installations;

(iv) to ensure a regular and equitable supply of ores and nuclear fuels;

(v) to prevent diversion and improper use of fissile materials;

(vi) to exercise the right of ownership over fissile materials (mainly uranium and plutonium);

(vii) to ensure wide commercial outlets;

(viii) to establish such relations as will foster progress in the peaceful uses of nuclear energy.

While major decisions (e.g. to establish and finance research programmes) are taken by the Council on the proposal of the Commission and after consulting the European Parliament, the management of Euratom is essentially the Commission's task. It is responsible for promoting and facilitating nuclear research, and to that end it is empowered to call for national programmes in order to co-ordinate and complement them. Having considered these programmes it delivers opinions, whose purpose is to discourage unnecessary duplication and direct research towards sectors which are insufficiently explored. It publishes at regular intervals a list of sectors requiring further research, and organizes conferences and symposia. It may also help states or undertakings to obtain nuclear ores and fissile materials, and may place installations, equipment, or expert assistance at the disposal of member-states, persons, or undertakings, either free of charge or against payment.

The Commission is entitled to details of all patents in this field, sought or

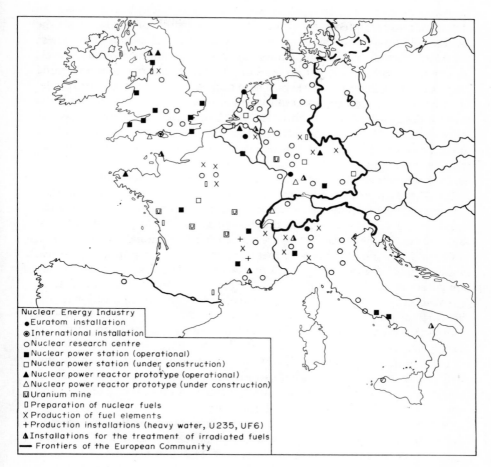

Fig. 10. Nuclear research and development in the EEC (By courtesy of the Publications Fund of the European Schools)

obtained in any member-state, and may in certain circumstances obtain licences to use them by a compulsory purchase procedure. (In practice this would be very difficult if not impossible to apply if the member-state concerned were unwilling to co-operate.) It is bound by the obligation of professional secrecy and obliged to compensate individuals and member-states for any damage caused by improper communication of confidential information thus obtained; there are also security provisions to ensure that the defence interests of member-states are not jeopardized.

The Council, acting on a proposal of the Commission, has the power to establish basic standards for protection of the health of workers and the general public against the dangers arising from ionizing radiation. These standards include maximum permissible doses, maximum permissible levels of exposure and contamination, and the fundamental principles governing the health surveillance of workers. These standards may be revised or supplemented at the request of the Commission or of a member-state, and it is the duty of the member-states to enforce them. Extra health and safety measures may be imposed by the Commission if any state is to carry out particularly dangerous experiments, and its assent is required if other member-states may be affected by these experiments.

Every member-state is further required to establish whatever facilities may be necessary to carry out continuous monitoring of nuclear installations (this covers the risk of explosion as well as leaks and other sources of accidental exposure). The Commission has the right of access and inspection and must be informed of the checks which are carried out by national authorities and undertakings, and of the arrangements made for the disposal of radioactive wastes—this because contamination of water, soil, or air space may easily spread across national frontiers. It is also required to make recommendations as to the level of radioactivity in air, water, or soil. (In this connection it may be worth mentioning that there are a few places with high levels of natural radioactivity, and the Commission, of course, can do nothing about this: the Treaty only covers risks arising from man's activities.)

The Commission is also entitled to information about investment in this field, and is required to publish illustrative programmes showing production targets and types of investment required: the opinion of the Economic and Social Committee is to be obtained before publication.

An important aspect of the Treaty is the encouragement which it gives to the establishment of joint undertakings (e.g. nuclear power stations financed and operated by two or more member-states). The Commission is required to investigate and report on such project, and the Council then decides whether or not to grant them a special status which confers exemption from various taxes and duties, and enables citizens of any member-state to work there.

The Treaty also sets up a common supply policy, administered by the Commission through the Euratom Supply Agency. In principle all special fissile materials in the member-states belong to the Community and may only be bought or sold through this Agency (in practice this merely means that an EEC official countersigns all such transactions) and it also has a right of option on ores and other source materials produced within the Community. This policy, however, was drawn up at a time when uranium was thought to be very scarce: it later became more plentiful, while France, the one major producer within the Community, would not go along with these arrangements. It has therefore largely remained a dead letter. The Commission, however, does have the power to build up ordinary and emergency stocks and may make recommendations to member-states for the development of prospecting and exploitation. It is also entitled to take security measures (special fissile materials to be held by the Agency or in other stores which are or may be inspected by the Commission).

Since 1973 uranium has become increasingly valuable as a source of energy: interest in the Supply Agency has therefore revived and the development of nuclear power stations has become a matter of some urgency. As it involves risks to the environment and, indeed, to public health and safety, very expensive research is required as well as considerable investments in measures of protection. All this is beyond the resources of most individual member-states, and some of the work (e.g. on nuclear fusion) can only be undertaken by the Community as a whole. Hence the Euratom aspects of the Community, which tended for some years to be overlooked as the bigger member-states preferred to get on with their own projects, are coming into their own.

CHAPTER 13

Economic, Financial, and
Fiscal Affairs;
Credit and Investments*

The Community is in principle working towards *economic and monetary union*. This implies a single currency—possibly the present unit of account—and, until such a currency is accepted, a fixed rate of exchange between all existing national currencies. The nine governments would then lose the room for manoeuvre which they now have, and it would be just as impracticable for the British Government to uphold the British economy on its own, or even try to do so, as for the Californian Government to try and uphold the Californian economy on its own.

In practice the Community is as yet nowhere near this state of affairs. Six of the member-states, with five currencies (Belgium and Luxemburg share one), keep these currencies close together, so that there can never be an excessive difference between the number of marks you can buy for a given number of guilders on any one day and what you will get for them next week. In fact the mark and guilder are worth nearly the same: for 100 guilders you should always get between 96 and 98 marks; similarly, for 100 French francs, you should always get between 895 and 905 Belgian francs.† The five currencies all maintain a parallel relationship to the US dollar and other foreign convertible currencies (e.g. the Canadian dollar, the Swiss franc, the Swedish crown, and the yen). If you can get more of them for your French francs you will also get more of them for your Belgian, German, Dutch, or Danish currency. Conversely, if they become more expensive in one of these countries, they become more expensive in all. The six countries concerned buy and sell one another's currencies to keep them all on the same approximate level.

*This chapter covers three closely related fields for which two commissioners are at present responsible: economic and financial affairs; credit and investments; taxation and financial institutions. Three directors-general are also involved, as well as an entirely distinct institution, the European Investment Bank.

†See note at end of chapter.

This arrangement is known as the "snake in the tunnel", the snake being the five linked currencies which wriggle up and down together, and the tunnel being the other convertible currencies. The British and Irish currencies, which are tied together, are not in the snake at present (1976), nor is the Italian lire; but there is some possibility that Italy may join, and that the Irish pound may become an independent currency and also join the snake.

The finance ministers and the governors of the central banks of the EEC countries are in constant contact with one another and can get together very quickly in an emergency, as they did, for instance, when the dollar was devalued, when the mark was revalued, and during the 1973 oil crisis.

There continues to be quite considerable differences from one EEC country to another, both as regards the rate of inflation and in the price of goods. These differences are sometimes greater between two EEC states (e.g. Germany and Britain) than between the EEC as a whole and the rest of western Europe as a whole, or between Germany (in the EEC) and Switzerland (outside). The Commission is not happy about this state of affairs, though such differences also exist between one state of the United States and another. Price differences, however, are to some extent being evened out by inflation, since the high-inflation countries (the United Kingdom and Italy) originally started with lower prices for most products than Germany and France. If the process continues, however, Britain will become more expensive to live in than either of the low-inflation countries, and will then keep on getting more expensive all the time.*

Another matter of some concern to the Commission is that freedom of investment, as between Community countries, is far from complete. Several governments, the British and French among them, still impose restrictions of one kind or another, either on investments placed in their country by citizens of the other member-states, or the other way round. Furthermore, investment across the Community's internal frontiers is discouraged by different rules and practices within each member-state. Thus company accounts are not necessarily kept in the same way in Britain, France, Belgium, and West Germany. This means that a British investor, accustomed to reading British reports and balance-sheets, cannot tell at a glance what a French, Belgian, or German firm is really worth, how well or badly it is being managed, whether its reserves are adequate or not, what allowance is being made for the depreciation of machinery, and much else besides. A German businessman, who is thinking of investing in Britain, will have similar difficulties. The Commission has therefore proposed a directive for the standardization of

*It is already more expensive to live in Britain on British wages or salaries than in Germany on a German income. At present, however, most of the things one can buy in the United Kingdom cost less in marks, French or Belgian francs, or guilders (after conversion to sterling) than they do on the Continent.

company accounts, or rather for more comparable though not fully standardized accounts.

This draft directive defines the type of firms whose accounts should be made comparable, and requires them to publish a balance-sheet, a profit and loss account, and an annex explaining how the other two documents were drawn up. This annex must provide further information as to the number of shares, debentures, etc., and the rights conferred on their holders, the firm's commitments in so far as they do not appear on the balance-sheet, and help to give a clearer idea of its situation, a detailed breakdown of the firm's products, activities, and markets, the number of people employed in the course of the year, information about wages, salaries, and fringe benefits (if not shown on the balance-sheet), directors' fees, pensions and any loans made to them, and taxation. The balance-sheet must include some fifty items specified in the directive: a shortened form is allowed in the case of small firms.

At this point it may be worth mentioning the activities of the European Investment Bank. While it is a separate institution within the Community, located in Luxemburg City and with one governor from each of the member-states, its work ties in closely with that of the Commission's Economic and Financial Departments.

What it does is to make loans on commercial terms (whereas the European Development Fund, mentioned in Chapter 17, mainly provides grants and soft loans) for various projects, about 95% of them in the Community and the rest in associated states. It also guarantees existing loans on certain conditions.

These projects include:

   (i) developments in the less-developed regions of the Community, the modernization of industry in areas heavily dependent on traditional declining industries, and new industries in those areas;
  (ii) projects of priority interest such as nuclear power stations, high-technology industries, and measures to protect the environment;
 (iii) infrastructure projects of common interest to several member-states;
 (iv) other projects of special interest to the Community.

They must be helpful to economic growth; if put forward by firms they must be capable of showing a profit.

Firms and regional authorities as well as governments may apply for loans and guarantees. This is an important point since, as we have seen, the Regional Fund can only be used in aid of projects put forward by national governments.

Loans are usually between £1 million and £10 million. They are not intended to cover the whole cost of the project, but about 30% to 40%. The rest has to be found from other banks, the applicant firm's own resources, taxation (in the case of government and regional authority projects), or government aid. Repayment starts once the project is functioning, i.e. when the factory is producing goods, the road is carrying traffic, or the nuclear station is giving out electricity.

The EIB in principle aims to break even and gets its money from other banks. It publishes an annual report of its activities with details of the operations it has financed. For these operations it uses a unit of account which is not identical with the UA used for most other Community purposes or with the special "green" unit used for agricultural transactions. It is calculated by a rather complex method which involves adding together a given quantity of marks, guilders, Danish kroner, French and Belgian francs, Italian lire, and British and Irish pounds, changing all (except the Belgian currency) into Belgian francs, and so arriving at a sum which is usually around 46–47 Belgian francs. For transactions with countries other than Belgium and Luxemburg, this currency unit is changed to the appropriate national currency at the rate of the day. This means the whole process has to be repeated daily. The main Community UA is calculated by a similar method but on a weekly basis, every Friday afternoon.

Taxation raises many problems in connection with the rules of competition, the internal market, and the Community's own resources as well as non-discrimination between citizens of the various member-states. Without going into excessive detail, we may consider some of the main points:

(1) *Company taxation.* The essential problem here is that it varies quite substantially from state to state, thus distorting competition and making it more or less profitable to be a shareholder, depending on where any given company pays its tax. Not only is the level of taxation variable but the tax base itself is calculated in three different ways:

(i) The whole of the profits may be taxed to begin with, and there may be further taxation of the profits which are distributed as dividends to shareholders after company tax as such has been paid. As a result the shareholders may get very little in the end, depending, of course, on the rate both of company tax and of income tax.

(ii) The dividends which are distributed are regarded as part of the company's expenses in the same way as directors' fees and company tax is reduced accordingly but the shareholders then pay tax on them.

(iii) The shareholder is allowed to deduct some of the company tax from the dividends which he receives. That is to say, the dividends are considered as having paid some tax before he gets them, and he does not pay the full amount of income tax on them thereafter. If he receives £300 he is considered as having paid £200 on £500, and in the end, if he only has a small total income (e.g. an old age pension plus a few shares), he may even get a refund because his pension *plus* the £500 on which he is supposed to have paid £200 does not add up to an income on which he would normally pay £200 tax.

If, on the other hand, the shareholder receives £3000, he is considered as having already paid £2000 on an income of £5000. Assuming he has *no other income,* he may still have to pay a little extra in Britain and Denmark. If he has another £3000, e.g. from a job or a company pension, his total income will be regarded as £8000 on which he has already paid £2000; he will then have something more to pay in all the member-states, though not much in some of them.

The Commission has produced a draft directive which would make the third system mandatory in all the member-states. It goes into quite extensive details, and also specifies that company tax, on distributed as well as undistributed profits, shall not be less than 45% or more than 55%, though reduced rates or complete exemption may be allowed for reasons of economic, regional, or social policy after consultation with the Commission. Special provisions cover such cases as:

(a) a firm which pays company tax in one country pays dividends to share-holders who pay income tax in another country;*
(b) due to his or her small income, a shareholder in another country is entitled to a tax rebate;†
(c) dividends, which are taxed as specified in the directive, are paid to charitable institutions and similar bodies which are not liable for income tax;‡
(d) a subsidiary firm in one member-state pays dividends to its parent firm in another state.

This directive had not been adopted at the time of writing. It may run into some difficulties at Council level, in particular because it makes no difference between distributed and undistributed profits, and some states may wish to encourage firms to plough part of their profits back into reserves.

(2) *Personal taxation.* The main problem here is a very considerable variation in the rates of taxation, especially on higher incomes. This is an inducement to people to leave the United Kingdom and Denmark for

---

*In the absence of special arrangements, this would mean that the latter state would get very little money out of the whole transaction.

§In the absence of special arrangements, this would mean that the latter state has to pay a tax refund to the shareholder though it has collected no tax from the company.

†In the absence of special arrangements, charitable institutions in countries which now use system (ii) would lose money as dividends would tend to be smaller under system (iii).

Germany and Belgium if they have usable skills and the necessary languages. It may eventually create very serious economic and social problems in the high-tax countries, first because the sort of people who can earn high incomes also provide valuable services as doctors, engineers, business executives, etc., and, secondly, because the Welfare State will collapse if it cannot rely on a certain number of people who give consistently and substantially more than they receive.

The Community as such cannot interfere, however, each state being at present free to maintain its own way of life, and to encourage "solidarity" or "getting on" as it prefers. Nevertheless, the EEC would probably work better with a more unified system, and it is perhaps significant that Britain and Denmark, the two high-tax countries, have had the most serious economic problems in recent years.

Not only is the rate of taxation different, but so are the starting-points and the expenses that may be claimed against tax (e.g. travel, use of a vehicle, necessary books and equipment). All this makes it considerably more advantageous to work in some countries than in others. In the end it is likely that the Commission will have to make proposals, if not for a directive, certainly for some sort of agreed convergence of national policies in this field.

(3) *Indirect (consumer) taxation.* This comes in two main forms, VAT and excise duties (drinks, cigarettes, petrol, etc.). Both give rise to serious problems for the Community.

(i) *Value-added tax.* This is not levied at a uniform rate, thus distorting competition to some extent, though not very seriously; nor is it at present levied on the same goods, services, and persons throughout the Community,* exemptions being more widespread in Britain and in Italy than elsewhere.

Variable rates lead to substantial differences in the price of some goods *from state to state*, and therefore to continuing restrictions on goods taken across internal frontiers by tourists or by people moving from one member-state to settle in another. The actual price of the goods *within one member-state,* depending on their origin, is not affected to the same extent, since French, Belgian, and German refrigerators sold in Belgium, for instance, will all pay VAT at the uniform Belgian rate while the manufacturers in each country will all be able to reclaim the VAT which they have paid on anything they have to buy in order to make them. The only difference VAT will make to manufacturing costs is that it may affect the cost of living, and therefore wages, especially in Belgium where wages automatically go up with the cost-of-living index, so that goods produced in a high-VAT country will be less competitive, other things being equal.

---

*Strictly speaking VAT is levied on goods and services, not on persons. But it is paid by persons and firms which supply these goods and services, and pass the cost on to the customer, and in some cases small operators may be exempt or pay at a reduced rate.

The varying range of taxable goods and services means that the Community gets less than its share of VAT revenue from countries with more exemptions, since it is entitled to the equivalent of a 1% VAT across the board: anything beyond 1% (the average rate is, in fact, about 18%) goes to the member-states.

It should be noted, incidentally, that there are two types of exemption—non-taxability and zero rating. The practical effect is the same in that no tax is paid to the member-state or the Community. However, where goods and services are non-taxable, legislation is needed to make them liable to VAT. If they are zero-rated, they are taxable, but the Government has chosen not to tax them in the meantime. It may, however, increase the rate from zero to 5%, for instance, by a simple administrative measure, without having to wait for the budget or to pass special legislation if there is a law which allows it to make such variations. Furthermore, in the case of exempted goods and services, the person who supplies them cannot reclaim the VAT paid on any supplies he may have needed in order to sell the goods or do the work. An example would be a pensioner who makes an occasional income from translations, or a housewife who types authors' manuscripts every now and again. Because their income from such work is below a certain figure, they pay no VAT, but they cannot reclaim VAT on paper, typewriters, dictionaries, etc. (though they could charge this expenditure against income tax if they are earning enough to be liable). Where goods could be taxed but are not taxed (zero-rating), VAT may be reclaimed on any necessary supplies (e.g. paper for the production of school textbooks or materials for children's clothes). Hence the state bears a loss and so does the Community. Small farmers in some countries are in a similar position: they do not pay VAT but are allowed to reclaim a refund of VAT, assumed to be a fixed proportion of their turnover, for anything they have to buy.

The Commission has therefore made proposals for the harmonization of VAT (Draft Directive of 29 June 1973). These cover the definition of taxable goods, services, and persons, the place where tax is payable (this may involve problems where somebody lives in one country and delivers goods or provides services in another),* the time when tax becomes due, exemptions and deductions, special rules for small businesses and small farmers, a list of

---

*This is quite an important point. Several million of the Community's 255 million citizens live within ten miles of one of its internal frontiers, mainly along the northern and eastern edge of France from Dunkirk to the outskirts of Basel, and in densely populated areas of southern Belgium, Luxemburg, and Germany. Among the more sizeable border cities are Lille, Saarbrucken, Strasbourg, Aachen, and Flensburg, but there are dozens of smaller towns and hundreds of villages in a similar situation, which gives rise to other problems, e.g. workers entitled to French social security but contributing mainly to the German economy; motorists who buy all their petrol in Luxemburg so that the French and Belgian service stations (and tax authorities) lose out; farmers with fields in two countries, etc.

operations which may be considered as agricultural (and therefore liable to a low rate of VAT, or exempt in some cases), and various other aspects. They also provide for the creation of a VAT Committee, similar in its organization and *modus operandi* to the CAP management committees, but giving the Commission slightly less power. That is, the Commission cannot take a decision contrary to the Committee's advice, or in the absence of advice (this might happen if the majority either way were too small, or if too few members were present). In such cases the Council has to decide, but the Commission settles the matter if the Council fails to do so within three months.

(ii) *Excise duties.* Similar considerations apply. The range of excisable products varies, and so does the rate of duty. This perpetuates border controls on tourist and removals traffic, thus breaking up the internal market. It also affects the cost of living, and therefore wages and the conditions of competition. An added difficulty is that the purpose of these duties varies from state to state and product to product. In some cases it is simply to raise money. In others it is partly or mainly to discourage undesirable forms of consumption, which not all states regard as undesirable. In others again it may be a hidden form of protection, e.g. beer against wine, which the state with a high excise does not produce (Denmark) or only on a very small scale (the United Kingdom), or wine against spirits (France). Strictly speaking this is against the basic principle of having a Common Market, though similar differences exist from state to state in the United States. Again the Commission would like to harmonize, but the member-states want to preserve their "brand image"—their way of life, moral values, etc., and the excises are a means to that end as well as a source of revenue.

At the time of writing the French franc is no longer one of the "snake" currencies and its value is now approximately 8 Belgian francs, rather than 9. In other respects, however, the snake operates as stated on p. 130.

CHAPTER 14

The Internal Market and the Customs Union

This is basically what the Common Market is about (Fig. 11). The policy was laid down in the Treaty of Rome; the Commission merely applies it and tries to get the member-states to apply it, often with some difficulty due to the considerable business interests involved. Some of the directives which it has proposed have been awaiting discussion by the Council for several years.

The "internal market" and "rules of competition" aspects of the Commission's work overlap to some extent. Thus, the preference given by all governments to contractors in their own country is a problem which is handled, at Commission level, by the "internal market" department. But this preference could equally well be considered as a tacit agreement between national governments and firms which may be very substantial taxpayers, or between regional or local authorities and firms which may be very substantial ratepayers, that contracts will be placed with these national, regional, or local firms wherever possible, i.e. so long as their prices, delivery dates, and general reliability are not wholly unacceptable. This is certainly how things

Fig. 11.   Cartoon (La Communauté Européenne, Information Office, European Communities, Paris)

work out in practice, and for that reason public contracts have already been mentioned in Chapter 6.

Other limitations on the internal market, some of which the Community accepts (e.g. restrictions on the import of dogs, cats, and exotic animals into the United Kingdom) while the rest should, in principle, be abolished outright or gradually phased out, include the following.

(1) *Various customs formalities.* Thus some states require goods imported into or taken through their territory to be cleared with the help of a customs agent: this provides work for their own people and puts up the cost to the importers. In so far as these rules affect trade between member-states they are contrary to the Treaty and therefore illegal. In so far as they affect imports from third countries they merely lead to the same American car, for instance, being more expensive in one member-state than another, a result which may also be achieved through different rates of VAT.

(2) *Public health and safety requirements.* These may prohibit the sale of certain products (e.g. fireworks) in a member-state. More often than not, however, they lay down requirements to which motor vehicles, machinery, electrical appliances, foodstuffs, etc., must conform, if they are to be sold in a particular state. There is some overlap here with consumer protection and environment policy, but these requirements are best considered under the internal market aspect. Thousands of different products are involved, and in every case it is necessary that rules should exist; these rules are often considerably older than the Common Market itself, but even where they are quite recent they vary extensively from state to state. As a result, for instance, a British firm wishing to sell cars on the French market, or a German firm wishing to sell electrical appliances on the British market, must make them specifically for that market, or at least must make some parts of them for that market. In both cases it may be impossible to sell the product in Italy without further adaptation, as other rules are in force there. All this puts up their prices, reduces the choice available to consumers in each country, and protects firms producing exclusively for the domestic market.

There are several ways of dealing with this situation. One of them is to get the member-states to accept one another's safety requirements. This has been done, for instance, in the case of pressure vessels. They are not made to quite the same specifications in each of the member-states, but a pressure cooker which is safe in Germany will also be safe in Britain, and vice versa.

Another way is to lay down certain requirements which must be complied with in every member-state. Individual states may then lay down additional requirements for products manufactured in their own territory, but these cannot be used as an excuse for keeping out products from other member-states which conform to the Community rules. Beer is a case in point. Certain additives are prohibited by Community law; in addition to this, however,

German law requires beer to be made with a certain kind of hops. English beer is made with other hops but may be imported into Germany, and vice versa.

In a few cases there is a single Community standard, in general as severe as that of the most demanding member-state or more so. This is mainly laid down where there is an imperative need to reduce pollution. Since considerable expenditure may be involved in adapting a product (and the machinery to produce it) or replacing it by another, a transitional period is always allowed after the relevant directive has been enacted by the Council and "translated" into national legislation. Even so, it can be very difficult to get these directives adopted in the first place.

(3) *Restrictions on the right of establishment.* Under the Treaty, member-states may reserve certain posts (Civil Service, army, teaching) for their own nationals. But other restrictions exist in practice through the need to have qualifications which can only be obtained in a particular country (e.g. a degree in Scots or Dutch law) and are generally obtained only by citizens or by foreigners who have been educated there. In some instances, where it is not legally necessary to obtain national qualifications, one nevertheless needs to know a great deal about the country's legal system and economic structure to be able to set up in business or even sell anything there, while knowledge of the language may be a statutory requirement (e.g. for doctors practising in the United Kingdom) as well as a practical necessity.

Various directives have been adopted or are in preparation to remedy this state of affairs in so far as it can or should be remedied (adequate knowledge of the language will always be necessary in practice, and may reasonably be demanded where lives are at risk). There are problems, however, in that qualifications may not be strictly equivalent from state to state; thus the medical degree course is shorter in Italy than elsewhere, and some of the smaller provincial universities may not be very demanding. Similarly, the actual work which people do, as solicitors for instance, may not be the same.

Thus a Scottish solicitor also sells houses, and this may be a very important part of his work. An English solicitor does not (though he co-operates with estate agents); both, however, prepare cases, while they can only plead in minor courts since advocates (in England barristers) are a separate profession. In Germany and France, on the other hand, lawyers may be advocates and solicitors at the same time, and many are, though some tend to specialize on the advocacy side. On the other hand, there are other people called notaries who handle wills and property matters and may have various functions devolved to them by public authorities but are not involved in court cases. Their work, in Britain and several other member-states, falls mainly or wholly to solicitors. The French notary is a public official (in part) and must therefore be a Frenchman. Similarly, Court of Appeal Advocates, in Belgium, hold the King's commission and must be Belgians, whereas "ordinary" advocates, (who double up as solicitors) are simply professional men who must know Belgian law but need not be Belgians.

(4) *The right to perform services.* Similar considerations apply, though what is involved here is the right of London solicitors or barristers, for instance, to go over to Brussels or Paris and assist clients there. The practical difficulties are not quite as great because the professional or businessman who comes over occasionally to perform services does not endanger vested interests to anything like the same extent; more often than not he will in any event have to work with somebody else who belongs there (e.g. a Belgian lawyer). There are tax and other problems, however.

(5) *Facilities for firms in one member-state to sell their products in another.* These are affected not only by health and safety requirements (see paragraph (2)) but by such things as different weights and measures, and different voltages and plug sizes. Britain is progressively going over to the metric system (but this may affect trade with America and with any Commonwealth countries that do not follow suit), and the Commission is working on the other difficulties.

(6) *Public contracts.* These have already been mentioned in Chapter 6.

(7) *Restrictions of company operations.* These include, for instance, various rules against undesirable mergers (going further than existing Community law in that they seek to prevent dominant positions from being established, as well as from being abused), rules about the amount of capital which a firm must have in order to start business or remain in business, and rules about the financial soundness and past record of directors. Thus in Britain you do not have a police record unless you have done something wrong, and where minor offences alone are involved, it is wiped out after three years. In France, on the other hand, you have one anyway and may be required to produce it in order to become a company director or to take up certain posts. These different rules may make it difficult for British or German firms, for instance, to set up French subsidiaries. The Commission is trying to alter this state of affairs; for social and political reasons several governments wish to maintain the *status quo.*

(8) *Patents and licences.* Here again the internal market and rules of competition departments overlap. In the past it was necessary to take out a patent for each member-state, and licences to manufacture patented goods were often granted in each state to a different firm. There are now two types of European patent, one valid for the Common Market only and the other for the whole of Europe including Communist countries. The system of national licensing, however, remains largely in force, but is not as exclusive as it was; thus the firm which manufactures a product under licence in Britain

cannot be prevented from exporting it to France, though it may still be required to make its main sales effort in the United Kingdom.

There are dangers in this practice of manufacture under separate licences in that a product may be sold under one name in one country and under a different name in another. It may then be found dangerous and banned under one of its names and yet circulate freely under another name. This, for instance, happened with thalidomide, known as *Contergan* in Germany, and banned there some time before the British realized it was the same product. Today this could not happen in the Common Market because if the German Federal Government or any other found a product dangerous and outlawed it, this would be made known to the Commission at once, and through the Commission to the member-states, who would then take the product out of circulation, referring to its chemical formula as well as its brand name. The EEC Pharmaceutical Products Committee would then discuss the matter at one of its regular meetings and add the product to the Community's black list. There is also a "white list", kept up to date by the same Committee, of products which have been thoroughly tested and judged to be safe. These may be sold throughout the Community, in any event until somebody finds there was something wrong with them after all, and again their chemical formula will be mentioned in each case.

At the time of writing the Common Market is not a complete Customs Union because duties are still being phased out between the six original member-states and the three which joined in 1973, while the new states are adjusting their external tariffs (e.g. on imports from America and Japan) to the Common Customs Tariff.

In addition, problems arise because, even with the CCT in force, incoming goods are not valued in the same way by all the member-states. The main difference, but not the only one, is that some states count the cost of transporting the goods (e.g. cars) from the exporting country as part of the total amount on which duty has to be paid, while others do not. The same car may therefore be regarded as more expensive by the Germans than by the Dutch, and pay more duty if it lands in Hamburg than it would at Rotterdam.

Again, there are different arrangements regarding products which may be imported duty-free for various reasons in some countries, but not others, e.g. some scientific equipment intended for research purposes (this problem, however, has now been settled) and products which are to be worked upon, or incorporated in other products, then re-exported from the Community. This affects quotas as well as the duty charged, since there may be a limit on the amount that may be permanently imported into the Community, and goods for outward processing are not counted on this quota. These problems will probably continue as long as Community policy in this field is applied by national rather than EEC-employed customs officials, but the Commission, as usual, is trying to harmonize.

Another quite serious difficulty has arisen, up till now, through trade between the two Germanies: they have free trade with each other for some purposes, but East Germany does not have it with the rest of the Community. In principle, therefore, goods coming from East Germany have a certificate of origin, which show them to be such, and pay duty on crossing into Benelux or France. In practice things are more complex.

(a) The original certificate may be discarded once the products reach West Germany, and a Zeiss camera from Jena, bought by the West German Zeiss firm, may then be resold in France.

(b) Russian and other East European products may get in on the act.

(c) East German products are very often *components* which are incorporated into West German products, and these, of course, circulate freely through the Community. This gives West Germany an unfair trading advantage, as East German wages are lower than those paid anywhere in the Community with the possible exception of south Italy, so that she can get these components cheaper than she or any other EEC state can make them.

The two Germanies, however, have now recognized each other as quite separate countries (though East Germans who make their way somehow to West Germany are still treated as citizens and not foreigners) and this arrangement will probably come to an end in the near future.

Yet another problem, now largely resolved, has been that of *Community transit,* i.e. goods passing through non-Community states from one part of the EEC to another (usually between Italy and Germany or Benelux through Austria or Switzerland, and goods passing through the Community between non-EEC states (usually Switzerland–Spain or vice versa through France). The main difficulty was to ensure that the products were not released on to the Swiss, Austrian, or EEC market while in transit or temporary storage. The problem, however, was simplified by the fact that Switzerland and Austria are both EFTA states, and therefore have industrial though not agricultural free trade with the EEC. As it happens they also have agricultural arrangements with the EEC whereby they undertake not to offer their products (mainly cheese and wine) at less than the Community threshold price; in return levies are not charged.

The Customs Union is managed by the Commission through a small self-contained service usually known as GUD (Gestion de l'Union Déuanìàre); this does not form part of any Directorate-General but comes under the same Commissioner as the Internal Market. GUD is assisted by a Management

Committee identical in structure and functions with those used for the Common Agricultural Policy: this Committee spends much of its time working out just where products should be fitted into the Community's Customs Nomenclature—a long list with over 1000 pages and some 30,000 products if not 50,000. The object is to make it possible for very similar products (e.g. a round bolt and a square bolt) to carry a different rate of duty if this is for any reason desirable. All products bearing the same number in the nomenclature (e.g. 24.05.06) pay the same rate of duty; but it would be quite possible for 24.05.07 to pay a different rate.

Another reason for this apparently tedious exercise is that new products are constantly coming on the market. If the Management Committee does not find them an appropriate place on the list, each country, or worse still each customs post, will arrive at its own decision. This may mean not only different rates payable in Germany and Britain, for instance, but quite possibly a higher rate of duty in Southampton than in Liverpool, as well as some time being wasted while local officials decide just where the product belongs.

Customs duties are collected by the member-states through their officials at the various rates laid down by the Community and on the products specified in the nomenclature, though (as we have seen) there can be some uncertainty as to the value and therefore the duty paid on the products themselves. The proceeds go to the Community, minus 15% which the member-states retain for their administrative costs in working the system: the variable levies on agricultural products are collected in the same way, again with the member-states retaining a percentage for administrative costs, and the same arrangement is used where export levies are charged (e.g. on scrap and on scarce agricultural products).

Co-operation with other countries, which is essential in this field, is made easier by the fact that the Customs Co-operation Council, a world body, also has its headquarters in Brussels. In addition the Community has an office in Geneva, the headquarters of GATT, and the representatives of its member-states hold co-ordination meetings there before any GATT meeting.

CHAPTER 15

Education, Science, and Research

The Community as such is not directly responsible for education except in so far as it runs a number of "European schools" briefly described below. But it is taking an increasing interest in educational problems especially those which have some bearing on employment and on the removal of obstacles to mobility and freedom of settlement. It is not much use allowing people to live, work, and provide services all over the Community if they are going to be seriously handicapped by language barriers or unable to make satisfactory arrangements for the education of their children. Furthermore, the Treaty of Rome has educational aspects in so far as it calls for the mutual recognition of educational and teaching qualifications (Article 57) and for the co-ordination of vocational training (Articles 118 and 128).

Some progress has already been made through the Council of Europe, to which all the member-states belong. Thus anyone who is qualified to enter a university in his or her own country is qualified to study in all nine states subject to the availability of places (some colleges and faculties can only admit a limited number of students) and subject, of course, to having sufficient knowledge of the language in which lectures are given and other activities (seminars, tutorials, etc.) are conducted. From this it follows that there are many foreigners in French, English, and German universities, but few in Italian universities and hardly any in Dutch universities, since nobody except a Dutch or north Belgian student will have learnt the language up to the standard required, whereas French, English, or German is the first foreign language throughout western Europe, and one of those three is usually the second.

Higher and lower qualifications, however, are not always interchangeable in this way. Thus the English O-level, the Scottish O-grade, the first half of the French *baccalauréat,* and the German-Scandinavian *Real Examen* are all roughly comparable, but it does not follow that you could walk into a German office with five O-levels and get the sort of job that requires a set of *Real-Examen* passes as a clerk or typist for instance. The same goes for university degrees: potential employers want to know just what courses you took, for how many years, and possibly also where (some German

145

universities and one or two in France are known for left-wing militancy and constant disruption of lectures, and many firms do not have a high regard for their diplomas). If you are a teacher they will also want to know about your training: English qualifications, for instance, are not necessarily valid in Scotland, let alone France. In any event, member-states are still allowed to reserve teaching posts for their own citizens and generally do so, though accepting a limited number of foreigners, usually on short-term contracts, to teach languages. The object of a French school is to produce Frenchmen and Frenchwomen, with French ideas and a French way of looking at things; similarly, the object of a German school is to produce Germans, and so on. The schools are the guardians of the nation's continuity and collective personality, as well as places where knowledge is put across and where pupils are taught to think and made to work, and the national governments remain very jealous of their sovereignty in this field (Fig. 12).

A serious effort is nevertheless being made to co-ordinate educational arrangements and to create a Community education policy, even though there can be no question, in the foreseeable future, of an European educational system except in the very limited sector of the "European schools". The principal landmarks on this road are the publication of the *Janne Report* (1973) and the Council Resolutions of 6 June 1974 and 9 February 1976.

Professor Janne, a former Belgian Minister of Education and Head of the Institute of European Studies at Brussels University, was asked by the Commission to consult a number of leading educationists and make proposals which should serve as a basis for discussion rather than as an actual draft policy. Regrettably, his panel of experts contained nobody who had been recently involved in primary or secondary teaching, and some of their suggestions would have been difficult to apply; but the report itself did not carry the weight of a formal proposal by the Commission, nor did Janne himself necessarily endorse everything they said: what he did, in general, was to quote the individuals concerned and add his own contribution in the form of a synthesis.

The decisive point which he made was that some existing Community policies, provided for in the Treaty, could not be effectively implemented without some kind of Community educational policy. He also stressed some vital political aspects, e.g. respect for national structures and traditions, the need to avoid a fresh upheaval in the German educational system, then undergoing extensive reconstruction, respect for the existing autonomy of schools and universities, and the desirability of involving other European states (e.g. Sweden and Switzerland) in whatever the Community might do.

The 1974 Resolution, strictly speaking, was not an act of the Council as such, but of the nine ministers of education meeting within the Council to

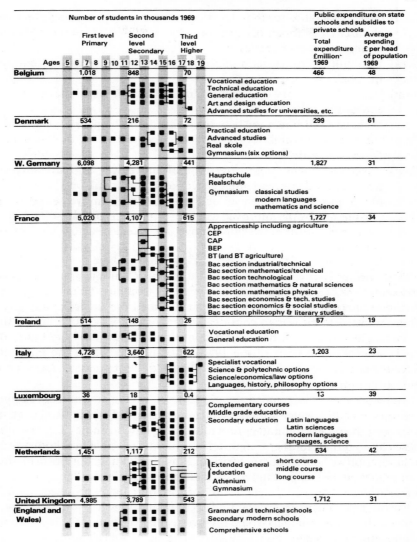

Fig. 12.   The basic education systems in the European Community (European Communities Information Service, London)

discuss co-operation. The technical distinction, however, was of no real importance since they were in any event agreeing to go home and do something, or rather a number of things, but not laying down rules that would be binding on anybody. They decided on the following priorities:

  (i) "better facilities for the education and training of nationals and the children of nationals of other member-states of the Communities and of non-member countries";

 (ii) "promotion of closer relations between educational systems in Europe";

(iii) "compilation of up-to-date documentation and statistics on education";

(iv) "increased co-operation between institutions of higher education";

 (v) "improved possibilities for academic recognition of diplomas and periods of study";

(vi) "encouragement of the freedom of movement and mobility of teachers, students, and research workers, in particular by the removal of administrative and social obstacles to the free movement of such persons and by the improved teaching of foreign languages";

(vii) "achievement of equal opportunity for free access to all forms of education".

They further resolved to set up an Education Committee composed of representatives of the member-states and of the Commission and chaired by a representative of the country holding the Council Presidency at any given time. Its initial remit was to consider and report on ways to promote the objectives listed above; it has since become a permanent advisory body. Its report served as the basis of the 1976 Resolution by which the ministers agreed to implement these objectives as their action programme, and set out appropriate measures in some detail.

Under point (i), this included at national level "organizing and developing a reception system which would include intensive study of the language or languages of the host country; providing more opportunities for teaching these children their mother tongue and culture, if possible in school and in collaboration with their country of origin" and "providing more information for families on the training and educational opportunities available to them". It would also involve an "exchange of information and experience" as well as various research projects organized at Community level.

Point (ii) (closer contact) would involve regular meetings of the ministers of education and senior policy-making officials as well as study visits and exchanges, the development of national information and advisory services, contacts between teacher-training authorities, and "educational activities with a European content". The following possibilities are to be studied at Community level.

(a) *Extension of the practice of recognizing periods of study abroad.* Study abroad, for a semester or a year, is already an essential part of honours degree courses in Scotland and in some English universities: the ministers apparently envisage that it could be extended to other courses, e.g. law. It would, in any event, become mandatory for teachers of foreign languages.

(b) *Enabling teachers to practise their profession for a time in a Community country other than their own.* This would involve changes in national legislation and administrative practice, and it would be necessary to ensure that promotion prospects and pension entitlements are not adversely affected.

(c) *The setting up of European or international-type establishments following specific curricula and using several teaching languages.* This is really an extension of the system already operating in the Community-run "European schools", and would involve setting up similar establishments, possibly with a narrower range of languages, in the national capitals and other places where there would be a sufficient number of pupils of different nationalities.

(d) *The idea and means of introducing a standard school record card.* This is likely to involve serious practical difficulties as the age of primary–secondary transfer varies considerably from state to state, as do the subjects taught and the time allocation given to these subjects.

Point (iii) (documentation and statistics) is to be tackled by setting up in each member-state a national service on education in the Community. Once these are functioning, steps will be taken to organize work at Community level.

Several member-states have already been working for some time on these various aspects, especially the education of migrant children. This is mainly the concern of the state in which their parents work, and in which many of these children were in fact born. However, their parents' country may also be actively involved by arrangement with the host country: thus the Italian and Spanish governments run a number of schools in Germany, and there are several French and German schools in other member-states. In any event, special arrangements are often required. One has to consider whether these children should be fitted, first and foremost, for life in their own (or their parents') country of origin, or for life in the country where their parents are now working and where many will remain, or whether to try somehow to keep both options open. The 1976 Resolution provides for all three possibilities.

If it is envisaged that they will in due course return home (and many are in fact sent back to their grandparents or other relatives at the age of 8 or so), it is obviously desirable to maintain continuity or at the very least contact with the system they will have to rejoin, though they also need to learn the language of the host country in the meantime. The French, German, Italian, and Spanish government-run "schools-in-exile" and the similar (but independent) British School in Brussels serve this purpose and also take care of children who started school in their own country and moved abroad with their parents: the possibility of setting up "schools in which teaching would be in more than one language", mentioned in the resolution and apparently distinct from "European or international-type establishments", which are mentioned later in the same document, also seems to be intended to help migrant as distinct from immigrant children.

If, on the other hand, integration is the aim, children may still need to be placed in "reception classes" and possibly taught through their own language until they have learnt enough of the host country's language to join normal classes. At the same time it may still be felt desirable that they should retain some contact with their parents' culture, and their parents are quite likely to insist on this, in some immigrant communities at least, even if the host country feels this may delay their integration. The ministers have taken this view, though cautiously adding the words "as appropriate", and have agreed that it would be better for this language and cultural teaching to take place within school hours. They have also recognized the fact that it should involve co-operation between the host country and the parents' country of origin (few British teachers can teach Urdu; fewer German teachers could handle Turkish, Greek, or Serbo-Croat).

If one wants to keep both options open, and incidentally foster the growth of a European consciousness, the most rational arrangement is that adopted in the *European schools,* which the Community itself runs in Brussels, Luxemburg City, and several other towns where it has research establishments, mainly though not (except in Brussels) exclusively for the children of its own staff. A similar school may be set up in Munich in connection with the European Patent Office, which will include all the EEC and EFTA states with a few others.

The nine ministers of education are, in theory, the governing body of these schools: in practice, since they cannot meet very often, they delegate their responsibilities to an inter-governmental committee on which the Commission is also represented. This body appoints the headmasters, while the nine governments each appoint a proportion of the teachers. Thus teachers on the English side are appointed by the British and Irish governments, teachers on the French side by the French, Belgian, and Luxemburg governments, teachers on the Italian side by the Italian government, and so on.

Each school has five or six sides (Danish in Brussels alone at present) and pupils can thus be taught mainly through their own language. But every pupil also learns a second language (English, French, or German) from the start, and eventually a third; in the middle and senior secondary forms he or she will be taught history through that language by a "foreign" teacher and in a mixed-nationality class. British pupils, at that stage, are taught history through German by a German, or through French by a Frenchman, south Belgian, or Luxemburg teacher, and will probably be a minority in their class, while the group which is taught through English by a British or Irish teacher, contains everything except British or Irish pupils.

The leaving qualification from the European schools is not "Highers", A-level, the *Abitur*, or any other national certificate, but the European *baccalauréat*, which gives admission to any university in the nine countries, and *also* serves as a job qualification equivalent to A-level and the rest, valid throughout the Community. In this respect it is more valuable than any of the national certificates since these, while giving access to universities throughout western Europe, are only valid, for career purposes, in the country where you have taken them. The reason is that the European *baccalauréat* guarantees that you have reached a high standard in your own language and a reasonable standard in two more as well as a few other subjects (e.g. mathematics, one of the sciences, and history or geography).

The European school in Luxemburg was set up in connection with the original ECSC and is therefore older than the Common Market itself; the others date back to 1960 or thereabouts, with an English side added in 1973. A more recent development is the *European Youth Forum,* which consists of leaders of students' and youth organization in the nine countries. It gives advice to the Commission on matters which are likely to be of interest to young people (e.g. job qualifications and training), either at the Commission's request or on its own initiative. The Commission meets all its expenses and provides secretarial services and interpreters as well as conference rooms. A weakness of this body, inherent in its very nature, is the rapid turnover of its members; as soon as they begin to know each other and are used to working together, they are no longer young and have to move on. Another weakness is that the ablest young people in each country, in the age group mainly involved, are too busy getting a good degree and establishing themselves in the adult world thereafter; hence they do not take an absorbing interest in "student" or "youth" activities as such, or at any rate not enough to get themselves elected to the representative bodies which might send them on to Brussels. The obvious remedy would be to enlarge this body by allowing each of the nine governments to nominate one or two young people, successfully active in some career or in adult politics, to sit alongside the elected youth and student leaders; but the elected members might not like this.

The Community is closely associated with two other ventures which, however, it does not directly control; the *College of Europe* in Bruges and the *European University Institute* in Florence.

The College of Europe, sixty miles from Brussels, is a small, high-powered institution taking 100 postgraduates through an intensive two-year course. Their curriculum includes political theory, the study of government and of international organizations, and ways to make a United Europe more of a reality. On completing course, many go into the Commission's "Civil Service" or into their own national administration, not necessarily in EEC member-states (there are also Swedes, Spaniards, or Turks among them); others teach or undertake research in universities. The College also organizes an annual symposium on some topic or group of topics connected with European integration. The activities of the European University Institute are more difficult to describe at this stage, as it will only start functioning in the autumn of 1976.

"European studies" in one form or another are now taught to a very limited extent at school and undergraduate level, and in greater depth at postgraduate level, in several member-states. The Commission helps in various ways but does not directly organize this work.

In secondary schools this teaching is largely incidental to civics, current affairs, "modern studies", history, or geography, and at the discretion of teachers. Belgium is the only country which gives it an official place on the curriculum. Through its Directorate-General for Information (DG X), the Commission makes pamphlets, slides, and other material available, and conducted tours of its headquarters are organized from time to time.

At undergraduate level, "European studies" are purely informal on the Continent and may, for instance, be fitted into a course in politics and economics if the professor and students are sufficiently interested. More formal work, however, is done in several British universities: details are available from the University Association for Contemporary European Studies, 12a Maddox St., London W1; several universities and polytechnics award degrees in European studies, or modern languages combined with European studies.

Whatever the description of the degree, the course always involves the study of two or more languages, and a stay abroad, normally one year.

Many shorter courses are available as part of a degree in Politics (e.g. at Aberdeen, Warwick, and York), Economics (London School of Economics, Liverpool, and Aberystwyth), Law (Birmingham, Edinburgh, and several others) or Social Studies. Some thirty universities and polytechnics run courses of this type which do not necessarily require languages (though this is obviously helpful) or a stay abroad. An interesting scheme, not listed as yet in the UACES Register, exists at Edinburgh; honours students in languages there may spend their year of residence abroad taking courses in law, economics, or politics in French, German, or Belgian universities, and study European as well as national institutions during that time. Again, the Commission helps by making information and material available; furthermore, several universities, on the Continent as well as in these islands, have been recognized as "depositories" for all Community publications (*Official*

Journal, Bulletin, and Supplements, etc.), which are sent free on condition that students shall have adequate access to them.

The main effort, however, is made at postgraduate level, especially on the Continent. Details are available from the Commission in its pamphlet *Postgraduate Degrees in European Integration*, for the United Kingdom they are also to be found in the UACES Register. Many different courses exist; typically with law, economics, and politics as their main thought not necessarily their only components: agriculture (e.g. at Reading), languages, and culture may also be involved, generally following from a first degree in law and/or economics, and leading to a master's degree or a doctorate.

While it has a supportive role in education as such, the Community is more directly active as regards scientific research and the development of whatever may be discovered; first because it has more powers under the treaties, and especially the ECSC and Euratom treaties, and, secondly, because the national identity and "brand image" of its member-states is not at stake in the same way as where primary, secondary, and higher education are involved. Moreover some of the research programmes under way are very expensive, and it is in everybody's interest that there should not be too much wasteful duplication. *Some* duplication is useful because two or three scientists working independently in the same field may each discover something that would otherwise have been overlooked. If they deliberately avoid covering the same ground, each of them in his own smaller area may miss something his colleague would have found. But to have ten or twenty of them on the same job is pointless, and probably means some other valuable piece of research is not being done because there is nobody to do it or no money to do it with.

Much of this work is carried on by national institutes under contract from the Community or from their own governments but backed up by Community finance; but a large part of it, especially in the nuclear sector, is undertaken by the Joint Research Centre (JRC) described below. Either way, the decision to promote and finance research is taken by the council on a proposal from the Commission and often after consulting a high-powered Scientific and Technical Research Committee, known as CREST, which is convened regularly to discuss projects and receive progress reports.

The JRC, set up under the Euratom Treaty but no longer concentrating exclusively on nuclear research and development, is directed by the Commission and consists of four establishments, together employing nearly 2000 people. By far the largest of these is the Ispra centre, on Lake Maggiore, about sixty miles from Milan. It is working on many aspects of nuclear science, including the chemistry of fissile materials, the behaviour of various metals and alloys used in reactors, shielding materials, and the prevention of accidents. But its nuclear work has led in other unexpected directions. Thus it is concerned with monitoring radioactive pollution of the lake and of its outlet, the Ticino River, irrigation channels flowing from the river, and rice-fields irrigated by them. Techniques developed for this purpose have been found useful in identifying other forms of pollution, and can further be employed to establish, for instance, soil moisture and acidity, and thus determine the suitability of a given piece of land for a particular crop; perhaps also to prospect for minerals or (in former battlefields) to locate unexploded shells, grenades, and bombs. Similarly, Ispra has several computers to assist its nuclear research, and scientists there have, incidentally, developed further use for them and for their other data-processing apparatus; a remarkable instance of this is their Russian–English translation machine.

A smaller establishment at Petten (Holland) is working essentially on the use of high-flux reactors and on the properties and behaviour of nuclear materials. What it does can only be explained adequately by a scientist to scientists, but is of extreme importance in any event, bearing in mind that nuclear plants are expected to provide half of Europe's electricity within the next twenty or thirty years, and that the Community may suffer from a permanent energy shortage if they cannot be safely used; on the other hand, if anything goes seriously wrong with the materials being studied at Petten, the consequences in and around the power station that uses them may be as disastrous as those of the Hiroshima bomb or worse, depending on where the accident occurs.

The Karlsruhe establishment shares its site with a German institute, itself considerably larger. It is concerned with the study of transuranium elements (plutonium and transplutonium), including their behaviour at high temperatures, and its work, again, has important safety implications.

Finally, the Geel establishment works on nuclear standards and measurements. It is situated in a small Belgian town, better known for the centuries-old tradition whereby mental patients from all over the country are placed as paying guests with local families, sharing in their day-to-day life.

"Non-nuclear" research, organized and at least partly financed by the Community, also includes work on new sources of energy (solar, tidal, geothermic), new means of transport (e.g. larger hovercraft than any now in use), oceanography, meteorology, and, as we have already seen, the protection of the environment. In some cases projects are not financed by the Community as a whole, but only by some of the member-states (and other states, such as Austria and Sweden, which may participate on an *ad hoc* basis), though they are approved by the Council and the work itself may be done or co-ordinated by one of the JRC establishments. The reason is that all the member-states are not equally interested; in some cases they are already running similar projects of their own in which the Community as such is not financially involved.

CHAPTER 16

The External Policy of the Community

The Common Market is not a country. Nevertheless, for some purposes it behaves like one and has dealings with other countries. It takes part, as a body, in many international conferences which its member-states, or most of them, also attend as nations in their own right. Furthermore, the representatives of the nine states, or such of them as are present, usually get together before every meeting in order to work out a joint line if they can.

This activity occurs mainly in four fields:

—(1) *Trade agreements and commercial treaties of all kinds,* as well as the overall regulation of international trade through the Customs Co-operation Council and GATT. Individual member-states are no longer allowed to sign *commercial treaties* with other countries whereby they undertake, for instance, to supply or accept a certain quantity of products or to reduce or abolish certain duties. Such arrangements can now only be made by the Community as a whole, and have to be negotiated between it and the foreign state or states concerned. In many cases their scope is further restricted by world agreements whereby the duties on certain products are fixed at a given level (this is the case for olive oil) or whereby any concession granted to one member of GATT must be granted to all.

Member-states, however, do sign *international agreements on commodities* whereby they undertake to buy a certain quantity of wheat, sugar, or coffee from producer countries taken as a whole. Each importing country is then committed to buying a certain amount, but without specifying from which producer country. A joint Community line is agreed on such matters, and the Community as a whole is represented by an observer at most of the conferences where this kind of business is transacted; alternately, one of the member-states (usually but not necessarily the one which currently holds the Council Presidency), is delegated to speak for the rest.

Member-states may also sign individual *co-operation agreements,* usually with developing countries which were once part of their colonial empire (e.g. France with Senegal, Britain with Nigeria, Belgium with Zaire), and such agreements may well have a commercial aspect, such as the supply of goods and services at reduced cost, or wholly at the expense of the European country involved, but to its advantage because it creates employment there and encourages subsequent purchases by the developing country which receives this aid. This is allowed under EEC rules, but the Commission has the right to know what is going on, and may object if the Treaty of Rome is being infringed. Thus if France agreed to supply Algeria with tractors but specified that they must be French tractors, that would be breaking the rules. In principle the French Government must advertise a contract and be prepared to buy German or British tractors and supply them to the Algerians. In practice it will probably advertise the contract and then award it to a French firm. British and German manufacturers know this and may not even bother to try; they will get their chance when their own Government makes a similar co-operation agreement with some other country.

(2) *Energy supply* (oil especially). The Community is heavily dependent on oil as its main source of energy, and nearly all of this oil has to be imported. It therefore does what it can to obtain a secure supply at a reasonable price. This involves some participation in international conferences, but most of the work is done behind the scenes by diplomatic contacts between the presidents of the Council and of the Commission, and the Commissioner for External Affairs, on the one hand, and Arab rulers and their ministers on the other.

This aspect of the Community's external policy has given rise to some complications. In the first place France has traditional links with Algeria, and Italy with Libya, both near neighbours to the south. Hence they are tempted to make a separate and better deal for themselves, get what they need, and ignore the others, who import from the Middle East, mainly round the Cape as the Suez Canal was closed until recently and cannot take very large tankers. Secondly, the Arab states require, as a counterpart for their goodwill, that the Community should take a pro-Arab line in their conflict with Israel. The governments, or most of them, do their best to oblige, but public opinion in all the EEC states is pro-Israeli, and in some of them overwhelmingly so, and nothing can be done about pro-Israeli demonstrations or newspaper articles in a free and democratic society. Moreover, in some European countries Arabs are disliked simply as Arabs, and quite apart from the merits of the Middle Eastern conflict. The Community's negotiators therefore have some difficulty in persuading the other side of their good intentions.

— (3) *United Nations aid to developing countries.* This is additional to the direct aid which the Community and its member-states provide. The Community has observer status at UNCTAD (United Nations Conference on Trade and Development) and FAO (Food and Agriculture Organization) the two UN bodies most directly concerned with this. All its member-states are also members of both organizations. At UNCTAD the Community promoted the system of generalized preferences, which makes it easier for developing countries to sell manufactured goods and the products of their craft industries (a very important item in some cases) to developed countries. In FAO it has helped to work out medium-term and long-term plans for increasing the world's supply of food; most of the Community's food aid, however, has been sent directly to the countries which needed it, to be distributed by their governments—but there has also been a contribution to international relief bodies such as UNWRA, which helps Palestinian refugees, and the office of the UN High Commissioner for Refugees (Fig. 13).

(4) *The fight against pollution* and defence of the environment in general. This had already been discussed in Chapter 11. Decisions in this field generally have to be taken by member-states rather than by the Community itself, and have to be co-ordinated not only between those states but with other countries, either neighbours whose activities may affect the Community's environment, and who may themselves suffer from pollution originating within the Community (Switzerland, East Germany, and Sweden being the most relevant from this standpoint), or major industrial powers with an impact on the world environment (USA, Soviet Union, and Japan). This requires extensive participation in committees and international conferences as well as co-operation with the Council of Europe and with OECD.

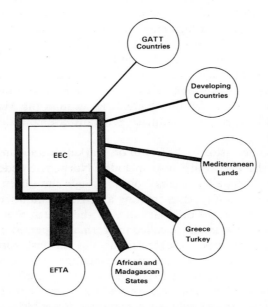

Fig. 13. The relationship between the EEC and the outside world (La Communauté Européenne, Information Office, European Communities, Paris)

Most countries (90 out of 140) now have an Ambassador or other diplomatic representative accredited to the Community as such. He often but not always doubles up as Ambassador to Belgium, Holland, or West Germany.

The Community as such does not have ambassadors. Its spokesmen are:

(1) the President of the Council of Foreign Ministers, holding office for six months;
(2) the President of the Commission, normally holding office for four years;
(3) the Commissioner for External Affairs;
(4) the other commissioners, in their respective specialities and in dealings with their home governments, of which they are of ten former members;
(5) the ambassadors of the state currently holding the Council Presidency, acting on instructions from their Foreign Minister, who is also the President of the Council;
(6) the representatives of the member-states at the United Nations and in its specialized agencies, again acting on instructions from home.

It does, however, maintain a number of missions abroad, e.g. in London, Paris, Dublin, Geneva, New York, and Santiago. These are at the same time information offices and co-ordination centres for dealing with any international organizations which may also be located there (UN in New York, UN, most of its subsidiaries, and GATT in Geneva, UNESCO and OECD in Paris, the Commodity Councils in London)..

While it would be impossible to go into all the details of the Community's foreign policy, we may look briefly at its dealings with other countries in Europe, and with non-European countries around the Mediterranean. Its relations with developing countries generally are considered in the next chapter.

Before their accession to the Common Market, Britain and Denmark were members of EFTA, which also included Norway, Sweden, Switzerland, Austria, and Portugal. The ideal solution might have been to merge EFTA and the old Community, thus creating a new Community of thirteen states (the same number as the original states of the United States and the Swiss cantons during what might be called the formative period of Swiss history). This, however, was impossible for a number of reasons. Norway voted not to join, mainly due to the absence of a satisfactory Regional Policy (urgent steps were taken to create one, spurred by the shock effect of her negative vote). Austria could not join because her State Treaty with Russia prevented her from acceding to any political or economic power block. Switzerland and Sweden did not wish to accede to any such block, though they would have been free to do so; in addition, Sweden was anxious not to break her links with Finland, politically independent and "Western" in constitution and outlook, but economically thirled to Russia. Portugal was not a democracy at the time and was therefore not eligible to join. Moreover, there were economic difficulties in her case. Her products competed with those of Italy, which already had considerable difficulty in selling them (wine, olive oil, citrus fruit). At the same time she was a developing rather than a developed country, and could not have fitted readily into the EEC's industrialized economy without a good deal of aid to place her on approximately equal terms with the others.

Special arrangements therefore had to be negotiated with all these states, on the following lines:

(1) They continued to have *industrial* free trade with the two states which were leaving EFTA to join the EEC, and were in due course to have it with the enlarged Community as a whole. Customs duties between them and the original member-states were to be reduced at the same time and by the same steps as between Britain and Denmark, on the one hand, and the Six Countries, on the other.

(2) A few products were subject to *quota restrictions* at the outset, but these were to be gradually relaxed and to disappear at the end of the five-year transitional period.

(3) *Agricultural free trade* as such was not provided for in these agreements. However, some of the EFTA countries concerned happened to apply an agricultural policy similar to the CAP and calculated to encourage home production, at some cost to the consumer, by means of import levies and export refunds. This made it possible to arrive at an arrangement whereby they undertook not to supply products below the threshold price at the Community frontier. In return, levies would not be charged on these products. Local free trade also continued between Geneva, a Swiss "peninsula" almost wholly surrounded by France, and neighbouring French rural districts.

(4) Complex *rules of origin* were set up to prevent misuse of these arrangements, e.g. duty-free imports from Russia through Sweden or from America through Portugal.

Similar agreements, but on a more limited scale, were made with Finland and Iceland, which were not part of EFTA, but were and are members of the Nordic Council along with Denmark, Norway, and Sweden.

As regards southern Europe the situation is more complex. Spain is simply a foreign country, though she has a trading agreement with the Community which she cannot join at present because of her political system. A different situation would arise if she became genuinely democratic. She could then be a tremendous asset, not only in her own right, but through her links with

Latin America, whose population now exceeds that of the Community itself. Portugal does appear to be reverting to parliamentary democracy, and may well have an acceptable system by the time this book appears, but there are economic problems (she is scarcely if at all more developed than some of the more prosperous African countries) and a very lengthy transitional period could be required. Greece *has* restored democracy, which she originally invented, after a brief but extremely unpleasant period of military rule. She has applied for membership and will most probably get in, again after a lengthy transitional period. In the meantime she has a Treaty of Association with the Community, signed before the colonels took over but suspended while they were in power. This involves trading arrangements similar to those made with the EFTA countries, *plus* political arrangements (regular meetings between Greek and Community ministers, ambassadors, and MPs).

A Treaty of Association is also in force between the Community and Turkey which is not, however, likely to join the EEC in the immediate future. Her accession, which the treaty envisages as a long-term prospect, would raise very serious problems.

In the first place it is not clear that she is *politically* eligible. Her system of government is democratic in principle, with parties and free elections, but the army is only just in the background, ready to take over whenever it feels the national interest demands its intervention. This has been the way since the time of Kemal Ataturk, himself a soldier-statesman, and the founder of the modern Turkish state.

Secondly, there is a massive gap in living and educational standards between Turkey and western Europe. Linked with this, there is the problem of "psychological acceptance". Whatever international organizations and the Common Market may think, most Europeans do not accept Turkish peasants and workers (the Turks they are most likely to see) as fellow-Europeans. Thirdly, free movement of Turkish workers into the Community would be quite unacceptable to West Germany and Belgium, which already have a large number. It would also leave Turkish agriculture and industry almost totally devoid of manpower if jobs were available in western Europe for all who wanted them. In present circumstances they are not, but there could still be a million Turkish migrants, and perhaps more, who would come and try their chance, as the Treaty of Rome allows, subject to being sent home if they found nothing within three months. This would create chaos at both ends.

Hence it is not certain that a Turkish application to join would even get a favourable opinion from the Commission. Without such an opinion the Council, though still free to consider it, would probably think it advisable to wait. So far she has not applied, and the feeling on both sides seems to be that it would be better to strengthen and improve the existing arrangement and develop the Turkish economy so that there may be more and better work for her people in their own country.

Yugoslavia is in much the same position as Spain. She has close trading links with the Community and many of her people work there, especially in West Germany (Spanish workers are mainly found in France and Belgium), but she is not politically eligible nor economically ready for membership. A different situation may arise when Tito is no longer there, as Slovenia could become a small democratic country similar to Luxemburg, and would then fit in quite readily, whereas it is difficult to visualize Bosnia, Montenegro, or Macedonia in the Common Market.

On the south side of the Mediterranean, Algeria, Morocco, and Tunisia all have traditional links with France and a special relationship with the Community as a whole. This involves both technical co-operation (a new and more pleasant term for aid) and duty-free or reduced-duty access for a limited quantity of their products. These limitations are necessary to safeguard Italian interests, since all three are major producers of olive oil and citrus fruit, and Algeria also exports considerable quantities of wine. The three Maghreb states make a useful income from European tourism, and Morocco is the world's largest exporter of phosphates, mainly to the Community. Similar agreements have been negotiated, or are being negotiated with Israel and her Arab neighbours in the south-east Mediterranean. Ideally, the Community would have liked to sign them at the same time, but in fact the Israeli agreement was ready first because it was more straightforward: Israel is a developed country with a European standard of living and way of life; the others are all developing countries, though better off than the ACP states and, of course, much closer to Europe geographically.

Other agreements have been reached and informal discussions conducted with many other countries all over the world, and this has involved the President of the Commission and the Commissioner for External Affairs in a great deal of travel. In particular there have been important contacts between the Community and its East European "counterpart", COMECON, as well as with the Soviet Union and other individual Communist states, or "state trading countries" as the EEC officially calls them. Until recently, there were various bilateral agreements in force between the member-states of the Community and countries on the other side. These have all run out and are being replaced by new agreements negotiated, on the western side, by the Community as a whole.

Trade with east European countries presents very special problems. One of them is that all buying and selling, on the eastern side, is conducted by state trading agencies, which are simply government departments. As a result, contracts are few and far between, and may take years to negotiate, but are very worthwhile if and when one gets them. Another is that the state trading agency may change its mind, for political reasons, without any fear of going bankrupt or being taken to court. A third is that eastern countries can make their money worth what they want it to be worth on the home market because it does not circulate internationally and because their domestic economy does not obey the ordinary laws of supply and demand: the Government simply decides what goods will be available, in what quantities and at what price, and proceeds to make and sell them. As a result, even a highly skilled accountant, trained in the western tradition, would have extreme difficulty in telling whether a particular transaction was being carried out at a profit or at a loss. Since these countries are very anxious to acquire western currency for a variety of purposes (possibly including that of unbalancing the capitalist economy) they are willing to sell their products well below cost price—in so far as the cost price can be established—to western countries, recouping themselves by making a massive profit out of their own citizens. East–west transactions are generally on a large scale, as we have seen, and this kind of dumping—as well as undercutting of freight rates by Soviet and other east European shipping lines—can be very damaging to western industry and commerce, which are unable to get away with the same sort of thing as they have to pay trade union wages and balance their books, and both have to be done in currencies whose value is known and cannot be doubled or halved overnight. The Community authorities therefore feel they have to keep track of what is going on, and watch this trade very closely.

So much for *Community* foreign policy in its present form. It is first and foremost an external trade policy, designed to safeguard the Community's interests as the largest exporter and importer in the world, and as the world's second industrial power (America produces more, but very largely for home consumption, and consumes more, but produces most of it herself). With this goes a feeling of responsibility towards developing countries, most of which were still British, French, or Belgian colonies when the Common Market was set up. In addition, the nine member-states co-ordinate their *national* foreign policies to an increasing extent, but at present in a largely informal way. Some would like to go much further, with Community foreign policy replacing national foreign policy, and various proposals have been made along those lines. For the moment at least they seem unlikely to be implemented, and there are several grave practical difficulties.

In the first place the Common Market consists of countries, as we have seen, and one of the differences between a country, however small, and a region, however autonomous, is that the former usually has its own Foreign Office and its own seat at the UN and elsewhere, while the latter does not. (The Ukraine and Byelorussia are exceptions, but larger than many countries.) On this count alone it is likely that several member-states would veto the scheme.

Secondly, these countries, or some of them, have separate interests which they will not readily give up. Britain has her links with America and the White Dominions; France, even under right-wing governments, tends to regard Russia as part of the balance of power in Europe rather than as the potential enemy against which the west must maintain a united front; Denmark remains part of the Nordic Council as well as of the Common Market and would probably choose the north if she had to choose.

Thirdly, the Community institutions in their present form are not adapted to conducting a full-scale foreign policy because the main decision-making body, the Council, has a rotating Presidency which is a serious obstacle to continuity.

A real Community foreign policy would require one of four things to be done.

(1) *The roles of the Commission and of the Council could be to some extent reversed.* The Commission would then become a kind of European Government and the Council a kind of Senate. The Commissioner for External Affairs, with a four-year term of office, renewable for another four years, would then have time to develop a consistent policy. But the Council would not wear this.

(2) *The nature of the Council itself could be changed.* Each of the member-states would then have its own Minister for European Affairs, who would have an additional speciality. Thus the Dutch Minister could also be in charge of agriculture, and the British Minister could take foreign policy as his domain. This would ensure reasonable continuity where a country does not replace its government too often, but the Commission might not be very happy about this scheme, which would seriously weaken its role.

(3) *A new institution could be set up* to co-ordinate national policies in matters not now under Community control. This body, tentatively known as the Political Secretariat in the "D'Avignon Plan", which runs along those lines, would take the real decisions in foreign policy, these being afterwards rubber-stamped by the Council and implemented by the nine governments.

(4) *The Treaty of Rome could be replaced by a European Constitution, establishing an entirely new set of institutions*, e.g. a directly elected European Parliament, a European Senate consisting of delegations appointed by the national governments or parliaments, and a European Government taking over from the Council and the Commission. Various proposals have been made more or less along those lines, but there is no immediate prospect of such far-reaching changes being accepted by all the member-states.

The Community's foreign policy, effective enough in its specialized fields, is probably the best that can be achieved with the Community as it is and its member-states as they are.

CHAPTER 17

The Community and Developing Countries

When the Common Market was first set up, two of the founder-states—France and Belgium—were major colonial powers, while two others—Italy and Holland—had minor but still quite significant responsibilities overseas.

The French colonial empire was larger than what remained of the British, excluding the White Dominions as well as India, Pakistan, and Ceylon, which had also become independent members of the Commonwealth. It formed a massive block extending, together with the mother country, from Dunkirk through Tamanrasset (already south of the Tropic of Cancer but still in Algeria and therefore part of France) to Brazzaville, 300 miles beyond the Equator. The French colonies were in general far more French than the British colonies and protectorates were British, this being due to a more thorough policy of assimilation, especially in the schools. Thus the standard history textbook used in Brazzaville was the same as in Dunkirk and began with the words: "Our forebears, the Gauls, were a warlike race."

Belgium had only one colony, the Congo (now Zaire), together with two small but thickly populated "trust territories", Rwanda and Burundi, taken over from Germany at the end of the First World War: these three, however, had eighty times the area and twice the population of the "mother country", whereas the French Empire, though about fifteen times the size of France (or five times, not counting the Sahara Desert), had a smaller population.

Holland had lost her East India empire (now Indonesia) some years earlier, but held on to a slice of Guyana and to several islands in the West Indies: Italy administered Somalia as a trust territory and maintained close links with Ethiopia, which had by then recovered its independence and taken over the former Italian colony of Eritrea.

All these colonies and other territories enjoyed free trade or trade on highly preferential terms with the "mother country", and in most cases there were other links. Thus a Frenchman could go anywhere in the French Empire without a visa, while Ivory Coasters, Senegalese, etc., could study in France or take up a job there without a permit. Dutch West Indians had completely free access to Holland if they could afford to get there.

All these territories were brought within the framework of the Treaty of Rome, continuing to enjoy free trade with their respective "mother countries" and, through the latter, gradually coming to have it with the Community as a whole (complete free trade within the EEC was to be achieved over a transitional period of twelve years) while the freedom of settlement already given (for instance) to Frenchmen in Senegal was extended to the citizens of the other five member-states.

Subsequently there were two important developments. In the first place the vast majority of these territories became independent between 1960 and 1963, the only exceptions being the Dutch colonies and some of the smaller French possessions, several of which were and are legally part of France. Secondly, the Common Agricultural Policy was set up, and this created problems where colonial products competed with those of the European mainland. In most cases they did not, but cane-sugar from the French and Dutch West Indies competed with beet-sugar from all the member-states, and anything which grew in Algeria, except dates, also grew in Italy and southern France.

The Treaty of Rome had been signed in the knowledge that most of the colonies would soon be independent, and provided for association treaties or agreements between them and the Community as a whole. At this stage complete free trade was no longer possible because (a) the newly independent states relied on customs duties for a large part of their revenue (most of their people being too poor to pay income tax), and (b) their governments wished to create manufacturing industries which could not survive without some initial protection.

These agreements (Yaoundé I, Arusha, and Yaoundé II) therefore ran along the following lines, with slight variations:

(1) Tropical products from the African countries concerned (e.g. cocoa, bananas) generally enjoyed free access to the Common Market.

(2) In the case of competing products (e.g. sugar, oranges) the associated states were allowed a duty-free quota but not unrestricted access.

(3) Industrial and artisan products (e.g. leatherwear, metalware) from the associated states enjoyed preferential access to the Common Market, sometimes subject to quotas. The associated states were not obliged to give a similar preference to industrial products from the Community, but in practice they took the bulk of their imports from the former "mother country" (in some cases over 90%) and collected duties on them.

(4) The citizens of all Community countries were generally free to travel to all the associated states and to set up in business there, as well as to trade with individuals and firms in those states. The monopoly privileges hitherto enjoyed by certain French companies in West and Equatorial Africa thus came to an end. In practice, however, most of the Europeans in the former

French colonies are French, most of those in Zaire are Belgians, and the Germans have tended to renew their links with some of their former colonies, especially the Cameroons.*

(5) Individual member-states of the Community continued to provide various kinds of aid (often with strings attached) to their former colonies. In addition, however, Community aid became available, in the form of granted and low-interest loans, for development projects such as new roads, railways, bridges, hydroelectric dams, and power stations, etc., in the associated states.

(6) Institutional links were created at three levels, involving meetings of ambassadors, MPs, and ministers, between the Community as a whole and the associated states, either individually or as a group. These meetings were largely informal, taking no actual decisions, but very useful nevertheless.

Yaoundé I linked the Community with the former French and Belgian colonies and with Somalia, and was replaced by Yaoundé II when it expired. The Arusha agreement was signed between the three English-speaking countries of East Africa and the Community; Nigeria signed a similar agreement even before Britain joined the Common Market. All these were due to run out after the United Kingdom's accession, and it would have created a very unfavourable impression in Ghana and Sierra Leone, for instance, and indeed in Britain, if the former French colonies had been given easier access to the British market than countries which had been part of the Empire for generations.

It was therefore decided that a new agreement should be negotiated between the enlarged Community and all the former European colonies in Africa, the Caribbean, and the Pacific. Asia was left out because manufactured products (textiles especially) from several Asian countries could flood the European market and because some of those countries might need far more aid than Europe could ever provide. The new convention took some time to work out, for several reasons.

(1) The total number of countries involved was now much larger—nine on the European side and forty-six on the other, as against six and eighteen previously. The forty-six ACP states had to negotiate not only with the Community but with one another, in general a slower and more difficult process.

(2) Nearly all the African states which had signed the Yaoundé Convention were basically "pro-European", this mainly due to the goodwill which existed between France and the French-educated élite in West and Equatorial Africa. In several of the former British colonies, on the other hand, there existed a strong undercurrent of hostility, and their leaders were on the whole more "Africa-conscious".

*Thus Cameroonian students frequently opt for German rather than French or British universities.

(3) Several of the English-speaking countries had a temperate climate or rather a highland tropical climate with monsoon rains as in the tropical low-lands but a temperature range similar to that of Mediterranean Europe, though narrower. Thus Nairobi may get down to 10°C (50°F) or up to 32°C (90°F) while Perpignan and Rome have occasional frosts with a maximum of 40°C (104°F) reached once or twice in a normal summer. The products of these countries—beef, maize, and wheat among them—were more likely to compete with those of the Community than the bananas, cocoa, groundnuts, etc., of the French-speaking states.

(4) A further problem was that the tropical side of the proposed association had grown much more than the European side. In terms of *area* it had more than doubled;* its *population* was easily trebled (Nigeria alone had more people than all the "Yaoundé" states put together) and its total *production* had increased by an even larger proportion since the original eighteen states included nearly half the Sahara together with a million square miles of jungle. The Community, on the other hand, had only grown from 190 to 255 million inhabitants (one-third). Hence the ACP states, as suppliers of tropical foodstuffs and raw materials were competing for a market which had not increased on anything like the same scale as their own production.

(5) There were also more people needing aid of one kind or another, but this was not a major problem, Asia having been left out of the arrangement largely for that reason. Most aid was provided by the original "mother country" rather than by the Community as such, and still is, while some at least of the former British colonies were relatively well off by African standards, Nigeria and Ghana being at least on a level with the poorest areas of Italy.

The negotiations succeeded nevertheless, because it was in everybody's interest that they should, and led to the signing of the Lomé Convention in January 1975. This followed the general principles of the earlier agreements but with two important differences:

(i) *Quotas* were more extensively used because of the greater competition between the ACP states as exporters of tropical products (too many bananas chasing too few Europeans);

(ii) individual ACP states were offered a *guaranteed income* from their main products in return for a *guaranteed supply* of these products to the Community. This would help Europe when commodity prices were high and the developing countries when they were low.

---

*The French Empire in 1957 was larger than the British Empire not counting independent Commonwealth countries. But this included Algeria (well over 1 million square miles with its share of the Sahara), which was not a party to the Yaoundé agreements and is not now one of the ACP states, but has special arrangements with France and with the Community as a whole.

Various technical details were left to be filled in later.

Algeria (part of France until 1962) and Morocco and Tunisia (French protectorates until 1956) were not parties to the Yaoundé or Lomé conventions, but have special arrangements with France on her own and with the Community as a whole. The agreements with France provide for aid or "co-operation" in various forms, mainly educational and technical, for an abundant supply of Algerian oil and natural gas to France (which therefore scarcely suffered from the oil crisis in 1973) and for the right of North Africans to live and work in France, where they take on many of the rough unskilled jobs in Paris and other major industrial centres. The agreements with the Community also provide for aid and for trade on preferential terms, but North African workers do not have the same rights in the other EEC states as in France, though Belgium has taken a few thousand. North African products compete directly with those of southern Europe and are therefore restricted by quotas, but France, though the largest producer of wine in the world, is also a substantial importer of North African wines, which are blended with her own to increase their strength.

The Community has on the whole paid less attention to other developing countries, for instance in southern Asia and Latin America. Africa is nearer and Europeans have a greater feeling of responsibility towards it: moreover, though it is large, taken as a whole, it consists for the most part of countries with small populations, typically ranging from 1 million to 10 million. Nigeria, Egypt (not a party to the Yaoundé or Lomé conventions) and Zaire alone are much bigger, with 60 million, 35 million, and about 20 million, respectively. Because these countries are not overpopulated one feels something can be done for them, whereas the average European tends to regard India and Bangladesh at least as hopeless cases: anything one does for them will only mean more people needing help next time something goes wrong— which is fairly often. Latin America is seen as largely a US responsibility, though in fact many Argentinians, Mexicans, and others would prefer to have more to do with Europe and less to do with North America.

Roughly 75% of the aid provided by EEC states individually and by the Community as a body goes to the ACP states, and many people—especially in other developing countries—feel this is too much since their population is less than half that of India alone. Another criticism often made is that most of this aid is tied: Africans are being helped to buy European products which they could get more cheaply from Japan, for instance, and at the end of the day what the Europeans are doing is to subsidize their own industries. This criticism ignores the basic fact that all the Common Market countries are democracies and, indeed, they have to be (Communist and Fascist states are not eligible for membership): their workers, with 40% to 70% of the vote in each country, would never agree to subsidize Japanese industry via development aid. As it happens, Soviet, East European, and Chinese aid is even more closely tied than EEC aid, since it consists almost entirely of goods and equipment rather than money.

The aid which the Community as such provides comes mainly in three forms:

  (i) grants;
 (ii) low-interest loans (both from the European Development Fund);
(iii) training facilities for government officials, experts, and others who come to work at EEC headquarters as *stagiaires,* usually for six months at a time.

The grants and loans are intended to finance specific projects, some quite small, others more considerable, e.g. a 300-mile railway link from the Gabon coast to a mining district near the eastern border. These projects have to be submitted by the Government of the associated state concerned, or sometimes by two or three governments together, where they are of interest to several countries. They are then assessed by Commission experts, who have to consider whether they may be over-ambitious and whether they are likely to be of any real use to the country or countries concerned. Other relevant aspects include maintenance costs, once the project has been completed, and possible side-effects (a dam creates a lake which may encourage the spread of malaria and bilharzia).

Assuming the project is approved (and most of them are) the money is then made available all at once or over a period of years; it is used mainly to pay for any equipment which may have to be imported and for the work done by Europeans. Local workers' wages are usually paid by the Government of the state concerned. The Commission appoints one of its own officials or more usually someone else (e.g. an accountant or an engineer) to see that the work is actually being done and the money spent as intended.

There have been complaints from several African governments that they are still being treated too much like colonial subjects and have not been given an adequate say in preliminary discussions with Community officials to assess the projects before any decision is taken or in the management of the projects once they were under way. These criticisms have been recognized as largely valid and a greater effort is now being made to involve them at all stages.

The staff training aspect of Community aid is more important than one might think from the relatively small amount of money involved, because the people who are sent to Brussels for this purpose are generally likely to end up as senior civil servants, ministers, or ambassadors, often at quite an early age. They come from Africa already holding down a responsible job and go back to the same or an even more responsible post.

As we have already seen, the Community also provides food aid in emergencies, largely from intervention stocks. The most spectacular example was during the West African drought (1973) when 92,400 tons of food and other products were airlifted, and lorries were made available to carry these products from airports or military airfields to smaller centres.* This operation was on the whole very successful, in any event where the African governments played their part, which was to distribute the supplies once they had arrived. In one or two countries, however, there was a traditional rivalry between the sedentary black population and the Tuareg nomads who were the hardest hit by the drought, and the government was controlled by the sedentary tribes. It saw an opportunity to starve out the nomads or compel them to settle down, and therefore did not take the supplies to the places where they were most desperately needed. Another problem was that dried milk could only be used by children as African adults, unlike Europeans, cannot digest milk in large quantities unless they belong to herding tribes such as the Masai. The Community's prompt action nevertheless saved hundreds of thousands of lives, possibly millions. On this occasion the whole decision-making process was greatly speeded up, its Commission

---

*This aid was allocated as follows by three separate Council decisions:

Milk powder: 13,000 tons of which 1800 tons for the Upper Volta, 2100 tons for Mali, 1800 for Mauritania, 2500 for Niger, 2400 for Senegal, and 2400 for Chad. Serious difficulties arose in connection with this product, the first because there was in many places no suitable water to dilute it, and, secondly, because milk as such is indigestible to most Africans, other than young children and members of some pastoral tribes such as the Fulani and Masai. (Decision of 14 May 1973.)

Butteroil (dehydrated butter): 6000 tons of which 1800 for the Upper Volta, 300 for Mali, 1000 for Mauritania, 1450 for Niger, 1300 for Ethiopia, and 150 for Chad. (Decision of 28 December 1973.)

Cereals: 73,400 tons of which 5000 for Ethiopia, 14,900 for the Upper Volta, 20,000 for Mali, 5000 for Mauritania, 7500 for Niger, 15,000 for Senegal, and 6000 for Chad. (Decision of 14 May 1973.)

Of these countries, Senegal and Mauritania have satisfactory ports and were the easiest to help. Ethiopia has a coastline, but this was inaccessible from the interior due to fighting in Eritrea; in practice, therefore, she could be regarded as landlocked and as almost wholly dependent on air transport and on the Djibouti Railway which terminates in French territory at the time of writing. The Upper Volta, Mali, Niger, and Chad are landlocked.

In this emergency the Community undertook responsibility for transport not merely to the nearest seaport or airport, but within the countries themselves, to the main distribution centres, where national authorities and voluntary bodies generally took over. Under normal conditions the Community pays for transport to the country itself, if landlocked or otherwise among the least developed, while developing countries which are less badly off (Egypt, Nigeria, for instance) pay for transport but not for the products as such. Non-emergency supplies are normally sent by sea and thence by rail or road in the case of landlocked countries: this routine aid can amount to hundreds of thousands of tons each year and is one of the principal means of running down intervention stocks. The Community also makes supplies available to international bodies such as the World Food Programme, UNICEF, the UN High Commission for refugees, the Red Cross and Caritas, but this depends on their ability to handle such aid at any given time and in any given place. Most Community aid is in practice given to national governments.

and Council stages together taking no more than forty-eight hours, whereas the average for a regulation or a directive is anything between six months and two years. Another interesting feature of this emergency action was co-operation on the ground between the Community and the East Germans, who also airlifted a useful quantity of supplies.

All the ACP states have ambassadors accredited to the Community as such, often doubling up as ambassadors to Belgium or to other neighbouring countries. They maintain a joint secretariat in downtown Brussels, about a mile from the EEC headquarters, through which they keep in touch with one another and with the Commission. On the European side, one of the two

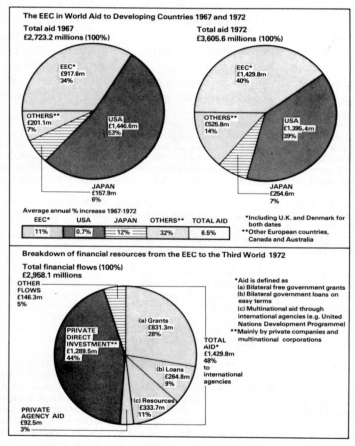

Fig. 14.   The European Economic Community and aid to the third world (European Communities Information Service, London)

French commissioners is at present responsible for relations with developing countries (the other is the President of the Commission) and there is a directorate-general which manages the European Development Fund and other aspects of co-operation. All nine EEC states are also members of the United Nations and of FAO, UNCTAD, and other UN subsidiary bodies, and at the General Assembly of these organizations they get together and try to arrive at a common policy on development aid, trade preferences for developing countries, special measures in favour of the least-developed countries (most of which are ACP states), and similar issues.

Note Since this chapter was written, Britain has assumed the Presidency of the Commission, with Mr. Roy Jenkins. The French Commissioner responsible for overseas development, Mr. Claude Cheysson, remains at his post, however. Ex-President Ortoli also remains as the other French commissioner.

CHAPTER 18

Conclusion

The Common Market may not be all its builders intended. It is a remarkable construction, nevertheless. The mere fact that it exists, after twenty years and in conditions very different from those which prevailed at the outset, is itself a solid achievement.

If it has not fully lived up to the expectations of its founding fathers—up to date in any event—we must remember that these expectations were very high. Konrad Adenauer, Joseph Bech, Alcide de Gasperi, Jean Monnet, Robert Schuman, and Paul-Henri Spaak were all in their sixties or early seventies when they brought their countries together: Adenauer, indeed, was even older. They had lived as grown men through two great wars, each of which had bled Europe white and diminished its weight in the world—wars that in retrospect looked like suicidal European civil wars. They were determined not only to save what they could from the wreckage but to ensure there could never be a third time, and they were prepared to make whatever sacrifices were necessary for that purpose—sacrifices of national pride and prestige, of economic interest, and of decision-making powers.

They felt European first and foremost because Europe had suffered so much and because most of them came from its internal borderlands, deeply influenced by their neighbours. Adenauer was from the Rhineland, with France and her culture no great distance away. Bech was a Luxemburger, born and bred within a few miles of Germany, France, and Belgium. De Gasperi came from the Italian-speaking half of south Tyrol, close to the language frontier, and had started life as an Austrian subject. Schuman had served in the Kaiser's army before his native province reverted to France. Spaak was a Belgian, from a country overrun and ruled in turn by Frenchmen, Spaniards, Dutchmen, and Germans. To all of them Europe was the essential reality, and they may have underestimated the strength of national instincts and loyalties—not that they ignored their existence at the time, but that they may have expected them to fade away. They saw only what had to be done, and did not fully appreciate the obstacles that barred their path.

The greatest of those who should have been among the founding fathers was missing, partly because age had worn him down more than his German

174

contemporary, partly because, having set his hand to the plough, he had looked back. The treaty of Rome would have carried even greater weight with Sir Winston Churchill's signature, but in the end the old lion had told his people that they should look to the open sea, and to their kinsmen beyond it, rather than to Europe. He had relinquished the cares of office, but his successor was of the same mind—if anything even more so—and the fourth pillar of the edifice had to be inserted fifteen years later.

Without Britain the Community got away to something less than an ideal start. But those in charge were determined to make it work, and it worked. There was a tremendous increase in agricultural and industrial production and, except in some fringe areas, a spectacular rise in the real incomes and in the living standards of its people. More important still, there was not only economic growth but a strengthening and deepening of human contacts at all levels, and a change in the attitudes of Frenchmen and Germans, in particular, towards each other. At the same time fresh links were created between newly independent African states and western Europe, links on the whole more satisfactory for both sides than those previously existing between colonies and colonial powers. When Britain joined, she joined a going concern: doubts as to whether the Common Market would survive, with or without her, had been among her main reasons for holding back at the outset.

Britain's accession to the Community required her acceptance of the Community's organization, rules, basic policies, and ways of doing things— the *acquit communautaire* as the French Foreign Minister, who chaired the most important meetings, called this complex of values, laws, and procedures evolved over a period of years. The interpreters—among them the author of this book—generally translated this expression as "the Community set-up" or "the Community patrimony", but there was no really adequate English term for something which had been thought out in French and generally in accordance with French ideas. In the British political tradition everything is adjustable and most things are negotiable, but this was a matter of going into the Common Market as it stood with concessions as to how quickly some of the rules would apply but no compromise on the fact that they were rules and would all apply sooner or later.

The organization itself caused few problems since it was and is based on the principle that the Common Market consists of states and that its authorities cannot override any one state's genuinely vital interests, and it was self-evident that Britain should have the same representation and voting power at all levels, and approximately the same financial obligations as the other major members.

Acceptance of the *existing* rules was more difficult because there were by then a great many of them, but the difficulty could be resolved (and was) by allowing various temporary concessions and a period of adaptation, in some cases exceeding the five years provided for the dismantling of internal customs barriers between Britain and the original member-states and for bringing external duties into line with the Common Tariff.

Acceptance of *future* rules did raise a difficulty, in principle insuperable. In the absence of a written British Constitution, putting international treaties before national sovereignty, the United Kingdom's representative at the Council table, approving a regulation or a directive, could not always guarantee that Parliament would in fact allow the regulation to be enforced or enact legislation in accordance with the directive. Should this happen with a directive, there would be deadlock, as has repeatedly occurred when the Italian Parliament refused to co-operate, but the Common Market has already shown that it can live with this kind of situation. A regulation, on the other hand, should become law throughout the Community when it is published, but British courts—English ones anyway—regard Parliament as supreme and would not enforce it if Parliament said it was not to be enforced. In fact this situation has not arisen so far and is unlikely to arise because British ministers have a very fair idea of what they can get through the Commons—possibly a better idea than their continental colleagues, who may not be MPs themselves. When in doubt they veto and make themselves unpopular in Brussels but avoid this particular embarrassment back home.

The real difficulty lay in a basic difference of philosophy on three vital points—agriculture, industry, and the tempo of the economy as a whole—and this was not apparent so much in the negotiations themselves as in parliamentary and public reactions thereafter.

In general terms, British farmers, though economically more efficient, were politically less powerful than their fellow-producers on the continent because there were relatively fewer of them. On the other hand, British trade unions carried more weight than continental ones because (a) they were older and more deeply entrenched, (b) they represented a larger slice of the total population and of the working population, and (c) they were not divided by political and religious tendencies. Their outlook on life was somewhat different because they were British.

What this meant in practice was that the Common Agricultural Policy was more biased in favour of the producers than British policy, which was based on keeping consumer prices down by cheap imports and by subsidies if necessary and making up the farmers' prices and incomes out of public funds so that they would stick around and be available if ever the country became more heavily dependent on them in a crisis. On the other hand, industrial policy was biased in the producers' favour in Britain and in the consumers' favour on the continent. So far as the United Kingdom was concerned, its primary objective was to maintain full employment, or as near full employment as one could get—but this went along with lower wages and lower productivity than were usual on the mainland. Lower prices—for food especially but also for most consumer goods—made these lower wages acceptable. Lower productivity meant there was a good deal of slack that could be taken up in an emergency, and this suited the Englishman's temperament. He often worked longer hours than a Frenchman or a German, and usually had shorter holidays; but he also took life easier between clocking-on and clocking-off time, and therefore did not wear himself out to the same extent; but if necessary he had considerable reserves of energy and strength which he put to good use. This was also true of the Scot, where he enjoyed reasonable security of employment, but he was generally less secure and may have tried a little harder, this being one of the reasons for Scotland's disproportionate share of the United Kingdom's earnings.

Accession to the Common Market made it difficult or impossible to maintain these differences. Wages and prices had to rise, which was hard on those who had to pay the prices but did not earn wages. People had to get used to the idea of paying for their food at the butcher's and the grocer's rather than (in part at least) at the tobacconist's or the petrol pump but, as it happened, cigarettes and petrol also became more expensive. At the same time it became impracticable to have the work of eighty men done by a hundred because one could no longer keep out products from France, where it *was* done by eighty men or from Germany, where it might even be done by seventy.

This in turn gave rise to further difficulties. A low-wage, low-productivity economy with few imports and a very high percentage of all production going on the domestic market may be quite viable so long as competing imports can in fact be kept out, though serious problems arise when one has to compete on the world market in order to buy essential foodstuffs and raw materials. It cannot be changed overnight into a German-type economy, because in getting rid of your extra producers so as to streamline your operation you are also halving the purchasing power of somebody else's consumers (the twenty or thirty men you lay off) and another firm, which is also trying to adapt, is doing the same to your consumers, its own surplus employees. The net result of its efforts and yours is that demand goes down all round, that you can both employ even fewer people, and that in the end you both go bankrupt.

The whole economic process requires consumers as well as producers—in fact it requires them even more than producers, who may to some extent be replaced by machines—and people do not make satisfactory consumers when they feel insecure about their jobs and their income or when they are dependent on social security benefits of one kind or another. Moreover, the welfare set-up is itself liable to collapse in the absence of money—taxes on wages, salaries and profits, and insurance stamps, paid for by those who are actually working or providing work, and VAT paid by those who can afford to buy something.

It also happened that Britain's adjustment to the Common Market had to be made at a time when the economy had to cope with other problems, essentially due to the sudden and spectacular increase in oil prices, whereas the original member-states had adjusted to one another at a time of rising prosperity, itself based on a plentiful supply of cheap oil.

Despite these difficulties the 1975 referendum showed that British opinion generally accepted membership of the Common Market, after the event if not at the time of joining, albeit with some reservations. To be more accurate, London and every English and Welsh county showed a substantial majority in favour of staying in. Every Scottish mainland region also gave a majority for staying in, generally smaller than in England, except in the Borders, which were above the UK average.* Orkney and Ulster also returned small majorities in favour. Shetland returned a small majority *against* the Common Market—53%, the same figure as Norway or, as some Shetlanders may have felt, the rest of Norway. The Western Isles had a very large adverse majority, mainly due to the influence of their local MP, though religion may have played a part. Even with its new member-states the Community is predominantly Catholic (on paper 64%, though a majority are non-practising); taking the original Six alone it is overwhelmingly so (about 76%). This no doubt pleased the people of Barra and South Uist, but those of North Uist, Harris, and Lewis were less happy about it. There was also an instinctive feeling that anything London wanted was probably bad.

In any event Britain is now in and in to stay: even if the United Kingdom breaks up it looks very much as though its component parts will all remain in the Community. We must now look at the future.

It has often been claimed that the Common Market must either evolve into a federal union or gradually wither away as national instincts and loyalties reassert themselves. There is some truth in this, but only to the extent that some of its common policies cannot be effectively applied in the absence of a federal government, and that its declared objective of economic and monetary union certainly cannot be achieved without one.

---

*The Borders' economy is based on farming, the production of expensive textiles, and· tourism, all of which stood to gain through Britain staying in and to lose heavily if we withdrew. A further consideration may have been traditional hostility towards England and a feeling that the continentals would help to keep the English in their place. As a result the Scottish Nationalists, who generally opposed the Common Market, were divided locally: the other three parties were all in favour at local level, though Labour were divided nationally, with the Government mainly in favour and the trades unions mainly against.

Economic union implies that the whole of the Common Market would form a single economy to the same extent as Scotland and England at the time of writing. Thus there is at present no means whereby English firms can be prevented from acquiring Scottish firms and closing them down unless the British Government itself (or exceptionally, the Commission) decides to intervene. Nobody knows whether Scotland has a favourable or an adverse balance of trade with England, or, indeed, with the rest of the world, nor even what the taxable revenue of Scotland is as distinct from the rest of Britain—this because many firms operating partly or mainly in Scotland are registered in England and pay tax there.

Monetary union implies that the whole of the Common Market would have the same currency or that national currencies would always change at exactly the same rate, the Unit of Account being permanently worth 50p, 50 Belgian francs, 2.50 marks or guilders, 5 French francs, etc. To be more accurate, the UA would be itself and the pound would be 2 UAs, the Belgian franc 2 Eurocents, the French franc 20 Eurocents, the mark and the guilder 40 Eurocents. It would become impossible for any national government to control the value of its own currency, which would in fact cease to be its own, and would merely be the national name for a given amount of the European currency. It would also be impossible for any government to control the inflow or outflow of money between the member-states, just as it is impossible for the Californian Government to control inflows from Oregon and outflows to Nevada.

The natural effect of economic and monetary union, other things being equal, is that more money flows from outlying areas to the centre than the other way round. Other things may not be equal, because an outlying area may have resources not available elsewhere—e.g. oil—and inflows from beyond the frontier may help to redress the balance. Thus Ireland attracts tourists from America, its nearest neighbour to the west, and would continue to do so even if the Common Market became an economic unit in the same sense as America itself. Perpignan, very outlying in relation to France as a whole, does very well out of Spaniards who come to get things which are not available in Spain. But the general effect is, as stated above, and EMU would considerably reduce the ability of national governments to remedy the adverse effects of this natural pull to the centre, a pull which occurs because it is cheaper to produce goods on a large scale where there are plenty of customers near at hand. Industry in outlying areas has the advantage of nearness and knowledge of the market in producing for its own area, but it cannot sell economically to the centre and beyond except by keeping wages down. It may not be allowed to do that, but even if it can, its workers will then move away if there is reasonably full employment in the centre. This, of course, runs down the local market even further.

Because local industry, except in specialized fields,* can only produce economically for the local market, its costs per unit are higher. It may still hold its own if transport costs are relatively high, so that goods produced nearer the centre are more expensive by the time they reach the area: it is for this reason that Sicily is marginally more prosperous than Calabria. But in that case one has monetary union without economic union, and this only happens if the local population is quite large, as in this instance.

The adverse effects of EMU, if it is genuinely implemented, can only be offset by the Common Market authorities themselves intervening in various ways much as national governments have intervened up till now—direct social spending, deliberate placing of contracts where employment is needed, investment grants to help suitable local specialization, the encouragement of trade between these local areas and countries beyond the frontiers of the Community, tourist developments, etc. If the balance of powers within the EEC remains as it is, however, with national governments having the last say, one may find that they will veto anything which imposes considerable expense on their own people to the advantage of the people in the outlying areas of other member-states: this, indeed, has happened and is the reason why the Regional Fund is not as large as it might be.

With a "Europe of the Europeans" rather than a "Europe of the nations (or states)" it is possible that the outlying areas would carry far greater weight politically, because the European Government of the day could not remain in office without their support. It is also possible that the Federal Government would deliberately favour them as a means of breaking up existing national loyalties and creating a more European spirit.

On the other hand, it may equally well be argued that the best way to counteract the adverse effects of EMU is not to have EMU or federation at all but keep the Common Market much as it is with its present advantages and disadvantages. The British Government, at the time of writing, appears to take this view. It may be the easy way out, and easy ways out are generally suspect, but it is not necessarily wrong.

The Common Market in its present form is not ideal but it works because it suits many millions of Europeans and others. There is room for improvement, but to dismantle it would be crass folly. It would involve huge traffic jams at the frontiers, the disappearance of hundreds of foodstuffs and consumer goods from every shop between Trieste and Galway Bay, the sudden closure of uncounted businesses and the return of whole armies of workers to their homeland where they would find no work nor even social

---

*Harris tweed and Border knitwear are obvious examples in Scotland. Both are produced for a minority market which is prepared to pay for quality. But the scope for this kind of industry is limited, and it is very vulnerable to fluctuations in the general economic situation. These are the products that people give up first when they are not sure what they can afford.

security benefits to keep them going because the resources of the state would be strained beyond its ability to cope. Even in the newer member-states there would be considerable disruption; in the original Six, whose economies are more fully integrated, there would be complete chaos. Yugoslavia, Greece, Turkey, and to a lesser extent the North African states and Spain, would also suffer heavily because western Europe could no longer provide employment for their surplus workers or a satisfactory outlet for their products. There would also be serious hardship to the forty-six ACP states, whose population is now exactly equal to that of the enlarged Community. Even the oil-rich states of the Middle East would be hit because their best customers would have been ruined and their investments in the European economy would have become largely worthless.

We may therefore be sure that the existing member-states will find some way to work together, at least so long as the Western type of mixed economy survives. If the economy itself collapses, the Common Market will go with it, but that is another problem, and largely one of political determination to survive, rather than of supply and demand. As much as anything else, it is a question of priorities. The Western system offers more freedom of choice and, for most people, a higher standard of living and a more interesting way of life: Communism provides greater equality and guarantees full employment at a relatively low level of efficiency and material comfort. If one regards any form of social injustice as the supreme evil one will probably opt for the Eastern system; if boredom and lack of liberty are even less tolerable than some injustice and indifference towards those who lag behind, our way makes better sense.

It is clear that at present more people in western Europe like the existing system than suffer from it, and there is no doubt at all about the verdict of those who have seen both, and who have left their homes, families, and friends, and sometimes risked their lives, in order to enjoy our way, despite all its shortcomings. Very few people have migrated in the other direction, even though there are no risks attached, and even though they at least can first go and look at the system as tourists, whereas those who flee to the West must take a leap into the dark. Western democracy will not vote itself out of existence in the foreseeable future: if it falls, it will be through subversion and betrayal or the use of force.

Barring this possibility, the Common Market looks like a permanent fixture—no less permanent than its present member-states and a great deal more so than Hitler's Third Reich, which was supposedly built to last a thousand years and in fact barely managed twelve. The Community has already done better, and its end is not in sight.

What is certain is that its purposes must evolve to some extent, as they are already doing. There will have to be a greater stress on conservation of existing resources: ever-increasing growth, in the sense originally envisaged in the Treaty of Rome, is impracticable both because these resources are finite, and because of the pollution which it would create even if they were inexhaustible. The main endeavour must be to make life more worthwhile, rather than to produce and consume more and more all the time. All this is clearly understood by the statesmen and politicians who set the tone and take the decisions, by the commissioners who try to guide and co-ordinate their thinking, and by the civil servants who run the machine. Whatever may be said against them—and they not merely have their own limitations but, in a context of political freedom, they must to some extent accept the limitations of the people around them and of the society in which they live—they are aware of the problems and of their urgency, and are making a determined effort to cope.

"With all her faults we love her still. . . ." That is what the Australian National Anthem has to say about Britain and that, perhaps, is how we can begin to feel about Europe and specifically about the Community. It is there, we are part of it, and though it is not a country it is more than just a convenient material arrangement. We may have our reservations and criticize various aspects of the whole set-up, but it is still *our* Community and we can no longer be indifferent to its fate.

Recent and Projected Developments

Up to this point we have only considered the Community as it is, its present organization, and the policies that are already being implemented. We cannot end, however, without a brief look at recent developments and projects in hand. The most recent of these are the Commission Memorandum and the Tindemans Report on a future European Union, and the arrangements made for the direct election of the European Parliament and for the issue of a European passport.

This last item would have essentially psychological significance: the scheme as adopted by the European Council at Dublin in April 1975 is that the passport would have the same outer cover, bearing the words "European Community" or "European Union" and the name of the holder's country of origin, but the contents would vary from country to country and the passport itself would be issued by the same authorities as at present, that is, by the governments of the nine member-states. As of now, the period of validity of these national passports is not identical, and the countries for which they are valid, with or without visa, also vary to some extent. The intention is that national passports in their present form will be gradually phased out and replaced by European passports when they fall due for renewal; but the more "European-minded" countries (e.g. Belgium) might call them in before they expire, so that it is quite conceivable that all Belgians would be carrying Community passports in 1980 while some United Kingdom citizens could still be travelling on traditional British passports in 1988.

The direct election of the European Parliament has also been approved in principle. A scheme put forward by its Political Committee, which envisaged a relatively large Parliament with 108–128 members from each of the four major member-states, was discarded because it would have given them excessive weight and because, in the event of further states joining the Community and being represented on the same basis (which could mean up to eighty MPs for Spain), the whole body would become quite unwieldy. In any event, with the present limited responsibilities of this Parliament, there did not seem to be much point in greatly enlarging it. If it were to become a legislature rather than a consultative assembly, it might be strengthened by

183

adding a Second House, representing the states as states, rather than by having more MPs.

The scheme currently favoured by the Parliament itself is based on the Patijn Report, drawn up by one of its Dutch members. It provides for the election of 71 German MPs, 67 British, 66 Italian, and 65 French, thus giving the four major states 269 members out of 355 (78%) as against 144 out of 198 (73%) under the present system, and 465 out of 550 (83%) under the discarded proposals of the Political Committee, the four states concerned having about 87% of the total population. For the smaller states, comparable figures are as follows:

	Present system	Discarded proposals	Parliament's own scheme
Belgium	14	24	23
Netherlands	14	31	27
Denmark	10	14	17
Ireland	10	10	13
Luxemburg	6	6	6

The Parliament's scheme provides that "Euro-MPs" could be members of their national Parliament at least in the meantime (some think this should be reviewed as the powers of the European Parliament are increased and more work is required of its members, but they would not have to be national MPs, senators, or peers as at present. On the other hand, they could not be national ministers (since this would make them potential members of the Council) or European Commissioners, nor could they be employees of any of the EEC institutions. Each member-state could, under this scheme, determine which parties, if any, should be banned from taking part in European elections (in Italy, for instance, it would probably remain illegal to stand as a "Fascist" though quite in order to be an MSI candidate) and whether independents would stand as such.

The European Council held in Luxemburg City in April 1976, which should have finalized electoral arrangements, ran into difficulties because some politicians were not really interested in direct elections and therefore insisted on principles which they knew would be unacceptable (e.g. the allocation of seats in strict proportion to each country's population, which would mean 700 MPs if Luxemburg were to be represented at all and 4200 if it were to retain six members). In the end France proposed that the present allocation of seats be retained, but that the 198 MPs be elected: most states were prepared to go along with this until a better scheme could be agreed by all, but Britain refused as this would make it impossible to provide for adequate representation of Scotland and Wales.

According to the Treaty of Rome the Parliament should be elected by a uniform method and on the same day throughout the Community. This, however, was found to involve serious practical difficulties, and it is now envisaged that, *as an interim arrangement* each member-state should use its own electoral system ("first-past-the-post" in the United Kingdom, second ballot in France, mixed constituencies and regional lists in West Germany, national lists in Holland, and various forms of proportional representation in the other states), and voting should be spread out over a few days to take care of the fact that France always votes on a Sunday while Britain never does. To prevent results in any one country from influencing voting in another, however, declaration would only take place once the whole Community has voted. In principle these elections should take place in the first week of May 1978. There is a problem, however, which is that elections are expensive (a United Kingdom general election or referendum costs about £20 million not counting the expenditure of the parties involved). Consequently some states would like to elect their Euro-MPs at the same time as their national MPs. This, apart from saving money, would result in a higher turn-out for the European election but would detract attention from European candidates and issues as such, and put a very considerable strain on individuals who happened to be candidates for both parliaments. Ultimately it is not impossible that the six original member-states will elect their Euro-MPs together, and possibly arrange for national elections to take place simultaneously for the sake of economy, and that Ireland, the most European-minded of the three new member-states, will fall in with this arrangement, while Britain and Denmark wait until national elections are due and elect their Euro-MPs at the same time. The second "European general election", however, would be fully synchronized, and by that time one might hope that a uniform method of election would have been worked out and that the European Parliament would have been given more adequate powers, which should lead to a higher turn-out even if the "European" election does not coincide with national elections.

Several other problems have yet to be resolved, for instance whether the election would be contested by European parties or by national parties having some sort of understanding and informal co-operation arrangements, and what should be the position of Community citizens living and working in a member-state other than their country of origin, e.g. the British in Belgium and Italians in Germany. There are several possible solutions: they could vote where they are (which would imply Britishers voting for Belgians and Italians voting for Germans); they could return home (but this would imply special arrangements for the British, who at present lose their place on the register if they are away for more than a year) or there could be a few extra-territorial constituencies (e.g. one for the British outside Britain, one for the

French outside France, one for the Italians in Germany and one for other Italians abroad). At present it seems likely that each country will work out its own scheme and that Community citizens will generally vote in their own country by post or returning home for this purpose, while foreign workers (Turks, etc.) will remain disfranchised as at present.

As regards the parties themselves, it should be borne in mind that Social Democrats, under one name or another, function in all nine states and Liberals in eight of them, the exception being Ireland. Christian Democrats, on the other hand, are absent from French and British politics, while in The Netherlands they are splintered between Catholic, Reformed, and Free Kirk parties. Conservatives as such only exist in Britain and Denmark, though the Christian Democrats are broadly similar in outlook while having a left wing which is parallel with the Social Democrats in some countries. This points to *ad hoc* arrangements such as already exist within the European Parliament, rather than official "Euro-Parties" a situation which might change if the powers of the Parliament were greatly increased.

The rate of progress towards a European Union has also been rather slow. The Commission submitted a memorandum to the Council on this subject in June 1975. Like the Tindemans Report, which is partly based on it, the Memorandum includes specific proposals, but does not set out to be a draft constitution. These proposals, however, go further than the Belgian Prime Minister subsequently felt it was possible to go at this stage.

In general terms, the Commission recommends that the Union should run everything which is now run by the Community, and should have added powers in the fields of monetary policy, budget financing, the improvement of social and regional structures, and foreign policy. Specifically, it envisages a centralized power of decision-making in monetary matters, exercised through an EEC Central Bank or a common system of central banks with pooled reserves. A new instrument should be created, initially for transactions between central banks; later this could also be used for transactions between public institutions and banks: it would probably be based on a weighted average of national currencies, like Special Drawing Rights. At the same time the Community budget should be made larger and more flexible—most of it is at present committed to automatic intervention under the Common Agricultural Policy and the rest is largely taken up by administrative expenditure. It could then be used to a greater extent as a means for the transfer of resources between national economies and between social categories (e.g. from Germany to Ireland and Italy, and from the well-paid to badly paid workers and those dependent on social security). But this increase in Community expenditure should also allow rationalization and savings in national expenditure so that the total cost should, after taking inflation into account, be no higher than at present.

The memorandum regards *regional development policy* as an essential field for Community intervention, which could take two forms:

(a) support for national programmes, as at present;
(b) direct intervention, with basic decisions as to objectives and projects taken at Community level.

There should also be an increased power of *social* intervention, in particular to help migrant workers, improve working conditions, and promote industrial democracy.

As regards *foreign policy* and *defence,* the Commission's recommendations are virtually identical with those of Mr. Tindemans, outlined below. The most distinctive part of the memorandum consists in the Commission's proposals for a complete reform of the existing institutions, going far beyond anything most of the present member-states are likely to accept at this stage. These proposals come in three versions, differing mainly in the powers that might be left with the present Council of Ministers or a similarly constituted body; but the scheme which the Commission favours would involve a two-house Parliament, one house being directly elected on a population basis while the other would represent the member-states in much the same way as the American, German, and Swiss senates.* Part of the Council's present remit, that of defending national interests, would then fall to this European Senate, or Chamber of States, while the rest (taking decisions) would fall to a European Government, which would make regulations and draft laws. This Government would also take over most of the Commission's present work, but the Commission might survive in a modified form as a "Committee of Wise Men", whose essential task would be to think on a high level and to act as guardians of the treaties, or rather of the new European Constitution which would have to replace them, since the changes proposed are too far-reaching to be implemented within the framework of the present treaties, even with amendments.

The memorandum was greeted with considerable diffidence, not to say hostility, by several governments, in particular those of Britain, France, and Denmark. It made a valuable contribution on the plane of ideas, as did other reports submitted by the European Parliament, the Court, and the Economic and Social Committee, but there was never any real prospect that it might serve as the basis for a unanimous decision—and the changes which it

---

*The American Senate has two members for each state, regardless of population. They are directly elected. The Swiss Senate, or Council of States, is elected in the same way, but the six half-cantons have one senator each, as against two for each of the nineteen undivided cantons. The German Senate, or *Bundesrat,* consists of delegations appointed by the governments of the eleven *Länder,* including West Berlin (but West Berlin has a special status and its representatives are voteless, as in the *Bundestag*). These vary in size but are not fully proportional to the population of the *Länder,* the smaller ones have a definite advantage.

proposed would have required unanimity in the European Council, ratification by all nine parliaments (in some cases with two-thirds majorities), and referenda in Britain, France, Italy, Denmark, and Ireland.

Mr. Tindemans, writing in a personal capacity as a member of the European Council for his fellow-members, was more cautious altogether, and started from the principle that, whatever might be desirable in the longer term (and he made it clear that he took the Federalist line), it was essential to stick at this stage to what could be done *within the framework of the present treaties and using the institutions as they stand.* Having been given a remit by his colleagues to define what should be understood by the concept of a European Union, he based himself on the memorandum and reports mentioned above and on a very wide range of personal contacts, pre-existing or established in the course of a series of visits to all the EEC capitals.

The Tindemans Report starts, like the Commission Memorandum, with a brief analysis of what is wrong with Europe as of now. Basically, it has run out of steam. Its own successes so far have caused it to be taken for granted: at the same time "our peoples are concerned with new problems and with values which the Treaties do not mention". Europe does not come up to the measure of their aspirations, and is unable to cope with such problems as the present unemployment crisis. The present state of affairs cannot last: "an unfinished building cannot stand up to the weather; it must be completed, or it will collapse. Today the Community's achievement is at stake."

What do Europeans want and expect from a United Europe? Tindemans summarizes the answer as follows:

(1) *A voice in the world.* There is a feeling of vulnerability and impotence, yet the will to make an active contribution is very strong: 100,000 young Europeans, working on overseas co-operation projects, give proof of this.

(2) *A new society,* which respects the basic values of our civilization and reconciles the rights of individuals and of communities; a new type of economic growth, with greater regard for the quality of life and of the environment; a better combination of economic and social goals, tending towards a post-industrial society which should make the best use of high technologies and of "Europe's grey gold" (intellectual capacity and know-how); participation by workers in decision making, control of undertakings and profits; greater freedom in the organization of work; more "transparency" (the decision making process to be more visible), decentralization, and consultation. The European Union should make up for the weakening grip of national structures and carry out reforms and checks which are often impracticable at State level. It should promote greater social justice.

(3) *Practical solidarity,* involving a greater effort to promote education and culture, information and communications, youth and leisure activities.

The European Council must now define the general scope of common enterprise during the stage of Union, which Tindemans regards as something more than the Community in its present form, but less than a federation. In due course a new legal text (a new or amended treaty) will be needed when this process has acquired its own momentum; in the meantime much can be done using the existing institutions with their existing powers. The main components of this process should be as follows:

(1) *We must be united in the face of the outside world.* This implies a common foreign policy at least in some major fields defined below.

(2) *The prosperity of our states is interdependent.* This implies a common economic and monetary policy, and common industrial and agricultural policies, as well as energy and research policies to guarantee our future.

(3) *Real and effective solidarity.* This implies social actions and a strong regional policy to correct the centralizing effects of other policies.

(4) *The European Union must have an effective impact on our daily lives.* This includes the protection of basic rights and the improvement of the context in which we live.

(5) *Effective institutions.*

(6) *Progressive construction by specific and carefully selected actions.*

Tindemans then expands on each of these points.

As regards *foreign policy* there should be a merger of the present "Community" and "political co-operation" aspects, so that the ministers, meeting as the Council, should be able to discuss everything that needs to be discussed, even if different procedures are used to some extent and the outcome is a joint decision in some cases and agreement to take parallel decisions in others. A common foreign policy should be set up, based on majority decisions, to cover in the first instance:

(i) a new world economic order (relations with developing countries);
(ii) relations between Europe and the United States;
(iii) security, including *détente*;
(iv) crises arising in Europe and its immediate vicinity.

As regards (i), the Community must present a united front in multilateral negotiations wherever they occur (GATT, UNCTAD, FAO, etc.), and its representatives should be appointed *ad hoc* after the ministers have agreed on a common line (they might be, for instance, the delegates of the state which currently holds the Council Presidency).

There should be a gradual transfer to the Community of a large share of the national credits intended for development co-operation, and a common position should be adopted on general economic problems arising in relations with the Third World.*

As regards (ii) a constructive dialogue with the United States is essential, and should include the discussion of defence. A member of the European Council should be delegated for this purpose.

Effective action on (iii) implies that Europe must eventually have a common defence policy. This is impracticable as yet, because different states assess the situation in various ways.† In the meantime there should be regular exchanges of views on these problems and on multilateral negotiations concerning security. There should also be co-operation in the production of armaments so as to reduce defence costs, increase the autonomy of Europe, and make her defence industries more competitive. The nine states should also continue defining common positions on *détente*.

As regards (iv) it is already normal practice for the nine states to have a common line on these issues. This should be made a binding rule, with a previous commitment to accept majority decisions.‡ Co-operation with other democratic countries in Europe is highly desirable, and their views should be taken into account in Community decision making.

While it has been agreed that there should be a common economic and

---

*An example of these problems is the transfer of low-technology, labour-intensive industries from developed to developing countries. This would undoubtedly help the economy of the latter but would cause very serious problems in Europe which has more workers than it could possibly employ at present in high-technology industries, and is naturally reluctant to become heavily dependent on imports of Asian or African-made clothing and footwear. Commodity prices are another and more important issue, and there it should be borne in mind that higher prices for copper may be very helpful to Zambia, but will do nothing for some of the poorer countries which depend on exports of groundnuts or bananas for instance. Similarly with other products, e.g. coffee and cocoa.

†Mr. Tindemans has been very cautious and diplomatic in his treatment of this point. The essential difficulties are that:
  (a) France has in the past adopted a "semi-detached" attitude to NATO, while Ireland is not a member of the Western Alliance and will not at present allow foreign bases on her soil;
  (b) there is a large body of opinion, especially among younger people, which feels that defence is pointless and that it is more important to spend money on other things;
  (c) some countries do not have National Service, while its length varies in the majority of states which do have it, and deferment and exemptions are easier to obtain in some states than in others.
A Common Defence Policy would imply a uniform proportion of the GNP spent on defence throughout the Community, and the restoration of National Service in those states which have abolished it, while the length and conditions of National Service would also have to be standardized, at least approximately.

‡This last point could give rise to serious difficulties in the event of another war in the Middle East. If the Community were to adopt a basically pro-Arab attitude in order to safeguard its oil supplies, it is almost certain that public opinion in Holland, Denmark and Scotland (if independent) would not allow the governments of those countries to go along with the common policy, the more so as Holland and Scotland are net exporters of energy (Scotland has oil and Holland can get it in return for natural gas), while Denmark can buy what she needs from Norway.

monetary policy, there is no political consensus to implement it, due to lack of mutual confidence, and no technical consensus on how to set about it. The recession has caused further practical difficulties (thus the French franc fell out of the "snake" after Tindemans had submitted his report), and the only way now is for the European Council to reactivate discussion and take some effective steps. Tindemans envisages this might be done by agreeing to move towards the same goal at different speeds, using and reinforcing the mechanism of the "snake" (see p. 130). Those states which can move ahead towards full integration of their economies would then be required to do so, while the rest (essentially Britain, Ireland, and Italy, together with Greece and Portugal if and when they join) would be helped in their efforts to catch up, and would meantime take part in the formulation of policy and the assessment of results.

At present the "snake" only covers monetary policy and is basically a mechanism for the mutual support and restraint of national currencies, preventing any excessive disparity between them. Its scope should be extended to involve rules governing:

(i) internal monetary policy (control of the money supply);
(ii) budgetary policy (size and financing of deficits);
(iii) the key elements of short-term economic policy and inflation control.

The mutual support obligations between "snake" countries must, in Tindeman's view, be made automatic and considerably strengthened, and these countries must progressively abolish obstacles to the movement of capital between themselves, especially those set up since 1970. These obligations should be suspended in the case of a "manifest crisis" occurring in a member-state and recognized as such by the Community as a whole.

Arrangements for the support of "non-snake" countries should be organized on an *ad hoc* basis and should include regional, social, industrial, and agricultural measures. All this should only be regarded as a beginning, further steps being the subject of debate within the Community institutions. The essential guidelines should be:

(a) global and interdependent solutions: measures of aid and acceptance of the rules must go together;
(b) an irreversible mechanism including major steps when necessary. It is not always possible to proceed by short steps.

As regards the sectorial policies, Tindemans makes the following points:

(1) The *Common Agricultural Policy* should be carried on but not conceived in terms of agricultural problems alone (it has important regional and social implications).

(2) The *Common Energy Policy* should include:

(a) a "solidarity mechanism" in times of supply difficulties;
(b) a Community definition of consumption and production objectives;
(c) the development, in the light of the above, of a programme of alternative resources on a Community basis;
(d) the development of additional production capacities by encouraging investment and taking measures to guarantee and protect investments if oil prices should fall (this would imply a kind of "intervention price" mechanism for North Sea oil, supported by levies on imported oil if need be);
(e) the mobilization at Community level of the financial resources required in order to implement (c) and (d);
(f) the establishment of a Community instrument for the organization of the energy market.

This should enable the Community to maintain a coherent policy and to negotiate from a stronger position.

Research policy has been hampered by difficulties with national institutes and industrial users due to a lack of confidence which must be overcome. The Community should concentrate on priorities established in the light of three criteria:

(i) research directly linked with a Community policy (e.g. environment);
(ii) research linked with a common activity in a given sector (e.g. alternative sources of energy);
(iii) research beyond the means of individual states (e.g. controlled thermo-nuclear fusion).

Resources must not be frittered away. They should be adequate in size and committed for a sufficiently long period, making it possible to achieve worthwhile results. There should be an exchange of information on national activities and results to eliminate wasteful duplication and make fresh knowledge available to all, and this research should allow the smaller states to participate in work that would not be justified on a purely national level.

Tindemans regards *Social Policy* as essentially a matter for the states, but with European objectives and specific European actions concerning:

(a) social security with special attention to migrants and disabled persons. There should be norms applicable in all states as regards wages, pensions, social security, and working conditions;
(b) concertation between employers, workers, and public authorities, organized at European level to fit in with the transfer of decision making powers to the Community institutions;
(c) workers' participation in the control of industry.

The Social Fund should be used along with regional aids to correct any imbalances that may arise. More sophisticated methods of European solidarity should be considered later, e.g. to deal with unemployment.

An effective *Regional Policy* is needed in order to compensate for the tendency of the market to concentrate capital and activity in the most profitable areas of the Community. Some of this correction will be made by national regional development policies as before. Much of it, however, will require use of the Community budget either directly (regional aids) or indirectly (action on economic structures in the context of the agricultural and industrial policies). The Regional Policy must therefore be gradually strengthened to keep pace with the results achieved in the convergence of the economic and monetary policies of the member-states. Its action must be concentrated in the regions of the Community where economic development is most backward.

Tindemans goes on to describe what he calls "the Europe of the citizens". "The construction of Europe is more than a form of co-operation between states. It is a bringing together of peoples who seek to adapt their societies together to changing world conditions, with due respect for the values which are their common heritage. Europe must be close to the citizen." The Community should protect the rights of Europeans where these can no longer be adequately guaranteed by national states. European solidarity should be given a visible form through outward signs such as the gradual abolition of frontier controls between the member-states,* easier transport and communications (including uniform rates for telephone calls, etc., across national borders), and simplification of the procedures whereby citizens of one member-state are refunded for medical expenses incurred in another.

There should also be protection of basic rights at European level involving the possibility of appeal to the European Court of Justice, and protection on a European scale of the rights of consumers, since the state is no longer always in a position to provide the necessary guarantees, where goods circulate more freely than before and their quality is difficult to check.

An interesting proposal is the establishment of a *European Foundation,* financed partly by the Community and its member-states, partly from private sources. Its task would be to promote anything that may lead to

---

*This recommendation may not be altogether acceptable to member-states whose frontiers are relatively easy to control (e.g. Italy, the United Kingdom) or to those which are most seriously concerned about terrorist activities. Under the Treaty they remain responsible for public order, and may feel that border checks are necessary for this purpose. Another problem is that they have different attitudes towards citizens of third countries. Thus Britain, France, and Belgium make entry easier for citizens of their former colonies than for other Africans; Germany will not have Arabs who are already in other member-states, and so on.

better understanding between the peoples of the Community, including youth activities, student exchanges, debates, and seminars.

The part of the report which has so far attracted most attention, however, deals with the strengthening of the Community's institutions. The basic principle is that the existing machinery should be used but the decision making process speeded up, which may in some cases require adaptation of the treaties. It makes the following main proposals:

A. *Parliament.* This should be directly elected and its powers strengthened, and it should have a certain right of initiative. This, however, would seem to be a right to have its recommendations discussed by the Council rather than a right to submit draft regulations and directives since it is not adequately equipped to work them out. It should also have the right to discuss all matters falling within the scope of the Union, whether or not covered by the treaties. (The Parliamentary Assembly of the Western European Union, as Tindemans points out, might then become redundant; its only advantage over the European Parliament is the fact that it can discuss defence, though it takes no decisions in that field or any other.) Finally, it should hold a number of major debates, including a "State of the Union" debate in which the President of the European Council and some other national leaders would be invited to take part.

B. *The European Council.* This body should decide on the main lines of Community policy arising from an overall view of problems. The Heads of Government should collectively use the authority which they have at national level to give the necessary impetus to the construction of Europe. They should act in accordance with Treaty procedures, in the presence of the Commission, when taking decisions in the field of Community policy. Otherwise their decisions should provide guidelines for those who have to implement them. The European Council should in every case indicate who is to give effect to a particular decision and specify a time-limit if necessary. Its meetings should be prepared by the Council of Foreign Ministers.

C. *The Council.* The Council of Foreign Ministers should be given a mandate to co-ordinate the activities of the other specialist councils (Agriculture, Finance, etc.). The distinction between Council and "political co-operation" meetings should be abolished; the same ministers should be authorized to discuss everything on the same occasion, though the distinction of powers should remain: in one case the Community decides to act in a certain field; in the other the ministers agree that their governments will take the same or very similar action in a field not at present covered by the treaties. Majority decisions should be the rule in the areas covered by the treaties and by the undertaking to pursue a common foreign policy. The duration of the Presidency (as also for the European Council) should be extended from the present six months to one year for the sake of greater continuity and consistency, but specialized tasks (e.g. discussions with America, mentioned earlier) should be remitted to the Commission, or a country, or to one or several individuals, independently of any changes in the Presidency, without in any way reducing the powers of the Commission under the treaties.

D. *The Commission.* Its powers should in general be upgraded to those of the old ECSC High Authority. Its President should be appointed by the European Council and his appointment should be subject to confirmation by the European Parliament. Thereafter he should appoint his colleagues, in consultation with the Council and having regard to the national distribution of seats laid down in the treaties (two commissioners from each of the major member-states; one from each of the rest).*

E. *The Court.* Its powers should be extended to cover any new areas falling within the scope of Community policy, and there should be a right of appeal to it by individuals against the Community institutions.

Tindemans also envisages a greatly enhanced role for the Standing Committee on Employment, which should be given much the same status as the Economic and Social Committee, with an automatic right to be consulted in matters of social policy, and a right of initiative, while some powers should be delegated to COREPER. Anything which is unanimously agreed there should be decided at that level (since its members act on instructions from home in any event) instead of being passed on to the Council as a non-controversial "Point A". The Political Committee should carry on as at present in preparing the diplomatic deliberations of the foreign ministers, while new bodies may have to be created as a result of administrative decentralization in the member-states. Tindemans is not very specific about this, perhaps in order to avoid offending French and other susceptibilities, but it would seem that he is thinking in terms of bodies which would deal direct with regional authorities to whom legislative and administrative powers have been devolved.

The general conclusions of the report are that it is necessary to define a political consensus as regards the objectives and characteristics of the Union; to establish the consequences of this choice in the various spheres of activity of the Union; to start a dynamic process by means of practical actions in each of these areas, and, finally, to strengthen the internal apparatus of the Community for this purpose. The Belgian Prime Minister stresses the declining weight and influence of European states in the modern world. Their grip on the controlling levers which make it possible to influence the future of our societies has been steadily reduced. They have less room to

---

*Tindemans does not explain what should happen if the European Parliament refuses, for any reason, to accept a President-designate of the Commission. A further point is that it might wish to know whom he intends to appoint before deciding to confirm him in office.

manoeuvre, and try to keep in balance in the face of pressures and factors, both internal and external, which they cannot control. There is a vicious spiral of impotence: by yielding to pressures they lose still more of their ability to resist further pressures. The construction of Europe is the only complete answer to this challenge. The Community was the first step: European Union must be the second. "Our way of life, and that of our children, will in the last resort depend on this."

It may be too early to judge this report, but its historical importance could be on the same level as that of the Spaak Report (1955), which served as the basis of discussion for the establishment of the Community as we know it. Public discussion so far has been less than adequate, though there has been considerable opposition from the British and Italian governments to the "two-speed" approach to economic and monetary union, which is one of its most important proposals. It does not, however, aspire to be a Grand Design, so coherent that no one part of it can be implemented separately from the rest, and that none can be omitted without jeopardizing the whole structure. For this reason it seems possible, at the time of writing, that some of the specific actions which it recommends will be put in hand—essentially those which do not involve any considerable sacrifice of pride (the "two-speed" approach, for instance, may be unacceptable in that it brands "non-snake" countries as second-class members of the Community) or any far-reaching surrender of national sovereignty.

In passing it may be worth noting that useful progress is being made as regards the mutual recognition of professional qualifications. Thus agreement has been reached, and a directive adopted and "translated" into national legislation, on the freedom of doctors to practise within the Community. Any Community citizen who has qualified in any of the member-states, by successfully completing a medical course of not less than six years, may now set up in private practice anywhere in the Community, even though he may not have adequate knowledge of the national language (one could imagine, in some places in Belgium and Germany, an Italian doctor practising exclusively in the large Italian population there). For public practice (e.g. in the National Health Service or in hospitals) added qualifications may be required, for instance knowledge of the national language or completion of an internship.

The position as regards lawyers is more complex, since the knowledge they require varies from state to state, whereas the content of medical knowledge is international, even though specific elements of it may not be taught in the same order: furthermore, as we have seen, the legal profession is divided in some countries and unified in others. In general terms, solicitors and advocates (barristers) may accompany their clients from their home state to another member-state, and help them in any litigation in which they may be involved there, co-operating for this purpose with locally based lawyers, but they cannot open up a practice, or chambers, in a country other than their own (e.g. an English solicitor in Frankfurt or a German *Rechtsanwalt* in London). It would be quite competent for the Englishman to set up in Germany, however (or vice versa) for the purpose of giving legal advice, which might be sought by British firms operating in Germany, or by local firms wishing to do business in the United Kingdom, but without conducting cases.

Other directives are in preparation, covering several other professional specialities: the general approach is to liberalize a speciality (e.g. giving tax advice or auditing the accounts of firms and public bodies), rather than to open up a profession as such (tax adviser, chartered accountant) because a particular kind of work may be undertaken by quite different people from one country to another (e.g. tax advice is given by specialists who do nothing else in Germany, by chartered accountants in Britain, and by lawyers in some other states).

As this book was going to press, the European Council reached an agreement, whose further details have yet to be worked out, on the main principles governing direct elections to the European Parliament. These are to take place for the first time in May or June 1978. The four major member-states are to have 81 members each: this, if Scotland and Wales are over-represented within the United Kingdom, would make it possible for Scotland to have as many members as Ireland and for Wales to have as many as Luxemburg. Holland will have 25 members, 1 more than Belgium; previously each had 14 while the four larger states had 36 apiece. Denmark will have 16 and Ireland 15 instead of 10. Luxemburg retains 6 members as before.

The principle of equality between the four major states is thus preserved: the Parliament's own scheme would have taken their different populations, ranging from 54 million for France to 62 million for West Germany, into account. Similarly, Belgium and Holland are treated as virtually equal, though the former has under 10 million and the latter nearly 13.5 million people, and there is a similar near-equality between Denmark (5.1 million) and Ireland (3.1 million). This confirms the French and British view that Europe consists of countries rather than of people: the Community is thus organized, as before, on the basis of states of the first, second, third and fourth order of magnitude. The fourth category at the moment comprises Luxemburg alone; but this also is where the Azores would fit in if they became independent and joined the Common Market; similarly, with Cyprus and possibly Slovenia, Scotland would quite clearly belong in the third; Greece and Portugal possibly in the second. The first-category states, however, acquire greater weight under this arrangement, with 324 members out of 410 (80%) instead of 144 out of 198 (73%).

Electoral arrangements (the actual method of voting, and the day, within a narrow range of a week or so) and the compatibility or otherwise of membership in the European Parliament with membership of the national Parliament, are left at this stage to the individual member-states. A more detailed agreement is to be drafted by the Council of Foreign Ministers and submitted to the national parliaments for ratification.

The European Council also appointed Mr. Roy Jenkins as the next President of the European Commission and agreed to implement two of the Tindemans Report recommendations. The new President will have a greater say in the selection of his colleagues and the allocation of their portfolios than his predecessors, and he is to conduct a thorough review of the staffing, structure, and political role of the Commission.

What this will involve is not clear as yet. It has been suggested that there are too many commissioners (13) at present, but one could equally argue in favour of having a few more, perhaps combining this increase with a slight reduction in the number of directors-general, so that there should be a commissioner as the political head and a director-general as the administrative head of each department. This would also make it possible to depart from a strict allocation of posts by nationality, allowing some of the member-states an extra commissioner or two if this would improve the quality of the team as a whole.

It might also be advisable to have more Commission officials working in the individual member-states, and some Community policies cannot be effectively implemented otherwise.

A further and very important point, which Mr. Jenkins will have to consider, is how to improve the cohesion of the Commission as a body without treading on too many personal, departmental, and national toes. At the time of writing it only meets once a week except in an emergency, and individual commissioners, with or sometimes without the support of their directors-general, may pursue individual policies which are liable to cancel out or in any event to obstruct each other. Thus some departments (e.g. Competition, Industry, and Technology) are apt to develop centralizing tendencies which others (Regional Policy, Social Policy) then try to counteract or mitigate as best they can, in the interest of the 100 million Community citizens who live in remote, mountainous, or otherwise disadvantaged regions.

Even where no direct conflict occurs, there is often a failure to consider the impact of one policy on the successful implementation of another: as Regional Commissioner, Mr. Thomson has more than once referred to this problem. At the very least, much closer liaison is required, even if continental traditions make it impracticable to establish anything like the British Cabinet system, with its doctrine of collective responsibility, the resignation of those who dissent on major issues and the preponderant role of the Prime Minister except where he encounters considerable opposition from his colleagues.

A new Commission took office on 1 January 1977, headed by Mr. Roy Jenkins and including several other new members, e.g. Mr. Christopher Tugendhat (United Kingdom), Mr. Henk Vredeling (Netherlands) and both the Italian representatives.

Mr. Claude Cheysson (France) remained in charge of Overseas Development, but some of the other Commissioners who stayed on moved to other departments; thus Mr. Finn Gundelach (Denmark), previously responsible for the Customs Union and the internal market, became Commissioner for Agriculture, ending the 20-year Dutch monopoly of this vital sector.

In some cases, responsibilities previously combined by one Commissioner were rearranged, but this did not affect departments such as Agriculture, Foreign Policy, Social Policy, and Regional Policy, which are not combined with any other; hence it did not seem necessary to reorganize the layout of this book. The arrangement of chapters continues therefore to be based, with the important exception of Coal and Steel, on the distribution of Commission portfolios in 1973–6. The coal and steel sector, though several Commissioners are responsible for its various aspects, is treated as a distinct entity because it comes under a different Treaty.

Following on the redistribution of Commission portfolios, there was a reshuffle of Directors-General: this because a Commissioner and the Director-General who works closely with him (on much the same basis as a Cabinet Minister with his Permanent Secretary) must not be of the same nationality. Thus Signor Ruggiero, previously DG for Regional Policy, moved to the Spokesman's Department, of which he became the administrative head, on the appointment of an Italian Commissioner. This reshuffle involved not only transfers within the Commission, as in this case, but the return of some DGs to their own country, and the arrival of others. The process will in due course extend downwards to the level of Directors and possibly Heads of Division, though relatively fewer of them will be affected, as the requisite balance of nationalities can be more easily maintained by the normal processes of retirement and promotion.

APPENDIX II

Suggestions for Further Reading

INTRODUCTION

S. de Madariaga, *Portrait of Europe,* Hollis & Carter, London, 1967.
D. de Rougemont, *The Idea of Europe,* Macmillan, New York, 1967.
Lord Gladwyn, *The European Idea,* Weidenfeld & Nicolson, London, 1966.
R. Mayne, *The Europeans,* Weidenfeld & Nicolson, London, 1972.

Chapter 1. HISTORICAL BACKGROUND

(a) *General*

Y. Brekilien, *Histoire Européenne de l'Europe,* Enseignement & Perfectionnement Techniques, Paris, 1965.
C. Dawson, *The Making of Europe,* Sheed & Ward, London, 1946.
O. von Habsburg, *Damals begann unsere Zukunft,* Herold Verlag, Vienna, 1973.
S. de Madariaga, *Portrait of Europe,* Hollis & Carter, London, 1967.
M. Mourin, *Histoire des Nations Européennes,* Payot, Paris, 1963.

(b) *Unification of Europe*

K. Adenauer, *Erinnerungen* (2 vols.), Deutsche Verlags-Anstalt, Stuttgart, 1965.
H. Brugmans, *L'Idée Européenne,* College of Europe, Bruges, 1965.
M. Camps, *What Kind of Europe?,* Chatham House, London, 1965.
M. Camps, *Britain and Europe, 1955–63,* Oxford University Press, London, 1964.
M. Camps, *European Unification in the Sixties,* Oxford University Press, London, 1967.
J. P. Gouzy, *Les Pionniers de l'Europe Communautaire,* Centre de Recherches Européennes, Lausanne, 1968.
W. Hallstein, *Die Europäische Gemeinschaft,* Econ Verlag, Düsseldorf, 1973. (This book in its present version only exists in German. An earlier version, *Die Unvollendete Bundestaat,* published by Econ Verlag in 1969, was translated into French as *L'Europe Inachevée* (R. Laffont, 1970) and into English as *Europe in the Making* (Allen & Unwin, 1972). Hallstein's book is also relevant to most of the chapters of *The Common Market and How It Works,* and is therefore repeatedly mentioned below.)
R. Mayne, *The Recovery of Europe,* Weidenfeld & Nicolson, London, 1970.
R. Schuman, *Pour L'Europe,* Nagel, Paris, 1964.
P. H. Spaak, *Combats Inachevés,* Fayard, Paris, 1969.

Chapter 2. THE MEMBER-STATES

(a) *General*

S. Holt, *Six European States,* Hamish Hamilton, London, 1970.
J. Meyer and I. Kermoss, *Elections in the Countries of the European Communities and in the United Kingdom,* College of Europe, Bruges, 1967.

(b) *Individual States*

   France

      J. Chappal, *La Vie Politique en France depuis 1940,* Presses Universitaires de France, Paris, 1966 (3rd Ed. 1972).

      M. Faure, *Les Paysans dans la Société Française,* Armand Colin, Paris, 1966.

      F. Goguel and A. Grossen, *La Politique en France,* Armand Colin, Paris, 1970.

   West Germany

      R. Dahrendorf, *Gesellschaft und Demokratie in Deutschland,* Piper Verlag, Munich, 1968 (a more recent paperback edition was brought out by Deutschen Taschenbuch Verlag, Munich, in 1972).

      A. J. Ryder, *Twentieth Century Germany,* Macmillan, London, 1973.

   United Kingdom

      J. P. Mackintosh, *The British Cabinet,* Stevens, London, 1968.

      J. P. Mackintosh, *The Government and Politics of Britain,* Central Office of Information, Britain, London, published annually, London, 1974.

   Italy

      C. Bibes, *Le Système Politique Italien,* Presses Universitaires de France, Paris, 1974.

   Belgium

      F. Huggett, *Modern Belgium,* Pall Mall Press, London, 1971.

   The Netherlands

      F. Huggett, *The Modern Netherlands,* Pall Mall Press, London, 1971.

   Belgium, The Netherlands, Luxemburg

      J. Karelle and F. de Kemmeter, *Le Bénélux Commenté,* Bruylant, Brussels, 1961.

   Denmark

      K. Miller, *Government and Politics in Denmark,* Houghton-Mifflin, Boston, US, 1968.

   (*with Finland, Iceland, Norway and Sweden*)

      N. Andren, *Government and Politics in the Nordic Countries,* Almqvist & Wiksell, Stockholm, 1964.

   Ireland

      B. Clubb, *The Government and Politics of Ireland,* Stanford/Oxford University Press, Stanford, California and London, 1970. Useful and up-to-date information on the individual member-states may also be found in the two annual Commission publications, the *General Report* and the *Social Report.*

Chapter 3. THE INSTITUTIONS OF THE COMMUNITY

(a) *General*

      ECSC Treaty, Articles 7–45, published by the European Communities.

      EEC Treaty, Articles 137–198, published by the European Communities.

      Euratom Treaty, published by the European Communities.

      Several important articles of the ECSC Treaty were repealed by the Merger Treaty and cannot be found in the combined volume which includes the ECSC, EEC, Euratom, Merger and Accession Treaties and various protocols. They are, however, to be found in the original Treaty as published on its own. The French text alone is authoritative. An English translation was published by HMSO.

      D. Coombes, *Politics and Bureaucracy in the European Community,* PEP, London, 1970.

      W. Hallstein, *Die Europaïsche Gemeinschaft,* Chapters II and III, Econ Verlag, Düsseldorf, 1973.

      M. Palmer and J. Lambert, *A Survey of the European Organisations,* Allen & Unwin, London, 1968.

      R. Pinto, *Les Organisations Européennes,* Payot, Paris, 1963.

      P. Pfimlin and R. Legrand-Lane, *L'Europe Communautaire,* Plon, Paris, 1966.

(b) *Individual Institutions*

Commission of the European Communities

A. Spinelli, *The Eurocrats,* Johns Hopkins University Press, Baltimore, 1966.

Council of the European Communities

S. Buerstedde, *Der Ministerrat der Europäische Gemeinschaften,* College of Europe, Bruges, 1964.

European Parliament

Sir B. Cocks, *The European Parliament,* HMSO, London, 1973.

PEP, *The European Parliament,* PEP, London, 1964.

J. Fitzmaurice, *The Political Groups in the European Parliament,* Saxon House and Lexington Books, Farnborough (UK) and Lexington (USA), 1975.

European Court of Justice

E. H. Wall, *The Court of Justice of the European Communities,* Butterworths, London, 1966.

L. J. Brinkhorst and J. D. B. Mitchell, *European Law and Institutions,* Edinburgh University Press, Edinburgh, 1969.

There are at present no outside-written books on the *Economic and Social Committee* or on the *European Investment Bank.* These institutions, however, have put out brochures describing themselves and their work, which may be obtained from their respective offices in Brussels and Luxemburg City.

Chapter 4. THE DECISION-MAKING PROCESS

W. Hallstein, *Die Europäische Gemeinschaft,* chapter IV, Econ Verlag, 1973.

(Symposium) *La Décision dans les Communautés Européennes,* Presses Universitaires de Bruxelles, Brussels, 1963.

Chapter 5. THE COMMON AGRICULTURAL POLICY

EEC Treaty, Articles 38–47.

W. Hallstein, *Die Europäische Gemeinschaft,* chapter V, Econ Verlag, 1973.

EEC Commission *General Report* (published annually since 1967; contains a section on each area of policy, with details of major developments in that field.)

EEC Council: Decisions of 4 December 1962 on the co-ordination of agricultural policies and setting up a standing committee on agricultural structures.

Directives: 72/159, *Modernization of Farms.*

72/160, *Encouragement to cease Farming.*

75/268, *Hill Farming and Farming in other Less-favoured Areas*
(this directive is also relevant to Regional Policy).

Directives No. 269–276 define areas in which aid may be granted.

OECD Agricultural Policy Reports, The Agricultural Policy of the EEC.
(The same series includes reports on UK agricultural policy before accession and on the agricultural policy of other developed countries.)

Chapter 6. THE RULES OF COMPETITION

ECSC Treaty, Article 67.

EEC Treaty, Articles 85–94.

W. Hallstein, *Die Europäische Gemeinschaft,* chapter V, Econ Verlag, 1973.

J. P. Dubois, *La Position Dominante et son Abus,* Librairies Techniques, Paris, 1968.

J. T. Lang, *The Common Market and Common Law,* University of Chicago Press, 1966.

D. Maclachan and D. Swann, *Competition Policy in the European Community,* Oxford University Press, London, 1967.

X. Roux and D. Voillermot, *Le Droit de la Concurrence dans les Communautés Européennes,* Joly, Paris, 1968.
EEC Commission: *General Report.*
    Competition Law in the EEC and the ECSC.

Chapter 7. SOCIAL POLICY

ECSC Treaty, Articles 56, 68–69.
EEC Treaty, Articles 117–128.
W. Hallstein, *Die Europäische Gemeinschaft,* chapter V, Econ Verlag, 1973.
EEC Commission: *General Report.*
    Social Report (annual report on the social situations in the Community).
    Supplements to the *Bulletin of the European Communities:*
    4/73, Guidelines for a social action programme.
    2/74, Social action programme.
    8/75, Employee participation and company structure.
    Comparative Tables of the Social Security Systems in the Member-states of the European Communities.

Chapter 8. REGIONAL POLICY

(a) *General*
    EEC Treaty, Articles 92–94.
    W. Hallstein, *Die Europäische Gemeinschaft,* chapter V, Econ Verlag, 1973.
    J. T. Lang, *The Common Market and Common Law,* University of Chicago Press, 1968.
    R. Petrella, *Le Développement Régional en Europe,* Mouton, The Hague, 1971.
    (Symposium), *Les Déséquilibres Régionaux en Europe,* ULB, Brussels, 1968.
    EEC Commission: *A Regional Policy for the Community,* 1969 (memorandum and draft decisions).
    Regional Development in the Community, 1971.
    Thomson Report, 1973, Com 73/SSO final.
    General Report (annual)
    EEC Council: *Regional Policy Regulation,* 724/75.
    Hill Farming Directive, 75/268.

(b) *Individual Regions*
    An interesting series, *Problem Regions of Europe,* has been published by the Oxford University Press (Ed. Scargill). At the time of writing it includes the following titles:
    Over-developed regions:
    Paris Basin, (I. B. Thomson).
    Randstad Holland, (G. R. P. Lawrence).
    North Rhine – Westphalia (J. D. Heller).
    Declining or underdeveloped regions:
    North-east England, (K. Warren).
    Massif Central, (H. D. Clout).
    Mezzogiorno, (A. B. Mountjoy).
    Scotland's Highlands and Islands, (D. Turnock).

Chapter 9. INDUSTRY AND TECHNOLOGY

W. Hallstein, *Die Europäische Gemeinschaft,* chapter V, Econ Verlag, 1973.
C. Layton, *European Advanced Technology,* Allen & Unwin, London, 1969.
C. Layton, *Cross-frontier Mergers in Europe,* Bath University Press, Bath, 1971.

C. Layton, Y. S. Hu, and M. Whitehead, *Industry and Europe,* PEP and Bath University, London, 1971.

EEC Commission: *General Report* (annual).

Bulletin Supplements:

7/73, Towards the establishment of a European industrial base.

14/73, Scientific and technological programme.

15/73, Multi-national undertakings and the Community.

1/75, The Community's supply of raw materials (also relevant to Chapter 16—External Policy).

Proposal for European Aerospace Industry.

Chapter 10. COAL AND STEEL

ECSC Treaty (preferably in original version, including the articles subsequently repealed).

W. Hallstein, *Die Europäische Gemeinschaft,* chapters I–III, Econ Verlag, 1973.

S. C. Constant, J. Ritter, and J. Laigroz, *L'Europe du Charbon et de l'Acier,* Presses Universitaires de France, Paris, 1968.

ECSC High Authority (subsequently EEC Commission):

General Report (annual)

General Objectives (at five-year intervals)

Chapter 11. THE COMMUNITY AND ITS ENVIRONMENT: CONSUMER PROTECTION: TRANSPORT

ECSC Treaty, Article 70.

EEC Treaty, Articles 74–84.

EEC Commission: *General Report* (annual)

Bulletin Supplement 3/73, Programme of environmental action.

EEC Council: Decisions 73/174, 73/176, and 73/180 EEC (concerning research projects on the protection of the environment and on new technologies in connection with solar energy and recycling).

Chapter 12. ENERGY POLICY

ECSC Treaty

Euratom Treaty.

EEC Commission: *General Report* (annual).

Bulletin Supplements:

4/74, Towards a new energy strategy.

5/74, Energy for Europe.

Chapter 13. ECONOMIC, FINANCIAL, AND FISCAL AFFAIRS: CREDITS AND INVESTMENTS

EEC Treaty, Articles 95–99, 103–116, 129–130.

W. Hallstein, *Die Europäische Gemeinschaft,* chapter V, Econ Verlag, 1973.

G. Denton (ed.), *Economic Integration in Europe,* Reading University Studies, London, 1969.

G. de Man, The EMU after four years, results and prospects, 12 *Common Market Law Review,* 193.

J. T. Lang, *The Common Market and Common Law,* Chicago University Press, 1966.

H. H. Maas, The powers of the EEC and the achievement of economic and monetary union, 9 *Common Market Law Review,* 2.

G. Magnifico, *European Monetary Unification,* Macmillan, London, 1973.
P. Salin, *L'Unification Européenne,* Calmann-Lévy, Paris, 1974.
EEC Commission: *General Report* (annual).
        Werner Report (OJ 1970 C 136/1).
European Investment Bank, *Annual Report.*

Chapter 14. THE INTERNAL MARKET AND THE CUSTOMS UNION

EEC Treaty, Articles 12–37, 48–73.
W. Hallstein, *Die Europäische Gemeinschaft,* chapter V, Econ Verlag, 1973.
G. R. Denton (ed.), *Economic Integration in Europe,* Reading University Studies, London, 1969.
M. Hodges (ed.), *European Integration,* Penguin, London, 1972.
J. T. Lang, *The Common Market and Common Law,* Chicago University Press, 1966.
M. Krauss (ed.), *The Economics of Integration,* Allen & Unwin, London, 1973.
L. Lindberg and S. Scheingold, *Europe's Would-be Policy,* Prentice-Hall Inc., Englewood Cliffs, NJ, 1970.
J. E. Meade, *Theory of Customs Union,* North-Holland, Amsterdam, 1955.
EEC Commission: *General Report* (annual).
        Bulletin Supplement 4/75, Statute for European Companies.

Chapter 15. EDUCATION, SCIENCE, AND RESEARCH

ECSC Treaty, Article 55.
Euratom Treaty, Articles 4–11.
EEC Treaty, Article 235 (enables the Council to take necessary action in fields not covered by the Treaty).
Janne Report (Bulletin Supplement 10/73, For a Community policy in Education).
A. J. C. Kerr, *Schools of Europe,* Bowes & Bowes, London, 1960.
A. J. C. Kerr, *Universities of Europe,* Bowes & Bowes, London, 1962.
    (These two books, by the author of *The Common Market and How It Works,* are now rather out of date, but describe the educational systems of all the EEC states and several others shortly after the Community came into being.)
E. King (ed.), Society, Schools and Progress Series, Pergamon, Oxford.
EEC Commission: *General Report* (annual).
        Social Report (annual, includes a section on Vocational Training).
        The Education of Migrant Children.

Chapter 16. THE EXTERNAL POLICY OF THE COMMUNITY

EEC Treaty, Articles 131–136, 228–231.
W. Hallstein, *Die Europäische Gemeinschaft,* chapter VI, Econ Verlag, 1973.
L. Tindemans, Report to the European Council, Bulletin Supplement 1/76.
E. Wellenstein, Free trade agreements between the enlarged European communities and the EFTA countries, 10 *Common Market Law Review* 137 (1973).
EEC Commission: *General Report* (annual).

Chapter 17. THE COMMUNITY AND DEVELOPING COUNTRIES

EEC Treaty, Articles 131–136, 228–231.
W. Hallstein, *Die Europäische Gemeinschaft,* chapter VI, Econ Verlag, 1973.
L. Tindemans, Report to the European Council, Bulletin Supplement 1/76.

EEC Commission: *General Report* (annual).
        Dossier Lomé (includes the text of the Lomé Convention).
        Bulletin Supplement 1/73, Renewal and Enlargement of the Association.

Chapter 18. CONCLUSION. Appendix I. RECENT DEVELOPMENTS

W. Hallstein, *Die Europäische Gemeinschaft,* chapter VII, Econ Verlag, 1973.
EEC Commission Report on European Union, Bulletin Supplement 5/75.
    European Parliament
    European Court of Justice   Reports on European Union
    Economic and Social Committee
European Parliament, *Direct Elections to the European Parliament.*
L. Tindemans, Report to the European Council, Bulletin Supplement 1/76.
    The above list is far from being exhaustive and there is a great deal more material available especially in the field of Community law. Without wishing to make any value judgements, the author regards the following as particularly important:

    The Treaties: these should if possible be read in more than one language, e.g. English, French, and German.
    Hallstein: preferably in the up-to-date German version published since the accession of Britain, Denmark, and Ireland.
    The Tindemans Report.
    The *General Report* and the *Social Report* published annually by the Commission.
    The Bulletin Supplements, also published by the Commission, and containing details of major policy proposals.

Additional Titles
    V. Giscard d'Estaing, *Démocratie Française,* Fayard, Paris. 1976.
    J. Monnet, *Mémoires,* Fayard, Paris, 1976.
    J. B. Noëlle, *Les Rouages de la Communauté,* Brussels, 1977.

Index